BROOKINGS-WHARTON

papers on URBAN AFFAIRS

2002

William G. Gale and
Janet Rothenberg Pack
Editors

BROOKINGS INSTITUTION PRESS
Washington, D.C.

BROOKINGS-WHARTON

papers
on
URBAN
AFFAIRS
2002

Purpose	The Brookings-Wharton Papers on Urban Affairs is an annual publication containing the articles and formal discussant remarks from a conference held at the Brookings Institution and arranged by the editors. The annual forum and journal are the products of a collaboration between the Brookings Institution Center on Urban and Metropolitan Policy and the Zell Lurie Real Estate Center at the Wharton School of the University of Pennsylvania. All of the papers and discussant remarks represent the views of the authors and not necessarily the views of the staff members, officers, or trustees of the Brookings Institution or the Wharton School of the University of Pennsylvania.
2002 Subscription Rates	Individuals and Institutions $24.95
	Standing order plans are available by calling 1-800/275-1447 or 202/797-6258. For international orders add $8.00 surface mail and $16.00 airmail.
	Send subscription orders to the Brookings Institution, Department 037, Washington, DC 20042-0037. Or call 202/797-6258 or toll free 1-800/275-1447. Or e-mail bibooks@brookings.edu.
	Visit Brookings online at www.brookings.edu.
	Brookings periodicals are available online through both Online Computer Library Center (contact the OCLC subscriptions department at 1-800/848-5878, ext. 6251) and Project Muse (http://muse.jhu.edu).

Contributors	Alberto Alesina *Harvard University*
	Stephen Calabrese *University of South Florida*
	Julie Berry Cullen *University of Michigan*
	Ingrid Gould Ellen *New York University*
	Dennis Epple *Carnegie-Mellon University*
	Teresa Garcia-Milà *Universitat Pompeu Fabra*
	Edward Glaeser *Harvard University*
	Andrew Haughwout *Federal Reserve Bank of New York*
	Vernon Henderson *Brown University*
	Robert Inman *University of Pennsylvania*
	Douglas Massey *University of Pennsylvania*
	Therese McGuire *Northwestern University*
	Derek Neal *University of Chicago*
	Thomas Nechyba *Duke University*
	Katherine O'Regan *New York University*
	Alice Rivlin *Brookings Institution*
	Amy Ellen Schwartz *New York University*
	Todd Sinai *University of Pennsylvania*
	Leanna Stiefel *New York University*
	Jacob Vigdor *Duke University*

Conference participants	Jan K. Brueckner *University of Illinois*
	Jerry Carlino *Federal Reserve Bank of Philadelphia*
	William Dickens *Brookings Institution*
	Anthony Downs *Brookings Institution*
	Joseph Gyourko *University of Pennsylvania*
	Pascale Joassart-Marcelli *University of California*
	Helen F. Ladd *Duke University*
	Amy Liu *Brookings Institution*
	Jens Ludwig *Brookings Institution*
	Janice Madden *University of Pennsylvania*
	Robert Margo *Vanderbilt University*
	Rebecca Menes *George Mason University*
	Edwin S. Mills *Northwestern University*
	Richard Netzer *New York University*
	Roger Noll *Stanford University*
	John Quigley *University of California, Berkeley*
	Steven Raphael *University of California, Berkeley*
	Thomas Romer *Princeton University*
	Michael Stoll *University of California, Los Angeles*
	Anita Summers *University of Pennsylvania*
	Susan Wachter *University of Pennsylvania*

Preface

The *Brookings-Wharton Papers on Urban Affairs* is devoted to bringing new research to bear on urban policy issues in an accessible manner. The collaboration between the Wharton School and the Brookings Institution in this endeavor represents an effort to draw on resources and personnel in both academia and the policy community. We hope and expect that the journal itself will be of interest and use to an even wider audience that includes policymakers and their staffs, interested parties in the private sector, journalists, students, and others.

The existence of this journal owes much to the efforts of key people at Brookings and Wharton. At Brookings, former president Michael Armacost, Robert Litan, the director of the Economic Studies Program, and Bruce Katz, the director of the Center on Urban and Metropolitan Policy, have avidly encouraged and supported all aspects of the project since its inception.

At Wharton, Peter Linneman and Joseph Gyourko, former director and current director, respectively, of the Samuel Zell and Robert Lurie Real Estate Center, have supported the journal both intellectually and financially with enthusiasm and energy. The dean's office has made its contribution by freeing some of Janet Rothenberg Pack's time to organize the conference and edit the volume. The Department of Business and Public Policy has in numerous ways encouraged her participation in this endeavor.

Several people made vital contributions to the publication of this volume and the conference on which it is based. Saundra Honeysett at Brookings organized conference logistics and managed the paper flow with efficiency and good cheer. Amy Liu and Jamaine Tinker provided valuable support at many stages. Gloria Paniagua and Catherine Theohary verified the papers. France Zak provided careful copyediting. The authors and discussants deserve special thanks for making extra efforts to draft their arguments in a clear and accessible manner.

Editors' Summary

URBAN AREAS FACE daunting economic challenges that have increased in scope in recent years. At the same time, cities provide exciting opportunities for growth and revitalization. The interplay of these challenges and opportunities creates important tasks for policymakers and researchers. The *Brookings-Wharton Papers on Urban Affairs* aim to address these issues by providing cutting-edge, accessible research on issues unique to urban areas, as well as on broad economic and policy topics that have special applications in an urban setting.

This volume of BWPUA contains papers and discussant comments from a conference held at the Brookings Institution on October 25–26, 2001. The papers are divided into two groups. A symposium of three papers examines metropolitan tax and fiscal policy. Stephen Calabrese, Glenn Cassidy, and Dennis Epple model and evaluate the effects of political mergers between cities and suburbs. Robert Inman and Andrew Haughwout examine the links between the economic vitality of cities and suburbs and ask whether suburban communities could make themselves better off by subsidizing central cities. Teresa Garcia-Milà and Therese McGuire present a new theoretical argument for firm-specific tax incentives for industry relocation and apply their model to Boeing's recent decision to move its headquarters to Chicago. In the other papers in the volume, Jacob Vigdor explores the impact of alternative measures of gentrification on lower income city residents; and Ingrid Gould Ellen, Katherine O'Regan, Amy Ellen Schwartz, and Leanna Stiefel explore the varying experiences of immigrant students in the New York City public school system.

Symposium on Metropolitan Tax and Fiscal Policy

Cities attract businesses and residents by providing high-quality amenities. But providing those amenities requires funding, and higher tax burdens increase incentives for city residents and firms to depart for lower tax locations. Balancing these considerations is an essential problem in urban public finance. The income disparity between most large central cities and their relatively wealthier suburbs makes these issues even more difficult and politically sensitive. In addition, the potential effectiveness of many fiscal options is unknown, and the connection between economic effectiveness and political feasibility is sometimes overlooked.

Metropolitan Consolidation

Large metropolitan areas in the United States are characterized by a very large number of local governments, with many urban areas containing more than 100 separate municipalities. The fragmentation of local government has led to concerns regarding the distribution of government services and the efficiency with which these services are provided. Central city mayors and some analysts have advocated political and fiscal consolidation, but annexation of developed suburbs has rarely occurred.

Stephen Calabrese, Glenn Cassidy, and Dennis Epple model voting behavior in multiple municipalities to evaluate the effects of mergers. Voters, who vary only in income, choose their preferred level of public services and redistribution, and the level and type of tax levied. They also choose their residential location based on these policies. In equilibrium, majority rule determines tax, public service, and redistribution policy; each municipality has a balanced budget; no one wants to move; and the housing market clears. The policy favored by the median-income voter will always be adopted. The model produces results consistent with observed patterns in cities: although both large and small municipalities provide public goods, redistribution occurs almost exclusively in large central cities. Small suburban municipalities depend primarily on property tax revenues to finance public services, but central cities use both income and property taxes. The policy choices result in income stratification across the metropolitan region. Low-income households with a preference for redistribution are more likely to locate in the central city, whereas wealthy households will choose suburbs with high levels of public service provision and less redistribution.

The stratification of municipalities by income implies that mergers are generally not politically viable. Residents of a poorer municipality, such as a central city, will support a merger with a wealthier suburb to obtain higher public good provision and redistribution, with lower overall tax rates. But residents of the wealthier suburb will oppose consolidation to avoid falling property values, reduced public good provision, and increased redistribution.

The aggregate welfare effects of mergers are more complicated. A merger between two jurisdictions will prompt the wealthiest individuals in the higher income jurisdiction to move from the consolidated city to a wealthier suburb in order to escape redistribution policies. These movers from the consolidated area will become the poorest residents in their new location and will purchase housing of less than the average value in that suburb. Housing prices in the new suburb will rise and public good provision will fall. This pattern will continue across suburbs in a domino effect. As a result, consolidation has negative externalities for surrounding suburbs as well as for the wealthier residents of the merged municipalities.

Consolidation might still raise aggregate welfare, if mergers benefit poor voters more than they harm wealthier ones. Where this is the case, governments wishing to encourage annexations could compensate suburban residents for their losses and still improve social welfare.

Besides providing new insights into the dearth of consolidations, this paper advances researchers' ability to model simultaneous decisionmaking across multiple policy choices and offers a systematic explanation for income segregation that arises even when households have no explicit preference for the characteristics of their neighbors.

Suburban Transfers to Central Cities

In the absence of political consolidation, financial transfers from suburbs to central cities are another, possibly more feasible, way to address metropolitan area public finance issues. But should the suburbs be interested in such an arrangement? Traditionally, proponents of such transfers have suggested that transfers are justified either because central cities fund public goods that benefit suburban residents, such as infrastructure, public education, and policing, or because central city poverty is a regional problem that should be addressed via transfers from the entire urban region.

In their paper, Andrew Haughwout and Robert Inman argue that neither of these arguments is compelling. They examine a new rationale for suburban transfers to central cities, based on two premises. The first is that cities create agglomeration economies. These economies occur because of the geographic concentration of firms within an industry and the resultant decline in transportation and labor costs, encouragement of innovation, and ease of spreading new ideas. These agglomeration economies reduce the cost of city-produced goods to both city and suburban residents. The second premise is that weak central city government—marked by a variety of financial practices and fiscal institutions—imposes costs on city residents and firms and induces them to relocate. The relocation, though, reduces the agglomeration economies available in the city and causes the price of city-produced goods to rise. If both premises hold, weak city governments hurt suburban residents, weak city finances *cause* poor suburban economic health, and suburban residents should be willing to pay to improve center cities' weak financial situation in order to preserve the benefits of agglomeration economies.

Haughwout and Inman demonstrate empirically that weak city finances are associated with negative city and suburban economic outcomes. In particular, they show that weak budgetary institutions, strong city unions, rising poverty rates, and declining tax bases are associated with lower income, population growth, and rates of home value appreciation in both cities and their surrounding suburbs. They also develop a structural simulation model based on Philadelphia's economy that builds in a link between city finances and suburban economic outcomes. The effects of city finances on suburban health in Philadelphia are found to be similar to those found in the aggregate data. In this simulation a causal relation is assumed by construction, and thus the model implies that a suburban family should be willing to pay between $100 and $250 annually to improve city fiscal institutions in order to realize the benefits of agglomeration economies in the city.

The conclusion that weak city finances reduce agglomeration economies implies that transfers from suburbs to cities would only protect agglomeration economies if the funds were used to strengthen weak city finances. Such transfers would be counterproductive if the funds were used to raise pay for city workers or increase constituent services. To avoid these problems and ensure that the funds are used appropriately, Haughwout and Inman advocate the use of a number of specific mechanisms for transfers, including using suburban aid to fully fund state poverty mandates, reforming local property tax rules, and making aid dependent on the adoption of competitive bidding practices for city service contracts.

Tax Incentives and Business Location

If city-suburb consolidations are rare and suburban areas are reluctant to transfer resources to central cities, as the first two papers suggest, a third fiscal option for urban economic development is large, firm-specific tax breaks aimed at attracting or retaining particular businesses. Such actions have been highly publicized in the past, ranging from cities recruiting professional sports teams to Alabama wooing Mercedes Benz in the early 1990s.

Despite the frequency of such actions, the research literature casts considerable doubt on the effectiveness of such incentives, on both theoretical and empirical grounds. One strand of the theoretical literature argues that under tax competition, all jurisdictions will select inefficiently low tax rates to prevent firms from exiting. This will result in a reduction of public service provision below efficient levels. Another strand of the literature argues that tax competition across communities results in an efficient allocation of resources, because people can choose where to live, and thus that specific tax incentives introduce distortions. This approach assumes that if no tax incentives are offered, cities tax corporations' capital at rates equal to the marginal benefit of the public goods provided to the firms. Neither approach justifies large tax incentives for particular companies.

In their contribution to the volume, Teresa Garcia-Milà and Therese McGuire challenge the conventional wisdom. They develop a model in which cities compete for a mobile capital stock and benefit from productivity-enhancing agglomeration economies. Under these circumstances, the efficient tax rates on new firms equal the difference between the marginal benefit to firms of the public services they consume and the marginal agglomeration benefits to the city of the additional capital brought by the firm.

The authors then examine Chicago's decision in 2001 to offer Boeing $50 million in tax incentives to relocate its corporate headquarters from Seattle. Chicago's pursuit of Boeing is puzzling, given that it involved only the relocation of Boeing's headquarters rather than its manufacturing plants. Moreover, since most of the headquarters' employees transferred from Seattle, few new jobs were created. In stark contrast, Chicago allowed a large local candy manufacturer employing nearly 1,000 people to leave the city without offering it tax incentives to stay. Garcia-Milà and McGuire suggest that Chicago planners believed that a management-oriented firm like Boeing would create greater potential for knowledge spillovers than would the retention of the manufacturing facility. The authors conclude that agglomeration of capital may have sufficient economic as well as political payoffs to justify firm-specific tax incentives.

Gentrification and Immigration

The other two papers in this volume provide new evidence on current issues in urban economics and urban policy. They demonstrate the breadth of topics that fall comfortably within the area of urban economics and the important insights that can be gained on urban issues from related fields of research, such as poverty and welfare or labor economics.

Does Gentrification Harm the Poor?

Although white flight to the suburbs during the second half of the twentieth century is often viewed as a causal factor in the demise of central cities, the return of affluent households to city neighborhoods sometimes elicits similarly intense criticism. Gentrification, or the influx of upper-middle-class or wealthy households into previously poor neighborhoods, is popularly seen as harmful to poor and minority residents. The closing of the Cabrini-Green Housing Project in Chicago and its partial replacement with townhomes, for example, produced an uproar among long-time public housing residents, who felt they were being driven from their homes despite city officials' reassurances that mixed-income housing developments would be beneficial to low-income as well as new middle-class neighborhood residents.

Jacob Vigdor's paper suggests that much less is known about the impact of gentrification on poor families than is commonly supposed. Rather than assuming there is a consensus definition, Vigdor begins by defining gentrification and makes the distinction between preference-driven and income-driven gentrification. In preference-driven gentrification, high-income households raise their valuation of the amenities available in poor neighborhoods. A common example is the two-earner family that decides it prefers a shorter commute and increases its willingness to pay to live in the more central neighborhood. Income-driven gentrification occurs when a change in the productivity of high-income households raises the demand for, and hence the price of, housing in upper-income neighborhoods. This forces some of the people in these neighborhoods to move to lower priced areas.

Under both types of gentrification, housing prices rise in the formerly poor neighborhoods, so that renters there either have to move or absorb the higher rental costs (and possibly higher amenities). One difference between the two lies in housing prices in the upper-income neighborhood, which fall under preference-driven gentrification but rise under income-driven gentrification. Vigdor proposes policy options that could reduce potential harm caused by gentrification both directly and indirectly. Rent subsidies or relocation assistance directly address rising costs of housing for low-income households. Job training or education subsidies could make poor residents more able to compete in the housing market.

Gentrification may also have effects on the poor apart from its impact on the housing market. Many of these effects are likely to be positive. Rising housing prices can raise property tax revenues, increase redistribution, and improve public services. An influx of higher income households might create job opportunities for low-income residents or relocate jobs closer to the neighborhood. Poor residents might benefit from improvements in neighborhood quality, such as lower crime rates.

Vigdor argues that most previous work on gentrification focuses too narrowly on spatial displacement and does not in fact demonstrate that displacement is caused by gentrification or that it causes harm. Using Boston as a case study, he finds that households with low educational attainment (who are more likely to be among the long-term poor) living in gentrifying areas are no more likely to move than other households in the area or than low-education households in other areas. Gentrification has not increased the segregation of Boston neighborhoods by socioeconomic class; in fact, gentrification seems to lead to more mixed-income neighborhoods.

Immigrants and School Segregation

The proportion of the U.S. population that is foreign-born, currently about 10.4 percent, is at its highest level since 1930. Research suggests that segregation among racial groups is significant and negatively affects children's educational attainment, but it is unknown whether the same holds true for immigrants. Peer effects—proximity to low-income, less-educated classmates—appear to have a negative impact on racial minorities, particularly for education and employment. Peer effects may have a different impact on the children of immigrants because although the parents generally have little education, immigrant groups often demonstrate a strong preference for educating their children. Similarly, although schools with large racial minorities have been found to receive less funding than average, no previous studies have investigated the impact of immigrant segregation on school funding. Indeed, segregation of immigrants may improve access to resources, as concentration of a group may make it more efficient for the government to provide particular services, such as classes in English as a second language.

Using evidence from the New York public schools in which 16 percent of students were foreign-born in 1998–99, Ingrid Gould Ellen, Katherine O'Regan, Amy Ellen Schwartz, and Leanna Stiefel evaluate the degree of immigrant segregation and its relationship to resource allocation and student performance. Having assembled a data set that contains information on the academic and socioeconomic characteristics of all children in New York City public schools in 1998–99, aggregated to school level, the authors find a relatively low level of segregation for immigrants overall.

Some groups of immigrant students, particularly students from the former Soviet Union and the Caribbean, are considerably more segregated than foreign-born students overall, but still less segregated than nonwhite students. The authors show that different immigrant groups, particularly Soviet and Caribbean immigrants, have substantially different peer influences and access to educational resources. Like native students, immigrant students are highly segregated by race. Racial segregation is accompanied by peer characteristics, teacher quality, and classroom and aggregate school spending patterns that have negative effects that overwhelm differences in educational attainment due to nativity. Soviet students who attend schools with high percentages of white students have higher quality teachers and higher achieving peers, while Dominican students in predominantly black schools are educated with students characterized by extremely high poverty rates and low test scores.

STEPHEN CALABRESE
University of South Florida

GLENN CASSIDY
Cassidy Policy Research

DENNIS EPPLE
Carnegie-Mellon University

Local Government Fiscal Structure and Metropolitan Consolidation

THE UNITED STATES has an enormous number of local governments. Even when the focus is limited to municipalities, as it is in this paper, the number is impressive. There were 19,372 municipalities in the United States in 1997.[1] Most large metropolitan areas in the United States are divided into a hundred or more distinct municipalities. Even metropolitan areas of moderate size typically have fifty or more distinct municipalities.

For much of the twentieth century, there appears to have been a relatively broad consensus reaching across disciplines that this multiplicity of local governments was undesirable—a manifestation of disorganization and a prescription for inefficiency in the provision of public services.[2] This consensus spawned a metropolitan government movement that met with little success and much resistance. At about the same time the political movement for metropolitan government was beginning to run out of steam, the intellectual underpinnings also came under challenge—thanks largely to the work of Tiebout, and Ostrom, Tiebout, and Warren.[3] The trade-offs between the benefits of decentralized choice and the potential gains from coordination have been the subject of debate ever since.

The lack of popular support for consolidation of metropolitan governments is mirrored in data affirming the permanence of municipalities. Municipal

We thank Janet Pack for suggestions that led us to investigate the topic studied in the paper, and we thank Alberto Alesina and Julie Cullen for their insightful comments. Support for this research was provided by the MacArthur Foundation and the National Science Foundation.

1. *Statistical Abstract of the United States, 2000,* table 491.

2. Stephens and Wikstrom (2000, ch. 2) provide an overview of the metropolitan government movement and document the breadth of support it once commanded.

3. Tiebout (1956); Ostrom, Tiebout, and Warren (1961).

boundaries, once drawn, are highly resistant to change. Vigdor reports that in Massachusetts, no new cities or towns have been created since 1920 and none deleted since 1938.[4] In Pennsylvania between 1980 and 1990, there were only eighteen annexations or mergers, involving less than one square mile and fewer than 500 persons.[5] Using data from the decennial boundary and annexation surveys of the 1970 and 1980 Census, Epple and Romer find that 98 percent of boundary changes are those in which an existing municipality adds *previously unincorporated* land.[6] Annexation of one municipality by another and mergers of municipalities have become increasingly rare. Nationwide there were an average of fewer than ten such consolidations per year in the decade of the 1970s.

Strong advocates of metropolitan consolidation remain, but they acknowledge that success is unlikely.[7] While efforts to promote metropolitan consolidation have largely disappeared, the outcomes that emerge under the current system of highly decentralized local government garner widespread criticism. Broadly, there are two issues. One centers on the distributional consequences of the tendency toward income stratification observed in U.S. metropolitan areas. One consequence is unequal quality of public services across municipalities, with quality inversely related to income. The other concern is that independently chosen tax and expenditures lead to large distortions at the metropolitan level, when central city governments engage in taxation for both redistribution and provision of public services. These issues are well articulated by Mieszkowski and Mills. They note the practical difficulties of maintaining a separation between the allocatable and distributive activities of governments. They point to the inefficiencies associated with redistributive taxation in the central city, and they offer the judgment that "tax and government service level considerations inhibit central city redevelopment."[8]

Recent years have witnessed growth of a body of research in political economy seeking to characterize equilibrium when both the populations of local jurisdictions and their policies are endogenous.[9] In these models, policy outcomes within jurisdictions are determined by "democratic federalism," to use

---

4. Vigdor (2001).

5. International City Management Association (1993).

6. Epple and Romer (1989).

7. Rusk (1995, 1999).

8. Mieszkowski and Mills (1993, p.146).

9. Ellickson (1971); Westhoff (1977); Epple, Filimon, and Romer (1984); Cassidy, Epple, and Romer (1989); Nechyba (1999, 2000); Calabrese (2001); Goodspeed (1989); Fernandez and Rogerson (1996, 1998); Epple and Sieg (1999).

the terminology coined by Inman and Rubinfeld; policies are chosen by simple majority rule.[10] Because of the well-known difficulties with characterizing equilibrium with multidimensional policy choices, each of these papers focuses on a unidimensional policy space.[11] Thus these models are unable to capture the tensions between public service provision and redistribution, and the associated impacts on housing markets, household location, and welfare that are at the center of the debate about the consequences of metropolitan fiscal decentralization.

Our contribution is to analyze metropolitan equilibrium when localities have multiple tax instruments and can engage in both public service and redistributive expenditures. Moreover, when voting, households consider the impact that these public policy choices have on housing prices and the population of the jurisdiction in which they reside. We do this by considering a class of preferences for which voting equilibrium exists in this multidimensional space.[12] Of course, adoption of a particular class of preferences entails some loss in generality, but we believe the sacrifice is well rewarded by the implications drawn from simultaneous consideration of the set of issues that arises in practice.

We characterize equilibrium analytically when there are multiple local jurisdictions. We then use functional forms and parameters that are consistent with American data to develop computations based on the multicommunity analytical model. The computed equilibria provide additional insights about the incentives facing different local governments on the choice of tax instruments and the allocation of revenues between services and redistribution.

We also use our computational multiple jurisdiction model to investigate the distributional and welfare consequences of fiscal consolidation through annexations and mergers. In most states, a merger of two communities or an annexation of one community by another generally requires majority approval in both communities. For instance, article IX, section 8, of the Pennsylvania Constitution assigns to voters the right to change boundaries of municipalities by initiative and referendum. A merger or annexation is permitted only if a

---

10. Inman and Rubinfeld (1997). Altruism is assumed to motivate redistribution in models by Brown and Oates (1987); Orr (1976); Wildasin (1991); Bucovetsky (1982); Johnson (1988); and Steen (1987) study the effects of exogenous changes in local government policies.

11. Typically a single tax instrument is considered and a single type of public expenditure. The government budget constraint then reduces public policy choice to a single dimension. Plott (1967).

12. Bucovetsky (1991) develops conditions for existence of equilibrium when the set of policies is multidimensional.

majority of the voters in each municipality involved in the consolidation approve.[13] Similarly, article 11 of the California Constitution states that except with approval by a majority of its electors voting on the question, a city may not be annexed to or consolidated into another.[14] The Texas Constitution, in reference to local municipal integration, states if at least 15 percent of qualified voters of each of two or more municipalities petition the governing bodies of their respective municipalities to order a consolidation election, the governing body of each municipality must order an election on the proposition.[15] In Florida, a charter for merger of two or more municipalities and associated unincorporated areas can only be adopted by passage of a concurrent ordinance by the governing bodies of each municipality affected, approved by a vote of the qualified voters in each area affected.[16]

We explore the political feasibility and general welfare effects of local fiscal consolidation by first investigating how equilibrium in our model changes if the central city annexes or merges with one or more suburban jurisdictions. We then calculate the change in welfare of each metropolitan household associated with the consolidation, which provides the information required to assess the political support and opposition to consolidation. We also calculate the aggregate welfare changes of consolidation and determine whether consolidation can possibly lead to a *potential* Pareto improvement even when it does not garner the necessary political support.[17] In the process of determining these distributional and welfare effects, we also investigate the importance of housing tenure choice (owner-occupancy and rental) on preferences for government policy and implications for consolidation. Our results make clear why the metropolitan integration movement could not gain purchase regardless of the potential aggregate welfare effects.

Our goal is to do more than write a belated obituary for the metropolitan integration movement, though that is potentially one way to interpret our analysis. Rather, our primary goal is to provide an improved understanding of municipal fiscal structure and its consequences for the efficiency and distribution of population in U.S. metropolitan areas. This in turn may help identify

---

13. Pennsylvania Constitution, article IX, Local Government, section 8: Consolidation, Merger, or Boundary Change.

14. California Constitution, article 11, Local Government, section 2 (b).

15. Texas Constitution, subchapter B. General Authority to Annex, § 43.021. Authority of Home-Rule Municipality to Annex Area and Take Other Actions Regarding Boundaries.

16. Florida Constitution, title XII, chapter 171, Municipal Annexation or Contraction.

17. Pareto improvement is a reallocation of resources that makes at least one person better off without making anyone else worse off.

policy changes that higher level governments may institute to preserve fiscal decentralization while limiting its adverse consequences.

Others have developed formal models to study various aspects of coordinated metropolitan government policy. Zodrow considers metropolitan tax base sharing in a two-jurisdiction model with a homogeneous population in which there is both business and residential property.[18] In his model, all individuals live in suburbs but consume services, such as police protection and transportation, in the central city. By contrast, our focus is on a multijurisdiction environment in which heterogeneous households reside in both central city and suburban communities, and we do not consider business taxation. Alesina, Baqir, and Hoxby consider the trade-offs arising from costly community formation on the one hand and the gains from tailoring the public goods to specialized tastes on the other.[19] To focus on fiscal incentives, we consider an established set of communities and consider how incentives for use of tax and redistributive instruments vary with size and population characteristics, such as income. The benefits of specialization of public good provision are reflected in our specification, however, since the desired level of public good provision varies systematically with income.

Others have also investigated choice of tax instruments. Nechyba considers choice of tax instruments when myopic voters set a local property tax and a sophisticated planner sets the income tax rate.[20] In our framework, voters choose all tax instruments and forecast the consequences of those changes employing the assumption that residents are utility-takers. Henderson develops a positive analysis of choice of revenue instruments by communities.[21] He analyzes choice among user fees, land taxes and property taxes, comparing outcomes with profit-maximizing communities to those with communities controlled by utility-maximizing voter-residents. By allowing heterogeneity among residents in both income and tenure choice, we highlight additional forces affecting choice of revenue instruments.

We necessarily abstract from many interesting aspects of the interaction of local governments. We assume that the government or residents of a jurisdiction do not cooperate with other jurisdictions when choosing policies. As Inman and Rubinfeld observe, the overall record with respect to cooperative federalism is not impressive, lending support to modeling jurisdictions as

18. Zodrow (1984).
19. Alesina, Baqir, and Hoxby (2000).
20. Nechyba (1997).
21. Henderson (1994).

pursuing independent policies.[22] The literature on cooperation among subnational governments contemplates cooperative arrangements that fall well short of the type of consolidation we consider here. [23] However, absent consolidation or legislation of enforcement powers to an overarching governmental entity, cooperative policies would require voluntary agreement of participating municipalities. Myers provides an interesting model in which there are incentives for voluntary intergovernmental cooperation.[24] In particular, with a homogeneous national population, he demonstrates that communities, acting independently, would voluntarily choose to make transfers to other communities that prove to enhance allocatable efficiency.

An interesting extension of our analysis would be to investigate whether voluntary transfers across communities would emerge with a heterogeneous population when policies of individual communities are chosen by majority rule. An attractive feature of our framework is that such transfers could be introduced as policy options for voters while preserving the existence of majority-voting equilibrium. In particular, in the income hierarchy of communities that emerges in our model, it would be quite natural to consider whether a community might choose to make such voluntary transfers to "adjacent" communities in the hierarchy. In this paper, a given municipality's policy choices have pecuniary impacts on other municipalities, but the framework could also be expanded to allow goods provision in a given municipality to create direct externalities.

Model and Properties

The economy of the model consists of a continuum of households that differ only in their endowed income y. The distribution of income is represented by a continuous distribution $f(y)$. All households have the same preferences represented by utility function $U(g, h, b)$, where g is expenditures on a publicly provided good, h is units of housing, and b is consumption of a numeraire bundle. We first develop properties of equilibrium for the case in which all household occupants are renters.[25] We then extend the results to the case of owner-occupants.

22. Inman and Rubinfeld (1997).
23. Donahue (1997); Stephens and Wikstrom (2000).
24. Myers (1990).
25. Our welfare calculations reported later take account of changes in land rent. When we analyze the preferences of voters of varying incomes, we do not explicitly allocate the rents

There are multiple local communities that may differ in land area. Each local government may impose a proportional income tax, m, on the income of its residents, and an ad valorem property tax, t, on the value of housing in the jurisdiction. Total tax revenue in each community may be used to finance expenditures on a publicly provided good, g, and redistribution of a lump sum grant, r, to each individual in the community. The parameters of a local government's budget, that is, the tax rates, m and t, and the expenditure levels, g and r, are determined by a majority vote of residents of the locality. Voting is conducted simultaneously on this set of variables.[26]

A household with income y faces the following budget constraint if the household locates in a particular community, j:

(1) $$y(1 - m^j) + r^j = p^j h + b \,.$$

The gross-of-tax price for each unit of housing is p^j. We denote the net-of-tax price p_h^j. The following identity relates the gross and net-of-tax prices: $p^j \equiv p_h^j(1 + t^j)$.

A household locates in the community with the tax-expenditure policy for which the household obtains the highest utility. We assume that g is separable in a household's utility from housing and numeraire consumption. This simplifying assumption implies that a household's demand for housing and the numeraire good are not directly dependent on the amount of g provided in a community. These demands are indirectly dependent on the expenditure on g through the taxes used to finance g. Thus let utility be represented by the function

(2) $$U(g, h, b) = f(g)[u(h, b) + \varphi] \,,$$

where φ is a constant.

Majority voting equilibrium generally does not exist when voting takes place simultaneously over multiple dimensions. However, we are able to prove the existence of voting equilibrium when it is assumed $u(h, b)$ in equation 2 is homogeneous of degree 1. This assumption is consistent with the empiri-

---

accruing to owners of rental properties. However, to the extent that such owners comprise a relatively small proportion of the population, the voting results would be little affected by allocating such rents.

26. While municipalities do not literally give cash grants to local residents, they do provide a variety of services to aid the poor. Inman (1995) identifies increasing poverty-related spending as the major source of increased per capita expenditure on goods, services, and supplies from 1973 to the onset of Philadelphia's financial crisis in 1990. Inman (1989) also emphasizes the importance of redistributive politics as a determinant of tax policy in his study of forty-one U.S. cities between 1961 and 1986.

cal evidence on housing demand that suggests the income elasticity of housing demand is 1.[27] This homogeneity assumption is widely used in the optimal taxation literature, in dynamic macroeconomic simulation models, and in a variety of other applications in economics.

Linear homogeneity assumption of $u(h, b)$ implies that the corresponding indirect utility function is linear in income:

$$(3) \qquad V(y) = f(g)\big[(y(1-m)+r)w(p)+\varphi\big].$$

In models of local public good provision with housing markets, it is frequently assumed that the slopes of indirect indifference curves (MRS) through any point in the (g, p) plane increases with income.[28] This "single-crossing" assumption implies that high-income households are willing to pay a higher price for each unit of housing than lower income households in order to obtain more g. Thus given two communities with the same m and r, this single-crossing assumption implies that the rich are willing to pay a higher housing price premium than the poor to live in a community with higher g. Our utility function in equation 3 with $\varphi < 0$ satisfies this single-crossing condition. If $\varphi > 0$, then the utility in equation 3 implies the opposite single-crossing condition. Note, however, even if $\varphi > 0$, communities with higher than average income may still provide more g than lower income communities because of the multidimensionality of the set of policy alternatives. Lower income communities will likely spend more tax revenue on redistribution and less on public goods than wealthier communities. If $\varphi = 0$, then the marginal rate of substitution in the $(g\ p)$ plane, MRS_{gp}, does not change with income.

While our framework can accommodate either direction of crossing in the (g, p) plane, we opt to consider the neutral case. Thus in the analysis that follows, we focus on the case $\varphi = 0$. Hence, from this point on, household y's indirect utility is represented by:

$$(4) \qquad V(y) = f(g)(y(1-m)+r)w(p).$$

Housing is produced by competitive firms in each jurisdiction from land and nonland factors via a constant-returns neoclassical production function. The price of nonland factors is assumed fixed and uniform throughout the metropolitan area. The housing supply function in community j can be represented by $H_s^j(p_h^j) = L^j h_s(p_h^j)$, where $h_s(p_h^j)$ is housing per unit of land in community

27. Harmon (1988).

28. Westoff (1977); Goodspeed (1989); Epple, Filimon, and Romer (1984); Cassidy, Epple, and Romer (1989); Ellickson (1982).

$j(C^j)$ and L^j is land area in community j.[29] Because $u(h, b)$ is homogeneous of degree 1, household y's housing demand in C^j can be represented by $(y(1 - m^j) + r^j)h_d(p^j)$. Housing equilibrium in C^j can thus be characterized by

(5) $$\theta^j(\bar{y}^j(1 - m^j) + r^j)h_d(p^j) = h_s(p_h^j),$$

where θ^j is the relative density in the community (households for each unit of land area), $\bar{y}^j$ is the mean income in the community, and

$$p_h^j = \frac{p^j}{1 + t^j}.$$

Equilibrium in this model is an allocation of households across communities such that

1. Within each community:

    a) the housing market clears

    b) the government's budget is balanced

    c) there is a majority-rule equilibrium determining the government's policy (t, m, r, g).

2. Each community is occupied, and no one wants to move.

We refer to the first part of the definition of equilibrium above as *internal equilibrium* and the second condition as *intercommunity equilibrium*. While we do not offer a proof of existence of equilibrium, we present conditions that must be satisfied for an allocation to be an equilibrium. In our computational analysis, we then verify an allocation is an equilibrium by checking that the conditions for equilibrium are satisfied. We begin by considering the necessary conditions for intercommunity equilibrium. We then characterize majority voting equilibrium, demonstrating that the median-income voter in each community is pivotal in determining that community's policy choices.

Intercommunity Equilibrium Conditions

The results that follow present necessary conditions for intercommunity equilibrium.[30]

---

29. Epple and Zelenitz (1981).

30. Formal proofs and details are presented in an earlier working paper version of this manuscript, available from the authors.

Result 1: Consider an allocation in which all communities are occupied and all households are not indifferent between any two communities. Necessary conditions for such an allocation to be an intercommunity equilibrium are:[31]

a) Income stratification among communities: Each community contains households with incomes in a single interval.[32]

b) Boundary indifference: Order communities from lowest to highest income levels. Between each pair of adjacent communities in this ordering is a household that is indifferent between the two communities.

To see the intuition for this result, let $x^j = (g^j, m^j, r^j, p^j)$ be the equilibrium-tuple characterizing community j, and similarly define x^i to be the equilibrium-tuple in community i. Let $V(y, x^i)$ and $V(y, x^j)$ be the indirect utility of household y in communities i and j respectively. From equation 4, the indirect utility function is linear in income for a given x. Thus $V(y, x^i)$ and $V(y, x^j)$ can intersect at most once, and in general they intersect exactly once. The point of intersection divides the set of incomes into two intervals, one interval preferring x^i and the other preferring x^j.

In understanding results to follow, it is useful to examine the value of the indirect utility function at $y = 0$ and its slope with respect to y. From equation 4 they are

$$V(0) = f(g^j)r^j w(p^j)$$

$$\frac{\partial V(y)}{\partial y} = f(g^j)(1 - m^j)w(p^j) .$$

Consider any two communities, C^j and C^k, with average incomes $\bar{y}^j$ and $\bar{y}^k$ respectively. Suppose $\bar{y}^j < \bar{y}^k$ and households with $y = 0$ are not indifferent between C^j and C^k. Comparing $V(0)$ for the two communities establishes the first condition below, and it then follows that the slopes in y must satisfy the second condition:

(6) $$f(g^j)r^j w(p^j) > f(g^k)r^k w(p^k)$$

(7) $$f(g^j)(1 - m^j)w(p^j) < f(g^k)(1 - m^k)w(p^k) .$$

If $V(0)$ for both communities are equal, then in equilibrium all households must be indifferent between C^j and C^k because if they were not, one of the

---

31. Proof of this proposition builds on the approach developed in Calabrese (2001).

32. More precisely, stratification is a generic property of equilibrium; there may be knife-edge cases such that households may be indifferent between a pair of communities.

communities would not be occupied. Thus if households with $y = 0$ are indifferent between C^j and C^k, the conditions shown in equation 6 and equation 7 become

$$(8) \qquad f(g^j)r^j w(p^j) = f(g^k)r^k w(p^k)$$

$$(9) \qquad f(g^j)(1 - m^j)w(p^j) = f(g^k)(1 - m^k)w(p^k).$$

Property tax is the predominant tax instrument used by local communities in the United States and is the tax instrument under consideration in most positive models of local tax-expenditure policy. Thus we consider it informative and useful for comparison with other models to first develop the intercommunity equilibrium conditions when it is assumed local communities do not employ income tax to generate revenue. We then consider the equilibrium conditions when income tax is included in the model.

Intercommunity Equilibrium Conditions without Income Tax

If local communities can only employ property taxes, then equations 7 and 9 and reduce to

$$(10) \qquad f(g^j)w(p^j) < f(g^k)w(p^k)$$

$$(11) \qquad f(g^j)w(p^j) = f(g^k)w(p^k).$$

The following result is derived from equations 6, 8, 10, and 11:

Result 2: Assume local communities do not employ income tax as a revenue-generating instrument. The following conditions are necessary for an allocation to be an intercommunity equilibrium:

(i) Descending lump-sum grants. The grant level is decreasing in average community income, that is, $\bar{y}^j < \bar{y}^k \Rightarrow r^j \geq r^k$.

(ii) If $g^j > g^k$ then $p^j > p^k$, and if $g^j = g^k$ then $p^j \geq p^k$.

(iii) If $p^j < p^k$ then $g^j < g^k$, and if $p^j = p^k$ then $g^j \leq g^k$.

Condition (i) accords well with intuition—low-income households migrate to the community with the highest level of redistribution. If community j also offers higher public good provision, then clearly the price must be higher in j, as stated in (ii). Alternatively, if the price in j is lower than in k, then public good provision must be lower in j than in k. Note that the above conditions do not rule out the possibility that the price in j is higher than in k and public provision in j is lower than in k. This can happen, for example, if the redistributive grant is substantially higher in j than in k.

Intercommunity Equilibrium Conditions with Income Tax

Introduction of an income tax increases the set of possible orderings of tax rates, expenditure levels, and housing prices across communities. Equations 6 through 9 imply restrictions on the combinations of possible orderings.[33] Some unlikely orderings are potentially consistent with equilibrium. For example, we would generally expect that the poorer a community, the higher the income tax rate and the level of redistribution. However, investigation of equations 6 through 9 reveals that this need not always be the case. For example, households in one community may choose a relatively low income tax rate and a relatively high per capita grant, while households in a higher income community choose a higher income tax rate, higher level of government services, and lower housing price. Many possible orderings of variables across communities are possible when communities have multiple tax and expenditure instruments.

Internal Equilibrium

Recall that in each community, the conditions for internal equilibrium are as follows: the housing market clears; the government's budget is balanced; and there is a majority-rule equilibrium on the parameters of the government's budget.

We define the set of combinations (t, m, r, g) perceived by voters to be feasible for community j as the *budget possibility frontier (BPF)*. The characterization of this frontier is detailed further below. For a given community, a point (t^*, m^*, r^*, g^*) is a *majority voting equilibrium* (MVE) if it is on the community's BPF and a majority of the community's residents do not prefer any other point on the BPF to (t^*, m^*, r^*, g^*).

33. Calabrese and Epple (2001).

Result 3: The MVE in each community is the outcome on the budget possibility frontier most preferred by the median-income voter in that community.[34]

This result follows from the linearity of the indirect utility function in equation 4. Given any pair of policy alternatives, the indirect utility functions are straight lines that intersect once, at most. Suppose the median income in the community is to the right of the intersection point. The policy preferred by the median will, by definition, be on the higher of the two lines at the median-income level. All those to the right of the median will also prefer the same policy, and they, coupled with the median, comprise a majority. A similar argument applies if the median is to the left of the intersection.

The condition that the housing market clear is simply the requirement that demand equal supply in the housing market:

$$(12) \qquad \theta^j(\bar{y}^j(1-m^j)+r^j)h_d(p^j)=h_s(p_h^j).$$

In order to complete the characterization of intracommunity equilibrium, we need to characterize the community budget possibility frontier. This in turn requires a characterization of voters' perceptions of how the private market equilibrium in the community will be affected by public policy choices. The latter is needed for two reasons: First, how voters perceive the effects of policy on the private market affects how they view the population to be served and the tax base. Second, voter utility depends on how voters expect policy changes to affect the price of housing.

There are many possible ways to characterize the BPF, depending on the degree of voter sophistication in anticipating the consequences of policy changes within a community. Our characterization of voting behavior draws on modern club theory and assumes that individuals are utility takers.[35] This means voters assume that the policy-tuples (t, m, r, g) and housing prices in all the other communities are fixed. Employing this utility-taking assumption, voters predict how the private market equilibrium would change in response to a prospective policy change. For example, a voter assumes the price of

34. The strategy of proof of this proposition is due to Cassidy (1990) who exploits the linearity of the indirect utility function in income to study voting equilibrium in a model with a flat grant financed by a property tax.

35. For an overview, see Glazer, Niskanen, and Scotchmer (1997) and references cited there. Empirical work by Epple, Romer, and Sieg (2001) rejects myopic voter perceptions such as the assumption that community tax base and population are unaffected by policy changes.

housing in his or her community is affected by changes in the government's budget through both changes in housing demand by current residents and migration into or out of the community, assuming policies and prices in other communities are fixed.

The income stratification result in result 1 implies that if community j's budget is balanced, then

(13) $$t^j p_h^j h_d(p^j)(\bar{y}^j(1-m^j)+r^j)+m^j\bar{y}^j = r^j + g^j.$$

Based on this utility-taking model of voting behavior, the possible (t, m, r, g) combinations for community j given $(t^{-j}, m^{-j}, r^{-j}, g^{-j})$ are the ones in which
1. The housing market clears in community j.
2. The government's budget is balanced in community j.
3. The stratification and boundary-indifference conditions of result 1 are satisfied.

The Contrasting Preferences of Owners and Renters

So far we have treated all of a jurisdiction's residents as renters. Suppose, by contrast, that all residents are owner-occupants.[36] They locate in a jurisdiction and purchase housing there before participating in the voting process that determines the structure of the jurisdiction's taxes and expenditures. There are no transactions costs in the purchase and sale of housing; households can adjust their level of housing consumption—that is, sell their current house and purchase another dwelling—in response to price changes without incurring transactions costs. As in the preceding model with rental housing, households correctly anticipate how their housing consumption will change in response to a change in the price of housing induced by a change in the structure of the jurisdiction's tax-expenditure policies. Households also anticipate the capital gain or loss they will incur if their jurisdiction's tax-expenditure policy is changed and a change in the net-of-tax price of housing results.

Let h_o be the amount of housing purchased at price $p_{h,o}$ by a household with endowed income y. When making decisions about whether to change his consumption bundle, the homeowner faces the budget constraint

(14) $$(1-m)y + r + (p_h - p_{h,o})h_o = ph + b,$$

36. Our formulation of the preferences of owners follows Epple and Romer (1991).

with h_0 and $p_{h,0}$ fixed. The third term on the left-hand side is the capital gain or loss from selling the household's existing dwelling.[37]

Capital gains or losses on housing due to changes in a community's tax-expenditure policy impact a homeowner's budget constraint. However, because transactions occur in equilibrium, the necessary conditions for inter- and intracommunity equilibrium for the renters' model continue to hold in the owners' model. This is shown in the appendix. However, while results 1 through 3 apply in the owners' case as they do in the renters' case, the equilibrium with owners will generally differ from that with renters. The reason is as follows: a change in a jurisdiction's tax-expenditure policy will, in general, change the net-of-tax price of housing. Since owners make their purchase decisions before voting, they experience a capital gain or loss if they vote for a policy change. Thus their utility will be affected by the change in the net-of-tax price of housing. Renters, by contrast, are affected by the gross-of-tax price but experience no capital gains or losses from changes in the net-of-tax price. This leads to differences in equilibrium outcomes when voters are renters compared to when voters are owner-occupants.

Development of more specific implications about the features of equilibrium requires more specific information about preferences, technology, the distributions of income and housing tenure, the number of jurisdictions, and the land area of each. We therefore turn to numerical computations to illuminate properties of the model.

Fiscal Structure and Integration

In this section, we develop computational or simulated equilibria based on the theoretical model above. The parameterization of the model is based on functional forms and parameter values that are broadly consistent with empirical evidence on housing supply and demand functions, government expenditures, and the distribution of income in the United States.

The utility function is taken to be

(15) $$U(g, h, b) = g^\beta h^\alpha b^{1-\alpha}.$$

This function is consistent with the assumption adopted above—that g is separable in a household's utility from housing and numeraire consumption.

37. We assume that the capital gain from housing is not taxed by the jurisdiction, but our analysis could easily accommodate allowing such capital gains to be taxed.

Also, utility is linearly homogeneous in h and b in this function, which ensures existence of majority voting equilibrium over tax-expenditures policies in each community.

In order to obtain values for β and α, we derived the demand functions for g, h, and b that would emerge if g were a privately provided private good:

$$(16) \qquad h = \frac{\alpha y}{(1+\beta)p}$$

$$(17) \qquad b = \frac{y(1-\alpha)}{(1+\beta)}$$

$$(18) \qquad g = \frac{\beta y}{(1+\beta)}.$$

The share of income spent on housing inclusive of property taxes is set equal to 1/3, which from equation 16 means:

$$(19) \qquad \frac{\alpha}{(1+\beta)} = 1/3.$$

The share of income spent on g is set equal to 0.1, which is approximately the share of GDP spent on local public goods.[38] Thus from equation 18,

$$(20) \qquad \frac{\beta}{(1+\beta)} = 0.1.$$

Based on equations 19 and 20, $\alpha = 0.37$ and $\beta = 0.111$.

The utility function in equation 15 implies the following indirect utility function for a household with income y renting in a jurisdiction j with housing price p, grant r, publicly provided good expenditure g, and income tax rate, m:

$$(21) \qquad V(p,r,g,m,y) = g^\beta \alpha^\alpha (1-\alpha)^{(1-\alpha)} p^{-\alpha}(y(1-m)+r).$$

The following constant-elasticity of housing supply function is adopted:

$$(22) \qquad H_s^j(p^j) = L^j(p^j)^\mu,$$

---

38. Data for this approximation are from the *Economic Report of the President* (1997, pp. 300, 304, 337, 391, 394).

where L^j is the land area of community j as a proportion of total land area in the economy, and μ is the ratio of nonland to land inputs in the production of housing. Based on available evidence regarding the share of land and non-land inputs in housing, this parameter is set equal to three. This supply function is implied by a constant returns to scale Cobb-Douglas production function.

The distribution of income is log normal with $\ln(y) \sim N(9.8, 0.36)$. This income distribution corresponds to the distribution in U.S. urban areas in 1980.

The benchmark model for the computations is a metropolitan area with five local jurisdictions. The metropolitan area consists of a large city and four smaller suburbs that have equal land area. The large city has 40 percent of the total metropolitan land area, and each of the suburbs has 15 percent of the land area. Result 1 above indicates there is income stratification among the communities. We assume that the large city is the poorest jurisdiction.

We also assume the pivotal voter in the city is a renter and the pivotal voter in each suburb is an owner-occupant. It is the case that a much higher percentage of residents in suburbs are homeowners than are residents in large cities. Hence given a political process based on direct democracy, tax-expenditure policies in large cities will tend to be more representative of the preferences of renters, and the tax-expenditure polices in the suburbs will tend to be more representative of the preferences of home owners. Our model implies that suburban tax-expenditure policies will reflect the consequences of those policies on the net-tax price of housing and concomitant effects on capital gains or losses.[39]

To investigate municipal consolidation, we allow merger of the central city with one or more suburban communities. We calculate aggregate welfare changes in the usual way—aggregate compensating variation plus aggregate changes in economic rent. We also wish to investigate how individual voters are affected by consolidation. For owners, we calculate the change in utility, taking account of the capital gain or loss as shown in equation 14.

We rely on results 1 through 3 to compute the equilibria presented below. First, the computational results for the benchmark model are presented. As mentioned above, this is the case with one large city and four small suburbs. In this model, every community can levy a property tax, t, and provide publicly provided goods, g, and a lump-sum cash grant, r. In addition, all the jurisdictions can levy an income tax, m, except the richest suburb. We adopt

---

39. In ongoing work, we are studying alternative characterizations of the aggregation of preferences of owners and renters in modeling voting within municipalities.

this restriction on income taxes in the richest suburb to add an element of realism. In our model, residents of all but the richest community can escape a burdensome income tax by relocating to a wealthier community. In practice, as we noted in our introduction, there are many small suburbs in most metropolitan areas. In addition, of course, the very wealthy may opt for tax havens elsewhere in the country or the world. Hence we assume an income tax rate of zero in the richest suburb to reflect the reality that the very rich can move to escape burdensome local taxes.

This benchmark model yields striking implications regarding the tax instruments that suburban communities would choose, were there generally no limits imposed by higher-level governments. While we believe that pursuing these implications is of considerable interest in its own right, this would draw us away from our primary focus. Thus we then proceed by restricting the choice of tax instruments to accord with the tax instruments used in practice. For instance, we assume that head taxes are not permitted by state constitutions, and negative property and income tax rates are also prohibited. These restrictions result in only the large central city imposing income taxes and undertaking redistribution.[40] We then explore how equilibrium changes when the central city merges with one or more of the suburbs. Based on the changes in equilibrium, we investigate the level of political support for fiscal integration and calculate the aggregate welfare effects of integration.

The Benchmark Computational Model

Column 1 of table 1 below presents the computed equilibrium results for the benchmark case with five communities and when all jurisdictions are permitted to use all the tax and expenditure instruments, except the restriction on income tax in the richest suburb. Community 1 is the poor large central city consisting of renters, and communities 2 to 5 are the suburban homeowner communities in ascending order of mean income.

In practice, while both large and small municipalities provide local public goods, expenditures for redistribution at the municipal level are undertaken

40. Under these conditions and with our chosen utility function, the stratification claim in result 1 is no longer a necessary condition for equilibrium. However, stratification would be implied if we were to append an arbitrarily small constant ϕ to our chosen utility function as in equation 2. The resulting computed equilibria would differ negligibly from the results we report. Thus our computational results, which assume stratification, can be thought of as having been derived incorporating a small value of ϕ.

Table 1. Simulation Results

	Benchmark model	Restricted model			
	Five communities	*Five communities*	*Four communities*	*Three communities*	*Two communities*
Variable	*(1)*	*(2)*	*(3)*	*(4)*	*(5)*
L^1	0.4	0.4	0.55	0.70	0.85
L^2	0.15	0.15	0.15	0.15	0.15
L^3	0.15	0.15	0.15	0.15	...
L^4	0.15	0.15	0.15	...	...
L^5	0.15	0.15	...	...	...
p^1	9.90	8.13	8.77	9.59	10.35
p^2	9.79	10.76	11.74	12.83	15.18
p^3	9.81	11.59	12.77	14.48	...
p^4	9.82	12.68	14.72	...	...
p^5	10.71	14.56	...	...	...
ph^1	7.43	6.1	6.58	7.19	7.76
ph^2	9.78	8.2	8.94	10.00	11.87
ph^3	9.81	8.92	9.85	11.69	...
ph^4	9.82	9.78	11.66	...	...
ph^5	10.01	11.53	...	...	...
r^1	1,642	1,729	1,771	1,881	1,607
r^2	-1,802	...	...	...	...
r^3	-2,507	...	...	...	...
r^4	-3,390	...	...	...	...
r^5	-4,018	...	...	...	...
g^1	1,176	934	1,117	1,225	1,656
g^2	1,876	1,208	1,521	1,895	3,272
g^3	2,548	1,548	2,010	2,969	...
g^4	3,454	2,087	3,233	...	...
g^5	5,281	3,314	...	...	...
m^1	0.171	0.22	0.19	0.16	0.12
m^2	0.0035	...	...	...	...
m^3	0.0016	...	...	...	...
m^4	0.0018	...	...	...	...
m^5	0	...	...	...	...
t^1	0.333	0.333	0.333	0.333	0.333
t^2	0.0013	0.312	0.313	0.283	0.279
t^3	-0.000012	0.299	0.297	0.239	...
t^4	0.00018	0.297	0.262	...	...
t^5	0.07	0.263	...	...	...
y^1	15,807	11,719	14,756	19,469	26,816
y^2	22,088	15,767	19,943	28,356	...
y^3	29,598	20,830	28,359	...	...
y^4	41,306	29,236	...	...	...
N^1	0.413	0.236	0.369	0.551	0.746
N^2	0.219	0.175	0.198	0.224	0.254
N^3	0.163	0.184	0.208	0.225	...
N^4	0.121	0.195	0.225	...	...

Table 1. Simulation Results (continued)

	Benchmark model	Restricted model			
	Five communities	Five communities	Four communities	Three communities	Two communities
Variable	(1)	(2)	(3)	(4)	(5)
N^5	0.084	0.210			
$\tilde{y}^1$	11,036	8,860	10,520	12,607	14,846
$\tilde{y}^2$	18,660	13,708	17,181	23,201	35,743
$\tilde{y}^3$	25,309	18,120	23,507	37,328	...
$\tilde{y}^4$	34,113	24,377	37,330	...	...
$\tilde{y}^5$	50,925	38,238	...	...	...

Note: L^i is community i's share of the total land area (i = 1,2,3,4,5). p^i is the gross of property tax price of housing in community i. $p_h{}^i$ is the net-of-property-tax price of housing in community i. r^i is community i's lump-sum grant. g^i is community i's per capital expenditure on the public good. m^i is community i's income tax rate. t^i is community i's property tax rate. y^i is the highest income in community i. N^i is community i's share of the total population. $\tilde{y}^i$ is the median income in community i.

almost exclusively by large central cities. This accords well with our computational results. Indeed, the results in the benchmark model indicate that the small rich communities not only do not redistribute, but there is incentive for the pivotal voters in these communities to use the lump-sum instrument, r, as a head tax to finance the public good. Additionally, because there is a strong preference among the wealthy communities to use a head tax to generate revenue, property tax rates, which in practice are the most commonly used local tax instrument, are very small and even negative in these computational results in the suburbs. Note also that the net-of-tax price in the city $[p_h^1 = 7.43]$ is substantially lower than net-of-tax prices in the suburbs, which range from 9.78 to 10.01. This is as one would expect, given that suburban voters are owner-occupants while city voters are renters.

As noted above, we proceed by imposing restrictions on the choice of tax instruments that accord with practice. Since head taxes are not observed in practice and are probably generally politically infeasible, we constrain our computational model so that head taxes are prohibited.[41] That is, we require r^j to be non-negative in all communities.

In addition, small municipalities tend to rely on property taxation, while large municipalities tend to use multiple tax instruments, including both income and property taxes. The results in our benchmark model also accord

41. User fees are observed for some local government services (Henderson, 1994). Our results for communities 2 through 5 indicate that, were it permissible, those communities would charge a user fee (head tax) essentially equal to the value of per capita public services. Of course, in practice, communities generally cannot charge user fees for major locally provided services such as education, police, and fire protection.

with this observation. The wealthy suburban communities that can impose an income tax in our model (communities 2 to 4) impose a very small income tax rate. Hence in order to reflect typical local fiscal structures even more accurately, we constrain the computational model so that all the rich communities, and not just the richest community, do not implement income taxes. As we see below, with these restrictions, a local fiscal structure emerges in which only the large city engages in redistribution and imposes income taxes. This is a particularly natural result for a "typical" metropolitan area in the United States—one containing a large city and many small suburbs.

Restricted Model Computational Results

The results for the restricted model with five communities are presented in column 2 of table 1. Before turning to a discussion of these outcomes, it should be noted that housing prices in our model should be interpreted as annualized implicit rentals for each unit of housing. Thus property tax rates, t, are expressed as a proportion of the annualized implicit rental value of housing services. Observed property taxes are, of course, expressed as a rate on the market value of housing, not on the annual value of services. If we use a real interest rate of 6 percent to compute the annual implicit rent for each unit of property value, the 33 percent rate on annual implicit rent for community 1, the large central city consisting of renters, is equivalent to a tax of 2 percent (0.06 x 0.33) on property values. This is the order of magnitude of property taxes observed in the United States.

One respect in which our computational results in table 1 are at variance with observation is the relatively high marginal income tax rate in the city. Note, however, that the net income tax payment, $(t^1 y - r^1)$, is not very high for most residents of the city. Thus the net income tax payments are not unrealistic. Nonetheless, the high marginal rate is not entirely satisfying. We think it likely that our model overstates the incentives for income taxation in the city by assuming the tax-expenditure policy represents only the preferences of renters.[42] In practice, of course, even central cities have a mixture of owners and renters participating in the political process. In future work, we envision extending the characterization of central city voters to embody an owners-renters mix that conforms to the observed mix in the United States.

42. This is likely due not only to assuming all residents are renters, but also because we do not consider business taxation.

The five-community computational results for both the benchmark model and the restricted model indicate that the higher the income level in the community, the greater is the amount of public good per capita provided. This is as one would expect, given the positive income elasticity of demand for g coupled with the higher per capita tax base in higher-income communities.

We now turn to investigation of municipal consolidation.

Impact of Municipal Consolidation on Local Fiscal Structure

Columns 3 through 5 of table 1 show the computed results when the central city progressively annexes or merges with the suburbs. A natural way—although not the only way—to characterize these consolidations is, at each step in the consolidation, to have the city merge with the poorest suburb. For instance, column 3 presents the equilibrium results after the central city merges with the poorest of the original suburbs, or community 2 in the five-community simulation. The city increases its share of the total land area from 40 percent to 55 percent through this consolidation. In column 4 are the equilibrium results when the central city and two suburbs consolidate, increasing the city's share of land area to 70 percent. Column 5 presents the equilibrium results after the third hypothetical consolidation, resulting in only two communities in the metropolitan area, a large city with 85 percent of the land area and one small suburb with 15 percent of the land area. We do not consider the case in which the city annexes all suburbs. In practice, a central city cannot establish a monopoly on all potential locations; there is always scope for residents, particularly wealthy residents, to move beyond the domain of any particular city. Retaining an independent suburb in all our simulations is a mechanism for reflecting this outside option.

We see that, after each consolidation, the highest income households in the merged suburb move into the next richest suburb. This creates a domino effect in which the richest households in each higher-income suburb move to the next richest community. To see the effect that consolidation has on the allocation of households among the communities, consider the equilibrium results for the five-community case as compared with the equilibrium after the first consolidation—the four-community equilibrium. This involves comparing the outcomes shown in column 2 with the outcomes in column 3. Originally, the city has 40 percent of the land area and 23.6 percent of the total metropolitan population consisting of all households with income below $11,719. Community 2 originally has 15 percent of the land area and 17.5 percent of the population, consisting of all households with income in the interval $11,719 to $15,767. If the merger induced no population movement, the post-merger income boundaries between the four communities would be $15,767, $20,830, and $29,236. Instead, we see the actual postmerger income boundaries are $14,756, $19,943, and $28,359. After the merger, almost a quarter of the population previously in community 2, those with incomes between $14,756 and $15,767, moves in order to avoid living in the city. This movement affects the remaining communities. About one-fourth of the population previously in community 3 moves to the next-wealthier community, and about 7 percent of the population previously in community 4 moves to the wealthiest community.

It is not surprising that the richest households in community 2 want to escape when their community merges with the city. These households would be the ones most burdened by the taxes used to finance redistribution and would experience a decrease in public good provision. They escape to the next richest suburb, driving up housing prices in this suburb. They also cause a reduction in per capita public good provision; they lower the per capita tax base by purchasing less than the average value of housing in the community, and they vote for lower public good provision. Therefore, the rich in this suburb have an incentive to relocate into the next richest suburb, creating the same effects on housing prices and per capita public good provision. This process occurs across all the suburbs. The ultimate result is that in the remaining suburbs, housing prices increase and public good provision levels decrease.

In the city, the per capita public good provision, lump-sum grant, and housing price increase, and the income tax rate decreases. In general, this trend continues for each successive merger. An exception is after the last consolidation when only a very large city and one small suburb are left. Each successive consolidation results in addition of some higher-income residents to the central city and some lower-income residents to the wealthier suburb. With the last consolidation, the new, wealthier pivotal voter in the central city prefers an increase in public good provision (to $1,656) and a decrease in the redistributive grant (to $1,607) relative to the levels ($1,225 and $1,881) in the central city before consolidation. Interestingly, despite the reduced income of the pivotal voter in the remaining suburb, the pivotal voter in that suburb also chooses a higher level of public good provision ($3,272) than before consolidation ($2,969). This change in the wealthiest suburb may reflect a desire by the pivotal voter for redistribution by way of public goods provision in the wealthiest suburb.

Political Feasibility of Fiscal Integrations

The consolidation of two or more municipalities generally requires the majority support of voters in each of the communities. As mentioned in the introduction, consolidations of municipalities in the United States have been relatively uncommon. In this section, we apply the computational model developed above to explicate possible reasons why there has been a lack of widespread popular political support for consolidations. We do this by calculating the effects of consolidation on the welfare of individual households. In this investigation we consider the importance of housing tenure choice (owner and renter) on the magnitude of these effects.

To illustrate who gains and loses from each successive consolidation shown in table 1, we first calculate the compensating variations for each household in the metropolitan area. Compensating variation measures the change in each household's welfare due to changes in consumption caused by changes in the local governments' tax-expenditure policies attending consolidation. In addition, each homeowner incurs a capital gain or loss when consolidation changes the price of housing in each community. Thus to fully capture a homeowner's welfare gain or loss, we also calculate welfare changes inclusive of capital gains or losses. This includes calculation of the capital gains for the absentee landlords in community 1. These welfare effects for each household are presented in figure 1.

It is not surprising that all the original residents of the large city are made better off when the city merges with one of the suburbs. After all, the city absorbs richer households and then is able to increase per capita public good provision and redistribution with a lower income tax rate and no change in the property tax rate. The original poor inhabitants of the city are much better off after the merger even though the influx of relatively rich households slightly increases housing prices.

What is surprising is that a majority of the households in community 2 (58 percent) are made better off in terms of their compensating variation. Every household with income below approximately $14,000 has a positive compensating variation. Every one of these households remains in the former suburb after it merges with the city.[43] These households mainly benefit because the lower housing prices allow them to increase their property hold-

---

43. To be sure, not all the households that remain in the former suburb have a positive compensating variation. All households in the income interval between $14,000 and $14,756 remain in the suburb, but incur a decrease in utility even before capital losses.

Figure 1. Individual Household Welfare Effects, First Consolidation

Compensating variation (dollars)

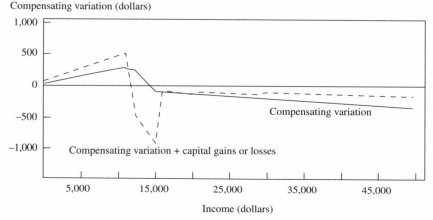

Income (dollars)

ings and private consumption without a dramatic loss in public good provision. However, the compensating variation numbers do not completely measure these homeowners' welfare changes. Although they now face lower housing prices, this also means they incur a capital loss on their housing and property. These capital losses are significant in that the net-of-tax price for each unit of housing falls from \$8.20 to \$6.58. When taking into account these capital losses, the merger makes all the original residents of community 2 worse off. If the residents of community 2 are sophisticated enough to realize what will happen to the value of their property if they merge with the city, they would never support the consolidation. Thus consolidation would never garner the necessary political support in the suburb.

It should be noted that the homeowners in communities 3 to 5 incur capital gains because the merger of communities 1 and 2 leads to higher housing prices in these three other suburbs, as discussed in the previous section. However, these capital gains do not offset the negative compensating variation of residents of communities 3 to 5. The influx of poor households into these communities leads to a decrease in per capita public good provision, which results in a greater loss in welfare than the increase due to capital gains. Therefore, even if a majority of residents in each municipality involved in a possible merger supported it, there could potentially be resistance to the consolidation from other noninvolved municipalities. The merger of communities creates potential negative externalities for other communities. These other communities may have an incentive to try to block the merger by lobbying a higher

Figure 2. Individual Household Welfare Effects, Second Consolidation

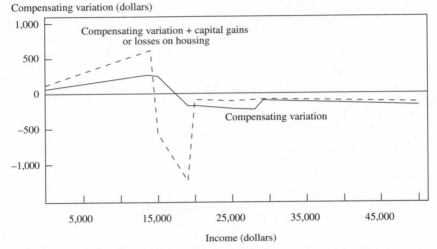

Compensating variation (dollars)

level of government that may have final jurisdiction over municipal consolidations, such as a state government.

The story revealed from examining the changes in the equilibrium results after the second consolidation summarized in table 1 is similar to the one from the first consolidation. The individual household welfare impacts for this case are summarized in figure 2. In this second consolidation, the city increases its share of total land area from 55 percent to 70 percent by merging with the poorest of the remaining three suburbs. Again, every resident of the city benefits from the merger, while almost every other household in the metropolitan area loses. Also, just as in the first consolidation, a majority of the households (53 percent) in the consolidated suburb incur positive compensating variation from the merger, but these gains are offset by capital losses on housing. Property values also increase in the other municipalities, but any benefits to the residents are offset by a less favorable municipal budget.

Figure 3 presents the welfare effects on each individual household that result from the third consolidation summarized in table 1. In this case, the city merges with the poorest of two remaining suburbs. A noteworthy difference between the outcomes of this merger compared to the other mergers is that the very poor households are actually made worse off. As figure 3 indicates, the compensating variation measures for households with income below $7,000, which make up the bottom 6 percent of the metropolitan income distribution, are negative. The consolidation does leads to higher average income and more

Figure 3. Individual Household Welfare Effects, Third Consolidation

Compensating variation (dollars)

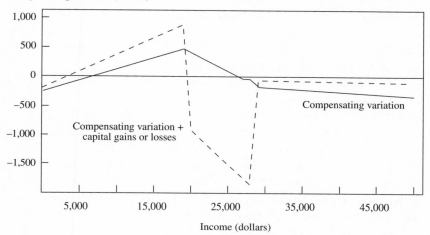

Income (dollars)

per capita public good provision in the city. However, the income of the pivotal voter is now so high that redistribution falls from the pre-merger level. This decrease in the lump-sum grant in combination with the increase in price of housing in the city makes the very poor worse off. Still, the merger makes all the rest of the households in the city better off, and thus a majority of the households in the city would favor consolidation. Again, the majority of households in the merged suburb are made worse off, due mainly to capital losses. Therefore, none of the three hypothetical mergers summarized in table 1 would have the necessary political support.

Aggregate Welfare Effect

The analysis presented directly above predicts that proposals for municipal consolidation would generally not garner enough political support in all the communities involved. The evidence accords well with this prediction in that municipal consolidations are relatively rare. However, this does not mean that consolidation could not result in an increase in aggregate social welfare. The change in aggregate welfare is measured not just by aggregating the households' compensating variations, but also by including any change in aggregate economic rent on land due to housing price changes. In the city, the

rents are paid to absentee landlords, who are outside the model in the sense
that they are sufficiently few in number that their effects on voting outcomes
can be neglected. However, we should include any changes in land rents that
accrue to the absentee property owners in the calculations of the social welfare effects of consolidation. We should also include changes in economic rent
that accrue to the homeowners in the suburbs.[44]

In addition, as shown in the individual household welfare calculations
above, the renter households in the city are usually made better off from consolidation, while suburban homeowners are made worse off. If the combined
aggregate gains of the city residents and property owners offset the aggregate
losses of the suburban residents, including land rents, then social welfare
would increase. If this were the case, then consolidation would lead to a
potential Pareto improvement for society. If the "winners" of consolidation
could somehow compensate the "losers," then everyone in all municipalities
could be better off through a merger of two or more of the municipalities.

Land rents in the metropolitan area are defined as the sum over communities of the producer surplus associated with housing production. Thus because
the aggregate population is normalized to one, from equation 22, per capita
aggregate land rents in these simulations, D, are given by

$$(23) \qquad D = \sum_{j=1}^{J} \int_{0}^{p^j} H_s^j \left(\frac{p^j}{1+t^j} \right) dp = \sum_{j=1}^{J} \frac{L^j \left(\frac{p^j}{1+t^j} \right)^{\mu+1}}{\mu+1},$$

where J is the number of communities in the metropolitan area.

Table 2 below presents the values for the aggregate change in social welfare resulting from each consolidation. The values in table 2 should be
interpreted on a per capita basis. The results in the table indicate that the first
consolidation leads to lower social welfare, while the other two consolidations
increase social welfare. These results arise primarily because the majority of
city residents benefit from consolidation.[45] The city's absentee landowners

44. When we derived individual household welfare effects of consolidation in the previous
section, we assumed homeowners incur capital gains or losses on housing structure when consolidation changes the price of housing. Of course, a housing price decrease that confers capital
losses on owner-occupants may be partially offset by benefits of lower housing prices to pur-
chasers of housing or to renters. Thus in the aggregate welfare analysis presented in this
section, we apply the standard definition of aggregate change in welfare and add the aggregate
total change in economic (land) rent to aggregate compensation variation.

45. As was discussed previously, households with incomes below $7,000, or about 11 per-
cent of the population of the city, are made worse off by the third consolidation. However,
aggregate welfare in the city increases.

Table 2. Per Capita Welfare Effects of Municipal Consolidations
Per capita dollars

Consolidation	Compensating variation	Change in land rents	Change in social welfare
First	-57.88	-4.86	-62.74
Second	11.77	-2.01	9.76
Third	92.06	-28.28	63.78

also benefit because consolidation causes the net-of-tax price of housing to increase in the city. Therefore, the larger the city is before consolidation, the greater the number of people that benefit. When the city increases in size from 55 percent to 70 percent of land area after the second consolidation, the benefits to the 37 percent of the total population that initially lived in the city, combined with the benefits to the city's absentee landlords, offset the losses of the other 63 percent of the metropolitan population, including decreases in land rents. The third consolidation leads to even greater aggregate welfare gains than the second consolidation.

The results in table 2 show that municipal consolidations can create positive aggregate social welfare effects even if they are politically infeasible. In these cases, the city's residents and landlords could, in principle, entice homeowners of a suburb to merge by offering to compensate them for their losses.[46] This compensation would produce a Pareto improvement. However, even when a merger would decrease aggregate social welfare, the benefits of consolidation to the city residents and landlords could possibly be greater than the losses to the residents of the merged suburb. In these cases, compensating the residents of the suburb to induce a merger would not produce a Pareto improvement for society. For instance, the city's residents' and landlords' aggregate benefits of the first consolidation are about $102. The aggregate losses caused by the first consolidation for the homeowners of community 2, including economic losses in land rents, are about $91. Therefore, the city residents and landlords could more than compensate the homeowners of community 2 for losses they would incur from a merger that would lower aggregate social welfare.

Another message from the preceding analysis is that the impacts on some households are quite large relative to the per capita effects found in table 2. For example, as figure 3 shows, the third consolidation produces losses ranging as high as $1,500 or more to owners whose properties are annexed. Thus the intensity of opposition to annexation from such households is likely to be

46. Consistent with this idea, the city absentee landowners could also attempt to manipulate the voting process by spending some of their "rents" in lobbying efforts and campaign contributions to pressure for ratification of consolidations.

very strong indeed. The gains are more widely and equally distributed, perhaps providing less motivation for organization in support of consolidation.

Conclusion

Our results highlight the importance of capturing the contending forces that determine local fiscal structure and the impact of the resulting fiscal structure on support or opposition to government consolidation. The results highlight the payoff from a framework that permits analysis of simultaneous voting on a set of community policy instruments. The overall picture that emerges from the analysis follows.

The lower a household's income, the more attractive is redistribution relative to publicly provided goods, and the less consequential are high tax rates. For lower income households, annexation poses a tradeoff. Annexation brings into the city higher income households whose preferences lead to a shift toward more public goods relative to the level of redistribution and to relatively lower tax rates. On the other hand, the higher income households bring an increase in both property and income tax base. As we have seen, the net effect on lower income households tends to be favorable. By contrast, higher income households, especially owner-occupants, find that annexation leads to unwelcome changes. While all suburban residents tend to be adversely affected by an annexation, the adverse effects are by far the strongest for residents of the suburb being annexed. As a result, annexation efforts routinely fail when subjected to a vote by residents of the suburb targeted for annexation.

The gains from annexation that emerge in table 2 are due to reduction in tax distortions. Annexation adds relatively higher income households to the city. These households both add to the tax base and add votes against redistribution. As evident from table 1, these two offsetting influences result in relatively little change in the per capita grant when annexation occurs. This coupled with the increased tax base results in a reduction in the income tax rate. The associated reduction in tax distortions is sufficient to offset the reduced ability of communities to tailor the public good level to heterogeneous preferences of residents. Ironically, the distortions present before annexation are responsible for the large adverse impact on households in a community that is annexed. Seeking to escape the high tax rates in the city, households bid up suburban housing prices. Annexation eliminates this housing price differential for the annexed suburb, causing large capital losses in the annexed community. Thus the distortions that give rise to the potential for benefits for taxation also create the conditions that give rise to strong resistance within a suburb targeted for annexation.

Appendix

This appendix explains why the necessary conditions for equilibrium in the owner-occupancy model are the same as the renter model.

The demand function for housing for a household owner, given that utility is linear homogenous over housing and numeraire consumption and based on the budget constraint given in equation 14, is of the form

$$h = (y(1-m)+r+(p_h - p_{h,o})h_o)h_d(p).$$

Substituting this demand function into the budget constraint and substituting both into the utility function yield the indirect utility function:

$$V(y) = f(g)(y(1-m)+r+(p_h - p_{h,o})h_o)w(p).$$

The housing demand function for a consumer with income y given $(p_0, r_0, g_0, m_0, p_{h,0})$ is

$$h_o(p_o, y(1-m_o)+r_o) = (y(1-m_o)+r_o)h_d(p_o).$$

Consider an owner y that purchased at $(p_0, r_0, g_0, m_0, p_{h,0})$. When voting, such an owner may contemplate voting for a change in tax-expenditure policy that would cause prices, taxes, and expenditures to change to (p, r, g, m, p_h). If such a change were to occur, the owner's utility at (p, r, g, m, p_h) would be

$$(24) \quad V(y) = f(g)(y(1-m)+r+(p_h - p_{h,o})((y(1-m_o)+r_o)h_d(p_o))w(p).$$

Thus when voting, owner y will vote for a change to (p, r, g, m, p_h) if the utility given in equation 24 is higher than it would be if the policy were unchanged and prices and tax-expenditure policy remained at $(p_0, r_0, g_0, m_0, p_{h,0})$. While renters care only about (p, r, g, m), it is clear from equation 24 that owners care about p_h as well.

Equation 24 above is linear in household income, y. This property of owners' utility functions can be used in a straightforward fashion to extend result

3 to the case where all households are owners. That is, the majority voting outcome when all households in a community are owners is the point $(p^*, r^*, g^*, m^*, p_h^*)$ that maximizes the utility of the owners with median income.

As is standard in static models, we assume that all transactions occur in equilibrium. Thus in equilibrium, households make transactions at $(p_0, r_0, g_0, m_0, p_{h,0}) = (p, r, g, m, p_h)$, and the majority voting outcome does not lead to a departure from (p, r, g, m, p_h). Note that equation 24 reduces to equation 4 when $(p_0, r_0, g_0, m_0, p_{h,0}) = (p, r, g, m, p_h)$. It follows that the results 1 through 3 of the renter's case continue to hold in the owner's case. Thus, necessary conditions for equilibrium in this owner-occupancy model are the same as in the renter's model.

Comments

Alberto Alesina: This is an ambitious paper, which asks a very important question: What is the purpose of having so many local governments in the United States, or, to put it differently, why is it that consolidation of local governments is so difficult and relatively rare? Does this multiplication of governments lead to inefficiencies?

The paper contends that consolidation would lead to income redistribution that wealthy suburbanites would despise. So the latter oppose annexation even in cases when it would be efficient in terms of public good provision and reduction of tax distortions.

I think the paper's contention is correct. The conclusion that rich suburbs do not want to be incorporated for fear of redistribution may not be overly surprising, but it is right. Researchers should be looking for what is accurate, not for what is surprising! In addition, there are many more results in the paper, concerning the choice of tax instruments, the amount of public goods, and so forth. The key contribution of the paper is in having both a public good and a redistributive motive in the analysis. The authors should be congratulated for addressing such a rich and complex problem.

Since I have very little to object to in the paper, what I would like to do in my comments is to make some remarks about the general topic and highlight some connections with the related literature. In doing so, I will shamelessly refer to my own work.

The paper begins by saying that there are many, perhaps too many, local governments in the United States. It would be useful to show some international comparisons. I mention this because in a recent paper, with Ed Glaeser and Bruce Sacerdote, we argue that one of the reasons why Americans choose to be governed in such a decentralized way is precisely because they dislike redistributive policies much more than the Europeans do.[1] The reason for this, we argue, lies in two main forces: a large proportion of Americans think that the poor are lazy, while Europeans think the poor are unfortunate. The second reason has to do with racial divides. Americans see redistribution as favoring (in part) members of different racial groups, so they oppose them more than they do in more homogeneous industrial countries. So, some international perspective might be useful here.

This leads to my second point: the paper by Calabrese, Cassidy, and Epple, like 90 percent of the related formal literature in urban economics, focuses on income as a determinant of local politics, and in particular, as a determinant of choice of residence and formation of jurisdictions.

In a series of papers I have written with several co-authors, I emphasize that, in fact, racial conflict may be an even stronger determinant than income of many aspects of local politics and formation of local jurisdictions. That is, individuals may be more willing to share a school, a government, and a social group with members of the same race but of a different income than vice versa. In other words, a rich white person may be more willing to share a local government with a poor white than with a rich black. My sense is that the urban economic literature has not paid enough attention to this point.

Let me publicize a bit my work in this area. Alesina, Baqir, and Easterly show that the provision of local public good is very much affected by racial fragmentation.[2] In more racially fragmented counties, cities, and metropolitan areas, local public spending is less focused on "core" productive public goods, like roads and schools. Racially fragmented cities spend more on law and order and on items that are likely to be patronage.

In Alesina and La Ferrara, we show that social capital is much lower in racially fragmented communities.[3] More specifically, participation in social groups is much lower in racially fragmented communities. In fact, we find that racial fragmentation is a much stronger predictor of social capital than income inequality. To put it differently, a wealthy white is much more likely to join a group that includes poor whites than wealthy blacks, even in cases when groups (like school associations) can decide on issues that have financial repercussions. In another paper we show similar results in regard to trust: trust is much higher in racially homogeneous communities.[4] In fact, as other experimental evidence shows, trust does not travel well across racial lines.

1. Alesina, Glaeser, and Sacerdote (2002, forthcoming).
2. Alesina, Baqir, and Easterly (1999, 2000).
3. Alesina and La Ferrara (2000).
4. Alesina and La Ferrara (2002).

A working paper I wrote recently with Baqir and Hoxby relates most directly to the one by Calabrese, Cassidy, and Epple. In this work we look at the determinants of a number of school districts (and schools) and a number of municipalities and special districts. The idea is that there are economies of scale in having large jurisdictions. The trade-off is against heterogeneity of the population, where the latter can be measured in terms of income, race, ethnic origin, religion, age, and so forth. I quote from the abstract of that paper: "Using both cross-sectional and panel analysis, we find evidence of a significant trade-off between economies of scale and racial heterogeneity. We find a weaker trade-off between economies of scale and income or ethnic heterogeneity. That is, it appears that people are willing to sacrifice the most, in terms of economies of scale, in order to avoid racial heterogeneity in their jurisdictions."[5]

Racial cleavages lead to a multiplication of jurisdictions in two ways. One is that people prefer to have social contact with individuals of the same race, and trust is higher among members of the same racial groups, so sharing a government is easier. The second reason is that members of different races may have different priorities about public goods and public policies.

The bottom line is that a very important factor which explains why the United States has so many local governments is because of racial fractionalization, and this point is missing from the paper. Incidentally, and this goes back to my previous point about international comparisons, if it is true that the United States has so many more local governments (and more powerful ones) than other OECD countries, then the question is: What makes the United States different? I think that racial fragmentation is the answer.

My second point concerns a similarity between some of the issues raised by the paper and issues discussed in recent literature on the size of countries, as in Alesina and Spolaore and Bolton and Roland.[6] This literature discusses a trade-off between economies of scale in country size and heterogeneity of preferences and in income. In that literature as well, one finds that a one-person one-vote rule may lead to a number of governments larger than the first best. Interestingly, these papers look at whether redistributive policies can be used to enforce the optimal number and size of jurisdictions. I was not quite sure whether this point could be handled in this paper.

My third point relates to higher levels of government. Many redistributive policies take place at higher levels of government, such as the state governments and the federal government. I wonder how much higher levels of

5. Alesina, Baqir, and Hoxby (2000).
6. Alesina and Spolaore (1997); Bolton and Roland (1997).

government can undo what local governments do (or vice versa). That is, if I were a wealthy suburbanite, I would wonder how much I could escape redistributive policies, given that the federal government could always, for example, make the income tax more progressive and devote more money to federal programs that favor the poor. I would like to understand better how much the global level of redistributive policies is affected by the fact that there are so many local governments in the United States, given that these local jurisdictions operate under higher levels of government.

My last point is a methodological one and reflects my perspective on empirical work. The paper begins with a very neat and simple model. Very soon, however, specific functional forms and assumptions are needed to advance the argument. Then the model gets even more complicated when voting is introduced, and more assumptions are needed. At the end, the paper presents some functional forms that are simulated, using parameters, defined as "realistic," based on other research. Given how many assumptions and functional forms are incorporated in the analysis, I am not sure the results become "realistic" because a couple of parameters are chosen based on empirical results of others! To put it another way, I am not sure how much weight I should put on the specific numbers in the simulations. Beyond looking at the sign, that is, the qualitative nature of the results, I would not put more emphasis.

This is, of course, a point of view on which reasonable people disagree. For instance, in macroeconomics, my "home field," two very different traditions are present. One uses numerical simulation of complicated general equilibrium dynamic models. The other uses simple regressions. I find the former approach, which is followed also by this paper, a bit of a "black box" so that it is hard to know exactly what drives what in the results.

Nevertheless, this is an excellent paper which goes very far in answering an important question about the organization of governments in the United States. Basically, all of my comments are in the category of "issues to be addressed in future research."

Julie Berry Cullen: This paper addresses an enduring theme in fiscal federalism. The fundamental question is which activities should be undertaken at what level of government, or under what degree of centralization or cooperation. There is an inherent trade-off between the potential gains from more decentralized provision due to the ability to better match individual tastes and the potential distortions that arise as localities compete for residents while providing both services and redistribution. In this paper, this classic tension is framed in the context of a city with surrounding suburbs. Each community provides local public goods (*g*) and per capita transfers (*r*) that are financed by a proportional income tax (*m*) and an ad valorem property tax (*t*). The authors develop a powerful model that allows them to explore the distributions of gains and losses as the central city expands through successive annexations, reducing some and exaggerating other distortions and inefficiencies as populations and policies endogenously evolve. One of the important insights provided by the accompanying simulations is the important role that capitalization plays in constraining political support for such annexations.

This paper also makes a significant contribution to the literature on political economy and local public finance. In developing the theoretical framework, the authors must tackle the thorny issues that arise with endogenous mobility and multiple policy instruments. Their goal is to characterize residential and voting equilibrium outcomes when voters choose communities based on the set of policies, and the set of policies within each community is chosen based on majority rule with attention to the potential impacts on the housing market and population. In this complicated setting, neither across- nor within-community equilibria generally exist. First, with sorting across communities based on tastes for local public goods, there is a tendency for the poor to want to live with the rich, since the rich subsidize the consumption of public goods for the poor (depending on the method of finance). To avoid cycling, where the poor move to be with the rich and the rich move to avoid the poor, previous studies have typically relied on restrictions on preferences (or explicit and implicit restrictions on tax instruments, including zoning). Second, since majority voting does not generally lead to consistent outcomes when there are multiple policy dimensions, most previous studies focus on single policies financed through a single mechanism. The authors of this paper solve both the sorting and voting problems by assuming that household preferences have a specific structure.

In their economy, there is heterogeneity across households on only one dimension: income. Households share the same preferences defined over a publicly provided good (*g*), housing (*h*), and consumption of a numeraire good (*b*). The publicly provided good is separable from private consumption in the household's utility function. Further, utility is linearly homogenous in *h* and *b*. These assumptions yield an indirect utility function linear in income. For renters, indirect utility can be expressed as $V(y) = f(g)(y(1 - m) + r)w(p)$, where *p* is the gross of tax price of housing.

For those who are relative outsiders to this literature (including myself), it is instructive to see how stratification by income across communities arises with preferences of this form. The mechanisms are easiest to describe for communities of renters. Imagine first that there are no per capita transfers or taxes, so that $r = 0$. In this case it is clear that all households will rank policy sets (g, m, r, t) and hence communities in the same way. Further, the premium that individuals would be willing to pay to purchase a unit of housing in a community with a higher level of g or lower level of m does not vary with income.[1] Since all individuals are willing to sacrifice the same percentage of income to live in one community over another (and the two tax instruments impose a burden proportional to income), there are no pressures pushing this economy toward a stable sorting equilibrium. The additive term r drives a wedge between willingness to pay to alter a given policy parameter for households of differing income levels. The relative value of a given increase in r is not equal across households since it is a larger share of income for low-income than for high-income households. The inclusion of the per capita transfer leads to single crossing conditions being satisfied in all of the two-dimensional policy planes (except for the g-p plane).[2] When the authors disallow these per capita grants, they assume that there is an additional linear constant (φ) that serves a similar purpose. The single crossing conditions lead households to self-segregate across communities with given sets of policies according to income.

Though the authors choose not to spend time developing the link between preferences and cross-community sorting, they do provide the intuition for how the assumed structure for preferences determines the sets of policies chosen within communities. As they describe, it is the linearity of the indirect utility function in income that guarantees the existence of a majority voting equilibrium. For any given pair of policy sets, the population can be divided

1. The way to show this more formally is to derive the slope of the indirect indifference curves (MRS) in different policy planes. For example, holding indirect utility and the other policy parameters constant, $dp/dg = ((f(w)/(fw') > 0$. Individuals will be willing to pay more per unit of housing in a community with higher levels of public good expenditure, though the premium is independent of income. Since housing demand is proportional to income, this implies that the share of income individuals are willing to trade for higher levels of g is also independent of income.

2. The MRS in different policy planes is no longer independent of income. For example, holding indirect utility and the other policy parameters constant, $dp/dr = (w/((y(1-m)+r)w') > 0$. The premium a household would be willing to pay per housing unit in a community with a higher per capita grant is decreasing in income (that is, the slope of the indirect indifference curve in the p-r plane (dp/dr) is steeper for lower income households).

into voters who prefer one set to the other strictly according to whether income is above or below some pivotal value. In simultaneous voting over the set of policy instruments, the set preferred by the resident with median income will be the majority vote outcome.

With these key difficulties surmounted, the authors are able to characterize populations and policies with multiple tax and policy instruments in a general equilibrium setting. The simulations based on specific functional forms and calibrated to U.S. data provide elegant results and generate many useful insights. The simplicity of the presentation and discussion is perhaps the paper's greatest weakness. The underlying mechanisms are quite complex and not always well explained. My remaining comments are dedicated to describing a few apparent puzzles that shed light on the type of issues that merit further discussion or exploration

The role of per capita transfer. I have described above the role that r (or an alternative additive term) mechanically plays in leading individuals to self-segregate by income. The authors further show that per capita transfers must be at least as great or higher in lower income communities in equilibrium, and find significant redistribution through the per capita grant occurring in the central city in the simulations. While it is clear why this necessary condition must hold for stability, it is less clear how higher levels of redistribution in low-income communities result from majority voting. Whether the pivotal voter desires a positive level of transfers should be a function of relative income. The median voter would like to redistribute if the ratio of median to mean income is less than one. With a log normal distribution, we are likely to see the opposite of this in the lowest income community that houses the lower tail. It is not clear to me whether interactions with the housing market and other policy variables or something else can explain why this intuition is incorrect.

The question also remains of whether we actually do observe higher per capita expenditures on the poor in central cities. Are central cities really in the business of local redistribution?[3] A further difficulty with evaluating how well the model matches reality is identifying what r is in practice. One way to think about the per capita grant is as any service that is provided that is a perfect substitute for income. Given that local governments are involved primarily in the provision of services, this characterization may not be too inaccurate for many types of expenditures. It is then empirically difficult to distinguish between g and r, since the per capita transfers may take the form

3. Another aspect of the simulation results that does not accord well with my expectations is the lower population density in the central city.

of publicly provided services that have private substitutes (such as recreation complexes or schooling).

The role of alternative tax instruments. The authors mention that one of their contributions is considering not only multiple policies but multiple tax instruments as well. They allow both for property and income taxation. In the absence of endogenous mobility, it is hard to explain why the median voter would ever choose to levy a property tax. Given the assumptions on preferences, demand for housing is proportional (or nearly proportional if r is non-zero) to income. This means that the property tax is equivalent to an income tax as far as the distribution of the burden of the tax is concerned. The only difference is that one distorts the allocation of resources across goods while one does not. It appears from this perspective that the property tax is dominated by the income tax. Exactly what the incentives are to levy property rather than income taxes is not obvious, though the capitalization and housing demand effects must explain why property taxes are attractive.

Commuting cost. The earlier literature in urban economics was built on models of monocentric cities. In these models, commuting costs play a key role. With differential tastes for housing by income, these costs lead to the predictions that the poor will live in the central city and the rich will live in the suburbs. When combined with commuting costs, the preferences described in this paper could generate pressures toward the opposite pattern of sorting. Commuting costs can be thought of as implying a higher income tax in outlying areas. If high-income households are willing to pay a premium for housing in communities with lower income tax rates (which is true when $r > 0$), then this would tend to lead them to choose to live closer to the city. This highlights how much the predicted allocation of individuals across communities is driven by the specific functional form choices, so that realistic extensions may not be easily accommodated without disrupting the system as a whole.

The above are examples of issues that are part of the background in this paper. Future work that pushes farther in linking this model and results to underlying principles and mechanisms has the potential to greatly increase our understanding of the formation of and interactions between jurisdictions.

References

Alesina, Alberto, Reza Baqir, and William Easterly. 1999. "Public Goods and Ethnic Divisions." *Quarterly Journal of Economics* 114 (4): 1243–84.

———. 2000. "Redistributive Public Employment." *Journal of Urban Economics* 48 (2): 219–41.

Alesina, Alberto, Reza Baqir, and Caroline Hoxby. 2000. "Political Jurisdictions in Heterogenous Communities." Working Paper 7859. Cambridge, Mass.: National Bureau of Economic Research (August).

Alesina, Alberto, Edward Glaeser, and Bruce Sacerdote. 2002. "Why Doesn't the US Have a European Style Welfare State?" *Brookings Papers on Economic Activity* (forthcoming).

Alesina, Alberto, and Eliana La Ferrara. 2000. "Participation in Heterogeneous Communities." *Quarterly Journal of Economics* 115 (3): 847–904.

———. 2002. "Who Trusts Others?" *Journal of Public Economics* (forthcoming).

Alesina, Alberto, and Enrico Spolaore. 1997. "On the Number and Size of Nations." *Quarterly Journal of Economics* 112 (4): 1027–56.

Bolton, Patrick, and Gerard Roland. 1997. "The Break-Up of Nations: A Political-Economic Analysis." *Quarterly Journal of Economics* 112 (4):1057–90.

Brown, Charles C., and Wallace E. Oates. 1987. "Assistance to the Poor in a Federal System." *Journal of Public Economics* 32 (3): 307–30.

Bucovetsky, Sam. 1982. "Inequality in the Local Public Sector." *Journal of Political Economy* 90 (1): 128–45.

———. 1991. "Choosing Tax Rates and Public Expenditure Levels Using Majority Rule." *Journal of Public Economics* 46 (1): 113–31.

Calabrese, Stephen M. 2001. "Local Redistribution Financed by Income Tax." *Public Finance Review* 29 (4): 259–303.

Calabrese, Stephen M., and Dennis Epple. 2001. "Local Government Tax Structure and State Mandated Tax Limits." Working Paper. University of South Florida.

Cassidy, Glenn. 1990. "Mobility and Choice: Three Essays on the Political Economy of Local Government." Ph.D. dissertation, Carnegie Mellon University.

Cassidy, Glenn, Dennis Epple, and Thomas Romer. 1989. "Redistribution by Local Governments in a Monocentric Urban Area." *Regional Science and Urban Economics* 19 (3): 421–54.

Donahue, John D. 1997. "Tiebout? Or Not Tiebout? The Market Metaphor and America's Devolution Debate." *Journal of Economic Perspectives* 11 (4): 73–81.

Ellickson, Bryan. 1971. "Jurisdictional Fragmentation and Residential Choice." *American Economic Review* 61 (2): 334–39.

Ellickson, Robert C. 1982. "Cities and Homeowners Associations." *University of Pennsylvania Law Review* 130 (3): 1519–80.

Epple, Dennis, Radu Filimon, and Thomas Romer. 1984. "Equilibrium among Local Jurisdictions: Toward an Integrated Treatment of Voting and Residential Choice." *Journal of Public Economics* 24 (August): 281–308.

Epple, Dennis, and Thomas Romer. 1989. "On the Flexibility of Municipal Boundaries." *Journal of Urban Economics* 26 (3): 307–19.

———. 1991. "Mobility and Redistribution." *Journal of Political Economy* 99 (4): 828–58.

Epple, Dennis, Thomas Romer, and Holger Sieg. 2001. "Interjurisdictional Sorting and Majority Rule: An Empirical Analysis." *Econometrica* 69 (6): 1437–65.

Epple, Dennis, and Holger Sieg. 1999. "Estimating Equilibrium Models of Local Jurisdictions." *Journal of Political Economy* 107 (4): 645–81.

Epple, Dennis, and Allan Zelenitz. 1981. "The Implications of Competition among Jurisdictions: Does Tiebout Need Politics?" *Journal of Political Economy* 89 (6): 1197–1217.

Fernandez, Raquel, and Richard Rogerson. 1996. "Income Distribution, Communities, and the Quality of Public Education." *Quarterly Journal of Economics* 111 (1): 135–64.

———. 1998. "Public Education and Income Distribution: A Dynamic Quantitative Evaluation of Education-Finance Reform." *American Economic Review* 88 (4): 813–33.

Glazer, Amihai, Esko Niskanen, and Suzanne Scotchmer. 1997. "On the Uses of Club Theory: Preface to the Club Theory Symposium." *Journal of Public Economics* 65 (1): 3–7.

Goodspeed, Timothy. 1989. "A Re-examination of the Use of Ability to Pay Taxes by Local Governments." *Journal of Public Economics* 38 (3): 319–42.

Harmon, Oskar R. 1988. "The Income Elasticity of Demand for Single-Family Owner-Occupied Housing: An Empirical Reconciliation." *Journal of Urban Economics* 38 (24): 75–85.

Henderson, J. Vernon. 1994. "Community Choice of Revenue Instruments." *Regional Science and Urban Economics* 24 (2): 159–83.

Inman, Robert P. 1989. "The Local Decision to Tax: Evidence from Large U.S. Cities." *Regional Science and Urban Economics* 19 (3): 455–91.

———. 1995. "How to Have a Fiscal Crisis: Lessons from Philadelphia." *American Economic Review Papers and Proceedings* 85 (2): 378–83.

Inman, Robert P., and Daniel Rubinfeld. 1997. "Rethinking Federalism." *Journal of Economic Perspectives* 11 (4): 43–64.

International City Management Association. 1993. *The Municipal Yearbook* (60). Washington.

Johnson, William R. 1988. "Income Redistribution in a Federal System." *American Economic Review* 78 (3): 570–73.

Mieszkowski, Peter, and Edwin S. Mills. 1993. "The Causes of Metropolitan Suburbanization." *Journal of Economic Perspectives* 7 (3): 135-147.

Myers, Gordon M. 1990. "Optimality, Free Mobility, and the Regional Authority in a Federation." *Journal of Public Economics* 43 (1): 107–21.

Nechyba, Thomas J. 1997. "Local Property and State Income Taxes: The Role of Interjurisdictional Competition and Collusion." *Journal of Political Economy.* 105 (2): 351–84.

———. 1999. "School Finance Induced Migration and Stratification Patterns: The Impact of Private School Vouchers." *Journal of Public Economic Theory* 1 (1): 5–50.

———. 2000. "Mobility, Targeting, and Private School Vouchers." *American Economic Review* 90 (1): 130–46.

Orr, Larry. 1976. "Income Transfers as a Public Good: An Application to AFDC." *American Economic Review* 66 (3): 359–71.

Ostrom, Vincent, Charles M. Tiebout, and Robert Warren. 1961. "The Organization of Government in Metropolitan Areas: A Theoretical Inquiry." *American Political Science Review* 55 (4): 831–42.

Plott, Charles R. 1967. "A Notion of Equilibrium and Its Possibility under Majority Rule." *American Economic Review* 57 (4): 787–806.

Rusk, David. 1995. *Cities without Suburbs.* 2d edition. Johns Hopkins University Press.

———. 1999. *Inside Game/OutsideGame: Winning Strategies for Saving Urban America.* Brookings.

Steen, Robert C. 1987. "Effects of the Property Tax in Urban Areas." *Journal of Urban Economics* 21 (2): 146–65.

Stephens, G. Ross, and Nelson Wikstrom. 2000. *Metropolitan Government and Governance: Theoretical Perspectives, Empirical Analysis, and the Future.* Oxford University Press.

Tiebout, Charles. 1956. "A Pure Theory of Local Expenditures." *Journal of Political Economy* 64 (5): 416–24.

Vigdor, Jacob. 2001. "Median Voters, Marginal Residents, and Property Tax Limitation." Sanford Institute Working Paper SAN01–07. Duke University.

Westhoff, Frank. 1977. "Existence of Equilibrium in Economies with a Local Public Good." *Journal of Economic Theory* 14 (February): 84–112.

Wildasin, David. 1991. "Income Redistribution in a Common Labor Market." *American Economic Review* 81 (4): 757–74.

Zodrow, George. 1984. "The Incidence of Metropolitan Property Tax Base Sharing and Rate Equalization." *Journal of Urban Economics* 15 (2): 210–29.

ANDREW F. HAUGHWOUT
Federal Reserve Bank of New York

ROBERT P. INMAN
Wharton School, University of Pennsylvania, and the National Bureau of Economic Research

Should Suburbs Help Their Central City?

SHOULD SUBURBS HELP finance their center city's core public services? This is a long-standing policy question in U.S. urban public finance and an issue of no less importance in other countries. Toronto recently merged its financing and governance with its surrounding suburbs. In configuring its new fiscal system, South Africa opted for a form of metropolitan financing that "twins" wealthy suburbs with less wealthy central cities. What are the arguments for suburb-to-city fiscal assistance, or stronger still, suburb plus city fiscal mergers?

Perhaps the most familiar argument is that suburb-to-city assistance corrects for the underprovision of city-produced public goods that benefit suburban residents, such as city subways and buses, airports, and museums.[1] When spillovers are significant and suburban residents benefit from city-provided public infrastructure, they should contribute to the financing of such infrastructures. However, efficient financing favors user fees and average cost pricing rather than intergovernmental transfers.[2]

Numerous colleagues have contributed to this research. Most important, Richard Voith generously shared his city and suburban data with us. We also thank seminar participants at the American Economic Association, Brookings, Colorado, Duke, Federal Reserve Bank of Philadelphia, the New School, Stanford University, and Wharton. We received very able research assistance from Silvia Ellis, Alison Glusman, and Minsun Park. The results and conclusions summarized in this paper are solely those of the authors and do not reflect official opinions of the Federal Reserve Bank of New York, the Federal Reserve System, or the NBER.

1. The spillovers from education, city police and fire protection, recreation, and trash removal are likely to be small. On education, see Acemoglu and Angrist (1999); on police protection, see Thaler (1978) and Hellman and Naroff (1979).

2. The possible exception to this rule may be financing of city streets where user fees may be difficult to collect. In this case, intergovernmental transfers to fund infrastructure might be appropriate; Small (1992). But even here, parking fees might be a useful "third-best" policy; Arnott, de Palma, and Lindsey (1991).

A second familiar argument is that city poverty is a metropolitan-wide concern and suburban residents ought to contribute towards meeting the needs of their city's poor. National programs define a common floor for income support, above which state and local governments can make supplemental contributions. In the presence of redistributive spillover benefits, however, city transfers will be too low relative to the efficient level of redistribution if individuals prefer to redistribute to lower-income households in close geographical proximity.[3] While theoretically compelling, this argument lacks a credible mechanism to reveal suburban preferences for redistribution to the inner city poor. To the extent we rely upon the political process to provide a measure of these preferences, current state funding for city poverty may be efficient. Furthermore, if there is a problem, an appropriate fiscal institution— state government—is already in place to correct it.

U.S. mayors have recently advanced a third argument for suburb-to-city fiscal assistance. The mayors argue that suburban residents need an economically vibrant central city to support their own real incomes, claiming, "Economies don't stop at the city's edge."[4] The mayors cite the now well-documented positive correlation between the average income of city and suburban residents in U.S. metropolitan areas. Their argument moves beyond correlation to causation, however. They maintain that a weak city economy *causes* a weak suburban economy and one of the central causes of a weak city economy is weak city public finance. A fiscally weak city has high tax rates and low public services that induce mobile firms and households to leave the city, undermining the city's private economy and thus, the mayors argue, the economy of the region as a whole. Suburb-to-city transfers that strengthen city finances will strengthen the city's economy, which enhances, in turn, suburban residents' private incomes. This paper seeks to evaluate the economic validity of this argument.

In the next section, we outline how weak city finances might adversely affect both city and suburban economic strength. Suburban residents benefit from production advantages due to agglomeration economies within the city that lower the cost of city-produced goods and services. Inefficiencies in the central city's public sector can counteract the benefits of city agglomeration economies by encouraging mobile firms and households to leave the city. Suburban households may prefer to transfer funds to their center cities to pro-

---

3. Pauly (1973).
4. See Eric Schmitt,"Cities and Their Suburbs Are Seen Growing as Units," *New York Times*, July 10, 2001, Section B, p. 10.

tect city agglomeration economies and maintain low-cost city-produced goods and services that support both city and suburban economic well-being.

The following section provides empirical evidence on these issues. First, we document the close interdependencies between central city and suburban economies for U.S. metropolitan statistical areas (MSAs). We then test for the effects of weak city fiscal institutions—strong public employee unions, weak mayors, poverty obligations, and redistributive tax structures—on city and suburban economies. We find that such institutions reduce the growth of city incomes, populations, and home values. More telling, we find those same *city* fiscal institutions also slow the growth of *suburban* incomes, population, and home values. These effects are statistically significant and quantitatively important.

We then examine these same issues using a structural model of a typical city-suburb metropolitan area. Using the best available microeconometric evidence of firm, household, and government behavior, we construct a general equilibrium model of an "open" metropolitan economy with central city agglomeration economies, residential suburbs, and fully mobile firms and households. The model allows us to simulate the effects of each weak central city fiscal institution on city and suburban incomes, populations, and land values. For plausible specifications of firm technologies, household utilities, and local politics, we are able to replicate the estimated adverse effects of each weak institution on city and suburban incomes, populations, and land values. These results suggest that claims that inefficient and redistributive city fiscal institutions can adversely impact suburban welfare must be taken seriously.

We conclude that when city agglomeration economies are important and city fiscal institutions lead to inefficient allocations or require significant fiscal redistributions, there is a plausible case for suburb-to-city aid. The final section offers some suggestions for how such assistance might be given.

A New Argument for Suburban Aid to Central Cities

There are two potential paths from the city economy to suburban residents' economic welfare: commuter jobs and wages and the market price of city-produced goods and services purchased by suburban firms and residents.[5] While potentially important, suburb-to-city commuting has declined over the

5. Voith (1993) presents evidence on how city commuter jobs impact suburban home values. We explore the second path in this article.

past thirty years, while the links between city and suburban economies appear to have tightened. For a typical suburban resident, the primary economic advantage of a strong city economy lies in the ability of city firms to provide valued goods and services at prices lower than (or equivalently, at a quality higher than) what might be available from suburban firms or firms outside the metropolitan region. City firms can supply low-cost goods and services to suburban residents if they have an economic or transportation cost advantage relative to suburban firms or firms in other cities.

Economic advantages arise from two sources: natural advantages, such as the city's proximity to an important production input, such as power, public infrastructure, or raw materials, or agglomeration advantages, facilitated by firm or household density within the city. For most U.S. cities today, agglomeration economies are the likely source. High firm density within the same industry—called Marshallian agglomeration in honor of Alfred Marshall's initial analysis of this advantage—leads to lower shipping costs for firm inputs when there are economies of scale in transportation.[6] Firm density may also lower labor costs in industries with firm-specific demand uncertainty but easily transferable labor between firms, such as in the fashion, entertainment, and "dot.com" industries. Having many firms in the same local labor market reduces the unemployment risk to workers with unique talents and therefore allows all firms to pay a lower wage. High firm density in the same industry may also encourage supplier innovation and specialization, again lowering firm production costs. Low-cost production technologies are likely to be more quickly copied when firms and workers are in close proximity. These idea "spillovers" may occur across industries as well as within industries, an advantage called Jacobian agglomeration for Jane Jacobs's insightful analysis of growing city economies.[7]

Household density within cities may give rise to agglomeration advantages in the provision of consumer services such as restaurants, theater, and sports and music entertainment. When city residential density provides sufficient numbers of like-minded consumers to sustain active center city dining and entertainment alternatives, suburban residents benefit from their proximity to these city-produced services. With this argument in mind, Edward Glaeser has suggested that the long-run economic future for many U.S. cities may lie in their ability to become successful providers of consumer services to city and suburban residents.[8]

6. Marshall (1890).
7. Jacobs (1969).
8. Glaeser (2000).

A growing body of empirical research demonstrates the importance of agglomeration economies within regional economies. Mark Beardsell and Vernon Henderson find that doubling industry employment density raises overall plant (total factor) productivity by 6 percent during the first year of the increase and by as much as 17 percent after four years.[9] Using county-level data, Antonio Ciccone and Robert Hall find that doubling aggregate employment density increases the productivity of all workers by an average of 6 percent. Ciccone and Hall also estimate that at least half of the variation in average labor productivity across states can be attributed to differences in industry density and the resulting advantages of agglomeration.[10] Ciccone finds results consistent with the Ciccone-Hall analysis for small economic regions in Europe.[11]

Increased firm density may stimulate higher outputs in the long run as well. Edward Glaeser and others, and Vernon Henderson, Ari Kuncoro, and Matt Turner find evidence that increased employment density leads to growing employment levels, particularly in high-tech industries.[12] Using a large national sample, James Rauch finds that after controlling for worker and house characteristics, both the average worker's wage and the average home's value are higher in MSAs with higher average levels of education and work experience.[13]

Current evidence also suggests that the benefits of agglomeration economies accrue within modest spatial boundaries, probably no farther than the geographical distance of a typical U.S. county. Although U.S. employment is becoming increasingly decentralized in metropolitan areas, the important exception to this pattern is "idea-intensive" industries whose employees have college and professional degrees and whose production process involves significant "face-to-face" interactions. Examples include the creative arts, finance and business services, science and technology, health care, and government.[14] These industries are disproportionately located within central cities. They are also the industries where agglomeration advantages are most important. Stuart Rosenthal and William Strange find that the locational advantages of agglomeration are strongest within one mile of the center of current firm concentration and are exhausted within five miles.[15]

9. Beardsell and Henderson (1999).
10. Ciccone and Hall (1996).
11. Ciccone (2002).
12. Glaeser and others (1992); Henderson, Kuncoro, and Turner (1995).
13. Rauch (1993).
14. Glaeser and Kahn (2001).
15. Rosenthal and Strange (2002).

Suburban Benefits from Agglomeration Economies

Suburban residents living near a productive central city gain from their ability to buy city-produced goods and services at comparatively low prices. If x_s^c is suburban consumption per resident of goods and services produced by central city firms, then suburban residents or retailers save the difference between the cost of buying these goods from city producers rather than from a less efficient suburban or "outside" producer. If k^o and k^c denote the production costs of a unit of a good provided by non-city and city firms respectively, and t^o and t^c denote the corresponding transit costs for non-city and city firms to ship to (or travel from) the suburbs, then the income or cost savings to suburban residents or retailers from an economically efficient central city will be

$$Z_s = x_s^c \cdot [(k^o + t^o) - (k^c + t^c)],$$

where Z_s is the average economic benefit enjoyed by the suburban residents or retailers living or conducting business near an efficient central city.[16] Changes in the city economy that either reduce x_s^c or raise k^c or t^c will reduce Z_s and make suburban residents and retailers worse off economically.

A potentially important determinant of x_s^c, k^c, and t^c is the efficiency of the central city's public sector. Just as firms may be drawn to a central city to be part of its efficient private-sector production network, they may be repelled by an inefficient or redistributive public sector. The effect will be a smaller city, lower city home values, and most likely lower city incomes. The smaller city economy means fewer exports to the suburbs ($x_s^c\downarrow$) and possibly higher production and transit costs ($k^c\uparrow$ and $t^c\uparrow$). The advantage of living in the suburbs is thereby reduced ($Z_s\downarrow$) and suburban population and employment, home values, and suburban incomes decline.

Figure 1 summarizes this argument more formally.[17] The profit curve denoted as $\Pi(\cdot) = 0$ and the utility curve denoted as $V(\cdot) = V_0$ show all the combinations of local land rents and local wages sufficient to hold local firm (excess) profits and resident utilities at their outside, next best options. Firms and households are freely mobile between all locations, within and outside the MSA. In equilibrium, firms must earn zero excess profits and households must receive the utility of V_0 in each location. This occurs at the intersection

16. See appendix A for the formal specification of this measure of suburban benefits.
17. A formal specification of the argument is provided below in "A Structural Analysis" and appendix C. The analysis here was first presented in Rosen (1979) and then developed fully by Roback (1982) and Gyourko and Tracy (1991b). See Haughwout and Inman (2001) for an application of the analysis to a wide range of city fiscal policies.

Figure 1. Rent-Wage Equilibrium in an Open Jurisdiction

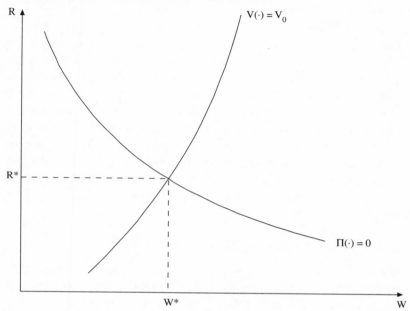

of the $\Pi(\cdot)$ and $V(\cdot)$ curves, which defines local land values (R^*) and local wages paid to resident workers (W^*) that are sufficient to keep firms and households within the location. In our analysis, the relevant locations are the central city and each of its surrounding suburbs.

Exogenous changes in the fiscal and economic environments of the city and its suburbs shift their respective $\Pi(\cdot)$ and the $V(\cdot)$ curves and lead to equilibrium changes in city and suburban land rents and wages. For example, inefficient or redistributive city finances will lead to higher taxes or possibly lower public services for city firms and households. Firms will only stay within the city if their rents and wages fall to compensate for weak city finances, represented in figure 1 by a downward shift in the city firms' $\Pi_c(\cdot) = 0$ curve. If all the adverse effects of weak city finances fall only on city firms, then only the $\Pi_c(\cdot) = 0$ curve shifts downward and in the new equilibrium rents and wages both fall. If the burden of weak city finances falls on city households, then a fall in rents or a rise in wages will be needed to hold residents within the city, represented by a downward shift in the residents' utility $V_c(\cdot) = V_0$ schedule in figure 1. Most likely, the city will share the burdens of weak finances across firms and households; thus both $\Pi_c(\cdot) = 0$ and $V_c(\cdot) = V_0$

shift downward. In this case, city land values unambiguously decline, but we cannot predict whether city wages will rise or fall.

Figure 1 also applies to any suburb, where now $\Pi_s(\cdot) = 0$ and the $V_s(\cdot) = V_0$ must be specified for each suburban community. The smaller and now more expensive city economy means less city output and higher average prices of city-produced goods and services for suburban residents and firms. Suburban retail firms' costs rise and profits fall and thus $\Pi_s(\cdot) = 0$ shifts downward. Suburban residents who shop directly within the city must now pay more for city produced goods and services or buy more goods from expensive non-city suppliers; thus, $V_s(\cdot) = V_0$ falls. The downward shifts in $\Pi_s(\cdot) = 0$ and/or $V_s(\cdot) = V_0$ imply an unambiguous decline in suburban land values. Suburban resident wages may rise or fall. If weak city finances matter, then we expect to see lower suburban land rents, fewer suburban residents, and possibly lower suburban wages and incomes.

Determinants of Central City Fiscal Performance

Four fiscal institutions seem particularly important for determining the fiscal performance of city governments: the city's poor population and state and federal unfunded mandates to provide city services to poor residents, bargaining rules for public employee unions, local electoral rules that define budgetary incentives, and the redistributive nature of the local tax structure.

First, city poverty affects mobile city households and business in two ways: Fiscally, city governments use redistributive public spending to contribute to the welfare of poverty households. For example, Anita Summers and Lara Jakubowski find that Philadelphia spending for state-mandated health and foster childcare services increased city taxes by 7.6 percent in 1995, up from 6.7 percent in 1985.[18] Thomas Downes and Thomas Pogue have estimated that the budgetary consequences of poverty range from 2 percent to as much as 25 percent of school spending to maintain test score performance in the average urban school district.[19] The important non-fiscal consequence of poverty is crime; higher rates of city crime discourage household and firm location.[20]

Second, a labor bargaining environment that favors city public employees imposes additional fiscal burdens on city taxpayers without compensating benefits. Since public employee unionization was in place in most large

18. Summers and Jakubowski (1997).
19. Downes and Pogue (1994).
20. Glaeser and Sacerdote (1999); Cullen and Levitt (1999).

cities by 1980, the large spending effects from conversion to unionization are no longer relevant. The issue today is how well the city's labor budget can be managed in a union environment. State rules governing local labor bargaining are key. Richard Freeman and Robert Valletta find that in states that explicitly require cities to bargain with their public employees, public employee wages are from 3 to 8 percent higher than in states that allow unionization but do not require bargaining.[21] Since payrolls constitute about 60 percent of most city budgets, strongly unionized cities will see an increase in current accounts city spending, and therefore city taxes, of about 2 to 5 percent.

Third, how city taxpayers elect their local representatives has important implications for city budgets. When budgetary powers are diffused, as in city governments run by neighborhood-elected city councils and institutionally weak mayors, budget agreements require coalitions of representatives. To reach agreement, governments often form "universal" coalitions in which each member is allowed to select a preferred level of spending for all projects that directly benefit his or her constituents, typically, recreation, streets, libraries, and school maintenance. Unfortunately, when benefits are localized but costs are shared among taxpayers throughout the city, there arises a "common pool" problem and a strong tendency for all representatives to select inefficiently large projects.[22] For a reasonable price elasticity of demand for neighborhood services, overspending may be as much as 40 percent of current neighborhood services or about 3 percent of the city's own source revenues.[23]

Fourth, the city's tax structure and its inherited tax base determine the degree of fiscal redistribution among city households and between the city's

21. Freeman and Valletta (1988) and Gyourko and Tracy (1991a).

22. This argument has been formalized and applied to budgetary politics at the federal level (Inman and Fitts, 1990); at the state government level (Gilligan and Matsusaka, 1995); at the local level for Los Angeles (Cox and Tutt, 1984); and for Philadelphia (Inman, 1995). Each study shows a clear upward bias to government spending as the problems of diffused budgetary powers become more pronounced.

23. A reasonable price elasticity of demand for neighborhood services is $-.40$ (Inman, 1979). The marginal cost for \$1 of services is \$1. The residential "tax price" defined as the ratio of resident's own tax base to the average tax base in the city ($= b/B$) is $\cong .50$ for middle-class city residents; see appendix B. Common pool budgeting reduces this tax price still further to approximately $(1/n) \cdot (b/B)$, where n is the number of district-elected city council representatives whose constituents share city taxes. In Philadelphia, n equals 10, so the tax price falls to .05 for these representatives; they form a majority on city council. This is a 90 percent fall in the price of residential services, which implies a 36 percent increase in government spending: $36\% = -90\% \times -.40$. In Philadelphia, this 36 percent increase in spending is approximately 3 percent of the city's own source revenues.

business and residential sectors. City tax structures, which are set by state law, define the nature of local tax redistribution.[24] City residents' and firms' tax prices determine the level of redistribution. Typically, a city resident or firm contributes to each dollar of city spending according to their "tax price," the ratio of their tax base, b, relative to the city's average tax base, B: b/B. City residents with higher-than-average tax prices subsidize consumption of city services by residents with lower-than-average tax prices, typically low-income residents. Thus, the tax costs to richer taxpayers increase with the percentage of the city's population who are poor. Using our sample of U.S. cities (described below), we find that an *increase* of one standard deviation in the city's percentage of residents living below poverty increases tax payments for our sample's average middle-class city resident by 2 percent.[25] The redistribution from city firms to residents is also important.[26] Capital-intensive manufacturing properties provide the most redistribution, and we find that a *decrease* of one standard deviation in the share of city manufacturing jobs increases city middle-class tax payments by about 2 percent.[27]

Taken together, the increase in a typical middle-class city household's total tax burden because of unfunded poverty mandates on city and school budgets (7 percent), public employee unions with strong bargaining powers (2 to 5 percent), weak mayoral control over budgets (3 percent), and redistributive tax structures coupled with declining economies (2 percent plus 2 percent) may be as much as 15 to 20 percent. The added tax burden on city businesses is likely to be as large. Haughwout and others estimate the elasticity of city jobs with respect to city tax rates at $-.2$ to $-.5$.[28] A 20 percent rise in city taxes implies a 4 to 10 percent fall in city jobs. If the lost jobs are in industries where production and consumption agglomerations are important, production efficiency and city output will decline significantly and the average price of

24. Inman and Rubinfield (1979); Inman (1989).

25. The city resident's tax burden is defined as the product of the resident's tax price times city spending: Tax burden = $(b/B) \cdot$ Spending. Appendix B provides a useful approximation for b/B: $b/B \cong 1/[1 - .6(\text{CPOV} + \text{COLD}) + (1.02 + .58 \cdot \text{CMAN})]$. Evaluated at mean values for the rate of city poverty (CPOV = .18), percent elderly (COLD = .13), and percent of jobs in manufacturing (CMAN = .14) implies a value of $b/B = .52$. Average city plus school spending in our sample is about $5,000 per household. Thus the typical resident's tax burden will be $2,600. A one standard deviation increase in CPOV to .24 implies a new tax price of $b/B = .53$ and new tax burden of $2,650, or an increase of 2 percent.

26. Ladd (1975).

27. Reducing the share of city jobs in manufacturing from its mean of 0.14 by one standard deviation to 0.07 changes the typical city resident's tax price from 0.52 to 0.53 and the resident's tax burden from $2,600 to $2,650—again a 2 percent increase. See footnote 25 above.

28. Haughwout and others (2000); see also Bartik's survey (1991).

Table 1. Correlations between the City and the Suburbs[a]

Year	Home value	Population	Income
1970	.311**	.547**	.559**
1980	.554**	.544**	.365**
1990	.696**	.526**	.398**
Growth rate between			
1970 and 1980	.712**	.493**	.678**
1980 and 1990	.849**	.420**	.600**

a. A city corresponds to the largest central city in each MSA, while the suburbs correspond to the balance of the MSA not in the central city. The full sample includes 252 MSAs.
** Significantly different from zero with 99 percent confidence.

city-produced goods and services will rise, harming both city and suburban residents and firms. Conceptually, the mayors who favor suburb-to-city transfers have an argument. In the following section we provide a more direct test of their conjecture.

Empirical Evidence

Table 1 presents strong evidence that city and suburban economic fortunes are tightly linked. Correlations between the levels of city and suburban populations, incomes, and home values for 252 U.S. metropolitan areas for 1970, 1980, and 1990 are all positive and statistically significant, as are correlations of growth rates of city and suburban population, income, and home values over the two decades for which we have data.[29] The increase in the correlation of city and suburban home values over the three decades is particularly striking. We find it suggestive that city and suburban home values became more closely linked over the same period that industries with agglomeration economies grew in economic importance.

Our empirical analysis seeks to explain changes within MSA private economies over the 1980s as a consequence of city finances. We regress the log values of city and suburban average home values, populations, and resident average incomes (denoted by the vectors $\ln Y_{crt}$ and $\ln Y_{srt}$ for city c or suburb s in region r and year t) on vectors of exogenous city (X_{crt}), suburban

29. We were unable to include city and suburban employment in our analysis because data on the spatial location of employment is only available on a county basis. Brooks and Summers (no date) have created a city-suburban employment series from U.S. Census *Journey to Work* files for sixty metropolitan areas and their work shows the same strong positive correlations between city and suburban jobs as we find for our larger sample for city and suburban populations, incomes, and home values.

(X_{srt}), and metropolitan-wide (X_{mrt}) determinants of area economic perform-ance.[30] The specification also allows for year and region fixed effects in seven national regions (New England, Mid-Atlantic, Midwest, Southeast, Plains, Mountain, and West Coast). We specify the model in first differences between 1980 and 1990 to control for city-specific and suburb-specific fixed effects:

(1) $\ln Y_{cr90} - \ln Y_{cr80} = \Delta Y_{cr.} = \Delta \Phi_{cr} + \gamma_c \cdot \Delta X_{cr} + \gamma_s \cdot \Delta X_{sr} + \gamma_m \cdot \Delta X_{mr} + \Delta \epsilon_{cr}$,

(2) $\ln Y_{sr90} - \ln Y_{sr80} = \Delta Y_{sr.} = \Delta \Phi_{sr} + \tau_c \cdot \Delta X_{cr} + \tau_s \cdot \Delta X_{sr} + \tau_m \cdot \Delta X_{mr} + \Delta \epsilon_{sr}$.

Remaining unmeasured effects that might influence city and suburban out-comes are specified by the vector of error terms $\Delta \epsilon_{cr}$ and $\Delta \epsilon_{sr}$, which we assume are uncorrelated with our included independent variables and which have means of zero and uniform constant variances unique to each dependent variable. We allow the errors to be correlated across each of the six depend-ent variables. The constant term in each of the first difference equations measures the average effect of the economic events of the decade 1980 to 1990 on city and suburban economies generally and in each of our seven regions.

We define changes in city finances (ΔX_{cr}) through four measures of the cen-tral city's fiscal institutions. The variables ΔX_{cr} appear as determinants of both city and suburban economic performance. We measure the fiscal conse-quences of poverty mandates by changes in the percent of the city's population below poverty. Our first difference specification should remove the fixed effects of federal and state unfunded mandates that existed in both 1980 and 1990 as well as control for level effects of having a differentially large city poverty population. Given mandates, an increase in the *city's percent in poverty* will increase aggregate redistributive city and school spending and thus taxation within the city. We expect increases in the rate of city poverty to adversely affect the growth rate of city population, city home value appreci-ation, and perhaps the rate of growth of average city incomes.

We measure the strength of public employee unionization in the city by an indicator variable equal to one if the city is located within a state with an explicit "duty to bargain" for police, fire, and blue collar employees, and zero, otherwise. Using state duty-to-bargain rules for police, fire, and blue-collar employees to identify a union fiscal effect requires the plausible condition that these rules have their primary fiscal impact only on city governments.[31] State rules creating *strong city unions* apply statewide, but the rules have important budgetary consequences only for central cities. Unionization of public

30. All monetary figures are in 1982 dollars.
31. Ichniowski (1988); Brown and Medoff (1988).

employees other than teachers is very limited in the suburbs. Most suburbs contract out services provided by blue-collar workers. Suburban police forces are generally small and not worth unionizing. Suburban fire departments are also small and often voluntary organizations. We expect the presence of strong city unions to have negative effects on city economies.

We measure weak city budgetary institutions by an indicator variable called *weak city governance* that takes a value of one if the city government budget is set by a city council with a majority of members elected from neighborhood wards and whose mayor is elected from the city council. Such city governments tend to fall prey to the problems of "common pool" budgeting, leading to inefficiently large spending for neighborhood projects. These projects typically favor low and moderate income residents over middle and upper income residents and businesses.[32] We anticipate the presence of weak city governance will have a negative effect on the city economy.

We use an approximation of the city's middle class residents' *tax price* for property taxation to measure the redistributive structure of city taxation. Tax price is the ratio of a middle class resident's home value (b) to the average value of property in the city (B):

$$(b/B) \cong 1/[1 - .6(CPOV + COLD) + (1.02 + .58 \cdot CMAN)],$$

where *CPOV* is the percent of the city's population who live in poverty, *COLD* is the percent of the city's population who are 65 or older, and *CMAN* is the percent of the city's workforce employed in the manufacturing sector.[33] In this specification, the middle-class taxpayer's burden rises with city poverty and the share of city residents who are elderly and declines as more of the city's job base is employed in the more capital intensive (and presumably property tax-rich) manufacturing sector. An increase in city tax price raises the cost of public services and drives middle-class residents and, for an analogous specification for businesses, firms from the city. We expect increases in the city property tax price to have adverse effects on city economies.

While our measures of inefficient and redistributive city finances are expected to depress the city's economy, their effects on the suburban economy are not clear a priori. An important methodological consideration for establishing causation from city finances to suburban economies is the exogeneity of our four city fiscal institution variables. We control for endogeneity of changes in the city poverty rate through the use of instrumental variable esti-

32. Inman (1995).
33. See appendix B for the derivation of this approximation.

mation (detailed below, table 3). The legal institutions creating strong city unions and weak city governance are well established and have been in place for decades before our sample period. We also respecify changes in resident tax prices to remove the effect of changes in city poverty and the percent of city residents who are elderly, leaving changes in the percent of jobs in manufacturing as the remaining source of variation in resident tax prices. City declines in manufacturing jobs is a historical trend based on past employment histories of the cities; we assume changes in this component of tax price are exogenous.

We also include in each regression changes in suburban (ΔX_{sr}) and metropolitan-wide (ΔX_{mr}) fiscal and economic variables to control for changes in city and suburban economic performance that are not related to city finances.[34] The ΔX_{sr} variables include changes in the rate of *suburban poverty* and the number of *suburban school districts* within the MSA. The ΔX_{mr} variables include: Changes in the MSA's ratio of state-to-local general revenue aid divided by all local governments' own source revenues as a measure of *state aid* support for local governments; an indicator variable of *suburban support* for county services for whether the suburbs and the city are part of a single country and thus share in the financing of county services; an indicator variable for whether the state enforces an explicit duty-to-bargain for local teachers creating *strong teacher unions*; the number of *airline hubs* at the MSA's airport(s); an indicator variable for whether the MSA contains both East-West and North-South *interstate highways*; 1980 *city population density* and *suburban population density* as controls for the availability of residential land in the city and its surrounding suburbs; and finally, the MSA's average annual number of *heating days* and *cooling days* as controls for climatic attractiveness.[35]

We define each city-suburban metropolitan area to include the counties of each central city's MSA for 1990. This holds MSA land area fixed in our analysis, allowing us to maintain a hypothesis of full market capitalization to interpret our coefficients in the home value equations as measures of city and

34. Appendix B lists the means, standard deviations, and sources for all variables included in X_{crt}, X_{srt}, and X_{mrt}.

35. In addition, we also include in each city and suburban regression the level of each *dependent variable lagged* (1980) from which changes for the decade are measured. A positive (negative) coefficient of the lagged dependent variable suggests high and low growth cities diverge (converge) over time. The inclusion of the lagged dependent variable in the estimation introduces a possible correlation between that lagged variable and the error term, however. When we correct for this possible endogeneity using 1970 or 1960 lagged dependent variables as instruments or by omitting the variable entirely, our results are virtually identical to those reported in tables 2 through 5.

Table 2. City Finances and the Suburban Economy[a]

	Home value appreciation		Population growth		Income growth	
	City	*Suburb*	*City*	*Suburb*	*City*	*Suburb*
Δ City percent poverty	-0.807*	-0.489	-0.173	0.684**	-1.027**	-0.304
	(0.450)	(0.389)	(0.279)	(0.293)	(0.173)	(0.205)
Strong city unions	-0.111**	-0.063**	-0.032	0.042*	-0.003	0.004
	(0.034)	(0.029)	(0.021)	(0.022)	(0.013)	(0.015)
Weak city governance	-0.044**	-0.059**	-0.008	0.012	-0.012	-0.024**
	(0.021)	(0.019)	(0.013)	(0.014)	(0.008)	(0.010)
Δ City tax price	-5.681**	-2.765*	-4.400**	-4.110**	-1.871**	-0.956
	(1.741)	(1.506)	(1.089)	(1.141)	(0.671)	(0.795)
Δ Suburban percent poverty	-0.345**	-1.364**	-0.017	-0.588**	-0.305**	-1.231**
	(0.153)	(0.133)	(0.095)	(0.104)	(0.059)	(0.070)
Suburban school districts	0.0003	-0.0003	-0.0001	-0.0001	-0.0004**	-0.0002
	(0.004)	(0.0004)	(0.0002)	(0.0002)	(0.0001)	(0.0002)
Δ State aid	0.536	0.599**	0.418**	0.288	0.054	0.020
	(0.338)	(0.292)	(0.211)	(0.220)	(0.130)	(0.154)
Suburban support	0.179**	0.0436	0.066*	0.033	-0.015	0.024
	(0.058)	(0.050)	(0.034)	(0.036)	(0.023)	(0.027)
Strong teacher unions	0.050	-0.036	0.067**	-0.012	0.033**	0.027
	(0.042)	(0.036)	(0.026)	(0.027)	(0.016)	(0.019)
Airline hubs	0.004	0.033	-0.006	0.036**	0.024**	0.015
	(0.025)	(0.022)	(0.016)	(0.017)	(0.010)	(0.011)
Interstate highways	0.038	0.025	-0.002	-0.0005	-0.003	0.005
	(0.023)	(0.020)	(0.015)	(0.016)	(0.009)	(0.011)
Pseudo R^2	0.726	0.783	0.571	0.710	0.897	0.915
F statistic for city fiscal variables	13.77	6.21	10.15	3.71	32.00	4.03
(*p* value)	(~0)	(~0)	(~0)	(0.002)	(~0)	(0.001)

a. The regressions controlled for the following variables: New England, Middle Atlantic, Midwest, Plains, Southeast, Mountain, West Coast, 1980 city population density, 1980 suburban population density, heating degree days, cooling degree days, and the 1980 log value of the dependent variable.
* Significantly different from zero with 90 percent confidence.
**Significantly different from zero with 95 percent confidence.

suburban resident welfare changes. We use seemingly unrelated least squares estimation to allow for correlation of error terms across all six equations.

The results in table 2 show that the four city fiscal variables are jointly significant and negative in the city and suburban home value appreciation, population growth, and income growth equations. The effects are strongest in the home value equations, in accordance with the predictions of figure 1. Finding negative effects of city fiscal variables (ΔX_{cr}) in both the city and the suburban home value, population, and income equations ($\gamma_c < 0$; $\tau_c < 0$) suggests city and suburban economies are more than simply fiscal competitors. Were fiscal competition the whole story, we should see negative effects of ΔX_{cr}

on the city economy but positive effects for these same variables on the sub-urban economy. If the effects of ΔX_{cr} on the suburban economy are negative, however, then the fiscally induced decline in the city private economy must have an adverse economic spillover on the suburbs that more than offsets the positive stimulus of any relocating city households and businesses.

The elasticities of city and suburban home values with respect to changes in the city's tax price are –2.95 and –1.44 respectively, while the elasticities with respect to changes in the city's rate of poverty are –.15 and –.09.[36] City and suburban home values also fell by 11 and 6 percent respectively over the decade in the presence of an explicit duty-to-bargain for city employees other than teachers and by 4 and 6 percent respectively because of weak city governance. In the income and population equations, the elasticity of mean city income with respect to city tax price is –.97 and with respect to city poverty is –.19. Weak city governance lowers suburban mean income growth by 2.4 percent. The effects of city tax price, strong city unions, and the rate of city poverty are negative but statistically insignificant in the suburban income equation. These consistently negative effects suggest that weak city finances undermine an economically valuable structural connection between the city and suburbs.

In table 3 we allow for the potential endogeneity of city poverty and, by extension, the city's tax price, whose estimated effects are likely to be biased towards zero without estimation by instrumental variables. To accommodate the endogeneity of the rate of city poverty, we first redefine the city tax price to omit *CPOV* from the specification:

$$(b/B)_{/CPOV} \cong 1/[1 - .6(COLD) + (1.02 + .58 \cdot CMAN)].$$

We then provide for instrumental variables estimation of the change in the rate of city poverty, using as instruments the seven regional indicator variables, the percent of the city's 1980 population who are black, the percent of the city's 1980 housing stock built before 1939, and the change in the Cutler-Glaeser-Vigdor index of racial segregation between 1980 and 1990.[37] The instruments (other than the seven regional variables) are jointly statistically significant ($F = 3.17$, $p = .02$). The most important instrument is the percent of city housing built before 1939; its effect is positive and highly significant ($p = .006$).

36. Elasticities reported throughout the paper are evaluated at sample means.
37. Cutler, Glaeser, and Vigdor (1999). Glaeser and Gyourko (2001) stress an old city housing stock as an important determinant of poor households' decisions to locate within the central city.

The elasticities of city and suburban home values with respect to the rate of city poverty now equal −1.20 and −.55 respectively, while the elasticities of city and suburban incomes with respect to city poverty are −.40 and −.25. The elasticities of home values with respect to the respecified city tax price are now −4.18 for cities and −2.63 for suburbs, while the new elasticities for incomes with respect to the new city tax price are −1.52 for city income and −1.23 for suburban incomes. In all cases the effects are individually and jointly significant. Strong city unions and weak governance remain negative and individually and jointly significant in both city and suburban home value equations; the magnitudes of their effects are similar to those reported in table 2.

Table 3 also reports estimates of omitting city poverty from the analysis, decomposing city tax price into its respective changes in the poor and elderly populations and in the share of city employment in manufacturing, and omitting city poverty and the components of tax price altogether. In this last specification, the only city fiscal variables that remain to explain city and suburban economic performance are strong unions and weak governance. We view these estimates as perhaps the strongest test of our hypothesis. Both strong unions and weak governance continue to have negative and statistically significant effects on suburban home values. The effects are similar in magnitude to previous estimates.

Our second extension directly examines the role of agglomeration economies by adding three additional indicator variables to our regressions. The first two variables indicate the presence of a *city research university* or a *suburban research university*. The third indicates whether the city's *cultural rank* from the *1985 Places Rated Almanac* places the city within the top quartile of a national ranking of all cities.[38] If city agglomeration economies are important, then we expect city research universities and the city's cultural rank to have positive effects on both the city and suburban economies. For example, research universities are incubators of ideas and a potential stimulus, if there is sufficient complementary industrial capacity, to Jacobian agglomeration economies. In our model, a suburban research university will have jointly positive effects only when there are significant suburban agglomeration economies.

---

38. The top quartile ranking ensures that the city's cultural institutions involve significant fixed costs and are not endogenous to contemporary economic growth or declines. Institutions included in the rankings are museums, colleges and universities for the performing arts, symphony, theater, opera, dance, and public libraries. The rankings include all cultural institutions in the city's metropolitan area, but the overwhelming majority of the rated institutions are located within each area's central city.

Table 3. City Finances and the Suburban Economy: Controling for Endogeneity[a]

	Home value appreciation		Population growth		Income growth	
	City	Suburb	City	Suburb	City	Suburb
Δ City percent poverty,	-6.536**	-2.953**	-3.250**	-0.925	-2.141**	-1.329**
predicted	(1.680)	(1.394)	(1.000)	(0.942)	(0.738)	(0.597)
Strong city unions	-0.124**	-0.083**	-0.026	0.051**	-0.008	-0.021
	(0.039)	(0.032)	(0.023)	(0.021)	(0.017)	(0.014)
Weak city governance	-0.039*	-0.054**	-0.014	-0.001	-0.013	-0.021**
	(0.023)	(0.019)	(0.014)	(0.013)	(0.010)	(0.008)
Δ City tax price,	-8.037**	-5.065**	-4.839**	-4.565**	-2.929**	-2.364**
without city poverty	(2.081)	(1.721)	(1.250)	(1.166)	(0.912)	(0.734)
Δ State aid	0.808**	0.707**	0.625**	0.294	0.342**	0.171
	(0.386)	(0.319)	(0.232)	(0.215)	(0.169)	(0.136)
Suburban support	0.125**	0.017	0.050	0.035	-0.038	0.016
	(0.061)	(0.050)	(0.035)	(0.033)	(0.027)	(0.022)
Pseudo R^2	0.703	0.758	0.571	0.759	0.854	0.940
F statistic for city						
fiscal variables	11.03	6.74	17.19	5.91	5.25	5.59
(*p* value)	(~0)	(~0)	(~0)	(0.0001)	(0.0003)	(0.0002)
Strong city unions	-0.116**	-0.065**	-0.035	0.042*	-0.007	-0.003
	(0.036)	(0.030)	(0.022)	(0.022)	(0.016)	(0.016)
Weak city governance	-0.034	-0.053**	-0.003	0.011	-0.005	-0.022**
	(0.023)	(0.019)	(0.014)	(0.014)	(0.010)	(0.010)
Δ City tax price,	-8.173**	-3.972**	-5.677**	-4.654**	-3.368**	-1.477*
without city poverty	(2.033)	(1.690)	(1.253)	(1.246)	(0.926)	(0.890)
Δ State aid	0.867**	0.779**	0.587**	0.288	0.307*	0.108
	(0.357)	(0.296)	(0.220)	(0.216)	(0.162)	(0.155)
Suburban support	0.158**	0.032	0.054	0.030	-0.029	0.019
	(0.062)	(0.051)	(0.036)	(0.036)	(0.028)	(0.027)
Pseudo R^2	0.685	0.770	0.525	0.712	0.835	0.910
F statistic for city						
fiscal variables	8.81	5.43	7.51	6.34	4.47	2.50
(*p* value)	(~0)	(0.001)	(0.0001)	(0.0003)	(0.004)	(0.058)
Δ City (% old +	-5.627**	-2.392*	-0.096	0.146	-1.060	-0.829
% poverty), predicted	(1.562)	(1.270)	(0.938)	(0.858)	(0.673)	(0.543)
Strong city unions	-0.135**	-0.086**	-0.031	0.052**	-0.013	-0.014
	(0.040)	(0.032)	(0.024)	(0.022)	(0.017)	(0.014)
Weak city governance	-0.041*	-0.055**	-0.015	-0.001	-0.013	-0.021**
	(0.024)	(0.020)	(0.015)	(0.013)	(0.011)	(0.008)
Δ % City employment	0.006	0.004	0.006**	0.005**	0.004**	0.003**
in manufacturing	(0.004)	(0.003)	(0.002)	(0.002)	(0.002)	(0.001)
Δ State aid	0.893**	0.749**	0.637**	0.309	0.366**	0.189
	(0.401)	(0.326)	(0.243)	(0.221)	(0.173)	(0.139)

Table 3. City Finances and the Suburban Economy (continued)

	Home value appreciation		Population growth		Income growth	
	City	*Suburb*	*City*	*Suburb*	*City*	*Suburb*
Suburban support	0.123**	0.016	0.065	0.041	-0.029	0.020
	(0.064)	(0.052)	(0.037)	(0.034)	(0.028)	(0.022)
Pseudo R^2	0.680	0.748	0.530	0.745	0.847	0.937
F statistic for city fiscal variables	6.65	6.76	1.24	2.91	0.94	3.33
(*p* value)	(0.001)	(0.001)	(0.29)	(0.06)	(0.39)	(0.04)
Strong city unions	-0.110**	-0.062**	-0.031	0.047**	-0.004	0.004
	(0.038)	(0.030)	(0.023)	(0.023)	(0.017)	(0.016)
Weak city governance	-0.031	-0.052**	-0.002	-0.004	-0.004	-0.021**
	(0.024)	(0.019)	(0.015)	(0.014)	(0.011)	(0.010)
Δ State aid	0.896**	0.795**	0.592**	0.305	0.319*	0.113
	(0.370)	(0.300)	(0.229)	(0.223)	(0.167)	(0.157)
Suburban support	0.140**	0.022	0.040	0.019	-0.036	0.016
	(0.064)	(0.052)	(0.037)	(0.037)	(0.029)	(0.028)
Pseudo R^2	0.661	0.734	0.481	0.693	0.825	0.909
F statistic for city fiscal variables	4.82	5.24	0.91	2.37	0.08	2.34
(*p* value)	(0.01)	(0.01)	(0.40)	(0.09)	(0.92)	(0.10)

a. Estimation is by seemingly unrelated regression, instrumenting for Δ city percent poverty in the first panel and Δ city (% old + % poverty) in the third. The regressions also controlled for the following variables: Δ suburban percent poverty, suburban school districts, strong teacher unions, airline hubs, interstate highways, New England, Middle Atlantic, Industrial Midwest, Plains, Southeast, Mountain, West Coast, 1980 city population density, 1980 suburban population density, heating degree days, cooling degree days, and the 1980 log value of the dependent variable.
* Significantly different from zero with 90 percent confidence.
** Significantly different from zero with 95 percent confidence.

Table 4 reports the regression results when the indicator variables for the presence of city and suburban research universities and for city cultural rank are added to the core specification in table 3, again allowing for endogenous city poverty and cross-equation error correlations. The semi-logarithmic specification used implies that the adverse effects of redistributive city finances on city and suburban economies will be greater in the presence of positive agglomeration economies.[39] The presence of a city research university and an important city cultural center add, all else equal, 8 to 9 percent to the decade's rate of appreciation of city home values and 3 to 4 percent to the decade's growth rate of a city's average real incomes. City research universities also add 5 percent to the decade's city population growth rate, but a strong arts infrastructure has no significant effect on city population. Most important, a city

39. With the logarithmic specification for Y_{cr}, we have $\partial Y_{cr}/\partial X_{cr} = \gamma_c \cdot Y_{cr}$. When agglomeration effects are positive, then Y_{cr} is larger and the marginal effect of weak city finances is larger as well.

Table 4. City Finances, Agglomeration, and the Suburban Economy[a]

	Home value appreciation		Population growth		Income growth	
	City	Suburb	City	Suburb	City	Suburb
Δ City percent	-5.934**	-2.610*	-2.831**	-0.699	-1.858**	-1.203**
poverty, predicted	(1.615)	(1.384)	(0.979)	(0.934)	(0.705)	(0.587)
Strong city unions	-0.117**	-0.082**	-0.026	0.055**	-0.004	-0.010
	(0.037)	(0.032)	(0.023)	(0.021)	(0.016)	(0.013)
Weak city	-0.045**	-0.058**	-0.019	-0.003	-0.015	-0.022**
governance	(0.022)	(0.019)	(0.014)	(0.013)	(0.010)	(0.008)
Δ City tax price,	-6.605**	-4.301**	-4.461**	-4.098**	-2.364**	-1.973**
without city poverty	(2.012)	(1.720)	(1.243)	(1.176)	(0.877)	(0.727)
Δ State aid	0.959**	0.792**	0.628**	0.330	0.390**	0.219
	(0.373)	(0.319)	(0.228)	(0.214)	(0.162)	(0.135)
Suburban support	0.129**	0.018	0.043	0.036	-0.039	0.017
	(0.058)	(0.050)	(0.034)	(0.032)	(0.026)	(0.021)
City research	0.088**	0.054**	0.048**	0.024	0.035**	0.021*
university	(0.030)	(0.025)	(0.018)	(0.017)	(0.013)	(0.011)
Suburban research	0.114	0.036	0.082*	0.057	0.076**	0.024
university	(0.073)	(0.062)	(0.044)	(0.042)	(0.032)	(0.026)
Cultural rank	0.076**	0.030	-0.004	0.027	0.032**	0.024**
	(0.034)	(0.029)	(0.021)	(0.020)	(0.015)	(0.012)
Pseudo R^2	0.732	0.767	0.596	0.767	0.870	0.944
F statistic for city						
agglomeration variables	8.83	3.46	3.53	2.34	7.73	5.01
(*p* value)	(~0)	(0.03)	(0.03)	(0.10)	(0.001)	(0.007)

a. Estimation is by seemingly unrelated regression, instrumenting for Δ city percent poverty. The regressions also controlled for the following variables: Δ suburban percent poverty, suburban school districts, strong teacher unions, airline hubs, interstate highways, New England, Middle Atlantic, Industrial Midwest, Plains, Southeast, Mountain, West Coast, heating degree days, cooling degree days, 1980 city population density, 1980 suburban population density, and the 1980 log value of the dependent variable.
* Significantly different from zero with 90 percent confidence.
** Significantly different from zero with 95 percent confidence.

research university and a strong city cultural presence enhance suburban home value appreciation and income growth as predicted by suburban proximity to center city agglomeration economies. Interestingly, there is no significant cross-effect on city home values and incomes of having a suburban research university. This is what we would expect if cities, not suburbs, are the primary centers of idea and production agglomerations.[40]

40. We repeated the analysis in table 4 by adding interactions between the indicator variables for a city research university and strong cultural centers and each of the four fiscal variables, tested one fiscal variable at a time. If agglomeration effects are the important channel through which fiscal variables influence the suburban economy, then these interaction effects should be negative and significant. The effects are negative but generally not statistically significant. The one exception is the interaction of city poverty and the arts infrastructure, which is negative and significant in both the city and suburban home value appreciation equations. The estimates imply that when the rate of city poverty is greater than 5 percent, the original positive effects on city home values of having a strong city cultural center are lost.

Our final extension follows the lead of Richard Voith and examines whether the economies of large MSAs—metropolitan regions with regional populations of 250,000 or more residents in 1970—reacted differently to changes in city fiscal variables than the economies of smaller MSAs.[41] We add an indicator variable for *Large MSA* and variables for *Large MSA* interacted with changes in the rate of city poverty and allow for endogenous rates of change of city poverty and for cross-equation error correlations.[42] Table 5 presents our results. Our four measures of weak city finances and our two measures of city agglomeration retain their joint statistical significance in each of the regression equations, and both the variable *Large MSA* and the interaction of *Large MSA* with the change in city poverty prove statistically significant and economically important as well. The larger MSAs show differentially higher rates of city and suburban home value appreciation, suburban population growth, and city and suburban income growth in the 1980s. Center city poverty has its strongest negative effects on city and suburban home values and incomes in the large MSAs. The implied elasticity of city home values with respect to the rate of city poverty is –.66 in small MSAs but –1.57 in large MSAs; the corresponding suburban home value elasticities with respect to city poverty are –.15 and not significant in small MSAs but –.82 and significant in large MSAs. A similar pattern holds for the elasticities of city incomes.

Since we are studying the case for, and ultimately the effects of, suburban-to-city fiscal assistance on the metropolitan economy, the effects on the city and suburban economies of the two metropolitan-wide aid variables are of particular interest. Using the estimates from table 5, the sample's mean rate of increase in the ratio of state aid (= .01) implies a $400 to $460 increase in average suburban and city home values, evaluated at the 1980 sample mean suburban ($50,589) and city ($48,706) home values. For our sample, a change in the ratio of state aid to own local revenues of .01 is equivalent to an average increase in annual real state aid of about $25 for each family. A $25 increase in annual state aid would imply an increase in home values of about $625 using the decade's real rate of interest of .04 (= $25/.04), a result plausibly close to the estimated increases in city and suburban home values.

While state aid benefits both city and suburban residents, suburban support for county government involves a fiscal redistribution from suburban to city residents. Cities that can share county expenditures, primarily poverty spend-

41. Voith (1998).
42. We also tested for the significance of the interactions of *Large MSA* with changes in the city's tax price and with the indicator variables for the presence of strong unions and weak governance. Those additional interactions were jointly insignificant in each of our six equations.

Table 5. City Finances, MSA Size, and the Suburban Economy[a]

	Home value appreciation		Population growth		Income growth	
	City	*Suburb*	*City*	*Suburb*	*City*	*Suburb*
Δ City percent	-3.553**	-0.820	-2.631**	-0.249	-1.237	-0.299
poverty, predicted	(1.719)	(1.490)	(1.075)	(1.014)	(0.773)	(0.632)
[Δ City percent poverty,	-4.896**	-3.592**	-0.402	-1.019	-1.192**	-1.615**
predicted] • Large MSA	(1.323)	(1.144)	(0.830)	(0.777)	(0.593)	(0.482)
Strong city unions	-0.113**	-0.079**	-0.026	0.057**	-0.002	-0.007
	(0.036)	(0.031)	(0.023)	(0.021)	(0.016)	(0.013)
Weak city governance	-0.043*	-0.056**	-0.019	0.001	-0.015	-0.022**
	(0.022)	(0.019)	(0.014)	(0.012)	(0.010)	(0.008)
Δ City tax price,	-7.469**	-4.878**	-4.509**	-4.532**	-2.464**	-1.966**
without city poverty	(2.000)	(1.725)	(1.267)	(1.180)	(0.894)	(0.726)
Δ State aid	0.953**	0.792**	0.626**	0.320	0.392**	0.227*
	(0.360)	(0.311)	(0.228)	(0.212)	(0.161)	(0.131)
Suburban support	0.131**	0.021	0.042	0.044	-0.039	0.017
	(0.056)	(0.049)	(0.034)	(0.032)	(0.025)	(0.021)
City research	0.079**	0.047*	0.047**	0.023	0.033**	0.018*
university	(0.029)	(0.025)	(0.018)	(0.017)	(0.013)	(0.010)
Suburban research	0.096	0.022	0.081*	0.049	0.071**	0.016
university	(0.070)	(0.061)	(0.044)	(0.042)	(0.031)	(0.026)
Cultural rank	0.059*	0.019	-0.005	0.019	0.030**	0.024**
	(0.034)	(0.029)	(0.021)	(0.020)	(0.015)	(0.012)
Large MSA	0.188**	0.132**	0.014	0.067**	0.038*	0.043**
	(0.048)	(0.042)	(0.031)	(0.030)	(0.022)	(0.018)
Pseudo R^2	0.750	0.778	0.597	0.773	0.872	0.947
F statistic for Δpoverty • Large MSA and Large MSA	7.77	5.49	0.13	2.76	2.05	5.71
(*p* value)	(~0)	(0.004)	(0.85)	(0.06)	(0.13)	(0.003)

a. Estimation is by seemingly unrelated regression, instrumenting for Δ city percent poverty. The regressions also controlled for the following variables: Δ suburban percent poverty, suburban school districts, strong teacher unions, air hubs, interstate highways, New England, Middle Atlantic, industrial Midwest, Plains, Southeast, Mountain, West Coast, 1980 city population density, 1980 suburban population density, heating degree days, cooling degree days, and the 1980 log value of the dependent variable.
* Significantly different from zero with 90 percent confidence.
** Significantly different from zero with 95 percent confidence.

ing and the costs of courts and prisons, with their suburbs (Pittsburgh, for example) will enjoy a fiscal advantage over cities that must meet these costs from the city tax base only (for example, Philadelphia). As expected, we find these favored cities have greater home value appreciation.[43] Suburban aid in the form of county cost sharing has a strong positive effect on central city home values worth about $6,380, again evaluated at the 1980 mean value for city homes ($48,706). Suburban home values appear to be unaffected by the

43. See table 5.

Table 6. Weak City Finances and Resident Home Values[a]

	ΔHV_s	WTP_s	ΔHV_c	WTP_c
ΔCity tax price = .01	−$2,468	$99	−$3,638	$146
	(873)	(35)	(974)	(39)
ΔCity percent poverty = .03				
Large MSA	−$6,696	$268	−$12,345	$494
	(2212)	(88)	(2460)	(98)
Small MSA	−$1,244	$50	−$4,997	$208
	(2261)	(90)	(2512)	(100)
Strong city union = 1	−$4,047	$162	-$5,358	$214
	(1563)	(63)	(1739)	(70)
Weak city governance = 1	−$3,035	$121	−$1,948	$78
	(946)	(38)	(1052)	(42)

a. Estimates of changes in city and suburban home values ($\Delta HV_{s,c}$) and willingness to pay ($WTP_{s,c}$), as well as associated standard errors, shown in parentheses, are based on coefficient estimates and standard errors reported in table 5.

transfer, and may actually rise by a small amount. This suggests fiscal transfers to the city from the suburbs provide a compensating benefit to suburban residents.[44] We propose that suburban aid allows the city to hold the line on taxes or to invest in city infrastructure, both of which protect city agglomeration economies and make the city's private economy more productive and suburban location more valuable.

Redistribution resulting from each of our weak city fiscal structure indicators imposes efficiency losses that reduce the value of both city and suburban properties. Table 6 reports suburban residents' potential willingness to pay to remove each of the city's adverse fiscal situations based on the esti-

44. An example makes the point. Consider an MSA with 500,000 center city families, of whom 20 percent are poverty households, and 800,000 suburban families, of whom 10 percent are poverty households, and where the state imposes mandated spending of $1,000 for each poor family, and center city poor families require an additional $1,000 for each family in added city spending. If the city and the suburbs meet their poverty spending on their own, then each middle-class city family must spend $500 (= $2,000 for each poor family x .25 poor families for each middle class family), while each middle-class suburban family must spend only $111 (= $1,000 for each poor family x .111 poor families for each middle-class family). If the city and suburbs share the costs of poverty, then the common expense for each middle class family in the metropolitan area would be $250. In this case, each middle class family living in the central city receives an annual net transfer of $250, while each middle-class family living in the suburbs loses $139. Discounting at the decade's real interest rate of .04 implies a gain in city home values of $6,250 (= $250/.04) and fall in suburban home values of −$3475 (= −$139/.04). The $6,250 gain in city home values is very close to what is estimated for our sample cities from shared suburban support. To match the estimated suburban home value gain of $1,062, there must have been a compensating benefit of $4,537 for each suburban family to offset the fiscal loss of $3,475. This gain of $4,537 is consistent with the estimated benefits to suburbanites from reduced city poverty spending. See table 6.

mated decline in city and suburban home values for our sample's average MSA because of adverse changes in the central city's finances during the 1980s. The estimates use our sample's mean change in city tax price between 1980 and 1990 (from .50 to .51) and in the city poverty rate (from .20 to .23) and the estimated effect over the decade of strong public employee unions or weak governance. The estimated changes in city and suburban home values are evaluated at the 1980 suburban and city sample means. The estimated change in suburban home values (ΔHV_s) provides a direct measure of the change in suburban resident welfare due to weak city finances.[45] Amortizing the loss in suburban home values at the decade's real interest rate of .04 gives a direct estimate of the average suburban resident's annual willingness to pay (WTP_s) to remove each of the city's adverse fiscal changes: $WTP_s = -.04 \cdot \Delta HV_s$. Our estimates suggest the average suburban homeowner might be willing to pay from $99 ($\Delta City\ tax\ price$) to $268 ($\Delta City\ percent\ poverty$ for Large MSAs) annually to reduce the adverse effects of weak city fiscal institutions on the suburban economy. Not surprisingly, city landowners will also be willing to contribute to reform the same weak city fiscal institutions.[46]

Three conclusions emerge from our empirical analysis. First, the fiscal institutions of our central cities offer one potentially important causal explanation for the observed correlations between U.S. city and suburban economies. Metropolitan areas whose city fiscal institutions allow significant redistributions from city taxpayers to poor city households and city employees will see lower city and suburban home value appreciation and income and population growth. Metropolitan areas whose cities control these fiscal redistributions will enjoy higher metropolitan-wide home value appreciations and income and population growth. Second, our estimates suggest suburban residents may be willing to make significant annual financial contributions to

45. Haughwout (2002b).

46. Table 6 shows these contributions are likely to be larger for city than suburban residents. The one exception to this pattern is for weak governance, where our estimates imply $WTP_c = \$78$ while $WTP_s = \$121$. If the suburbanites' WTP_s reflect only losses from higher private good prices for city produced goods and services and *if* a city resident's losses from higher city prices are at least as large as a suburbanite's losses—as would be the case if city goods are a larger share of city residents' budgets than of suburban residents' budgets—then our estimates imply weak city governance confers a *fiscal benefit* on city residents of at least $43 per year (–$78 = +$43 (+) –$121). This makes sense if weak governance favors city residents over city business by lowering resident taxes (or raising resident services) and by raising business taxes (or lowering business services) and if city zoning leads to separate residential and commercial property markets. Businesses still leave the city, lowering city agglomeration economies, but city residents now get a fiscal transfer that offsets, at least in part, the resulting rise in private goods prices. Suburban residents suffer only the burden of higher private good prices.

reform or at least ease the burden of redistributive tax structures, strong unions, weak governance, and, most important, rising rates of city poverty. Third, there is evidence that general fiscal assistance in the form of greater state aid and targeted suburban-to-city support will enhance the overall economic performance of both the city and suburban economies.

A Structural Analysis

The empirical analysis in the previous section establishes a link between city finances and suburban welfare for an average U.S. MSA. In this section we develop an open-economy structural model calibrated to approximate the economic structure of the Philadelphia MSA in 1990 in order to explore more formally the fiscal link between city and suburbs for one particular MSA. The analysis extends our earlier study of fiscal policy in an open central city economy by first allowing for agglomeration economies among city firms and then including a fringe of fiscally competitive suburbs.[47] Appendix C provides a brief description of the model's formal structure and outlines our solution algorithm.

Firms within our MSA are price-takers. They need to earn the competitive after-tax rate of return on their capital, and they sell their output in a competitive world market at an exogenous world price plus transportation costs. Households in the MSA are "utility-takers" and need to receive the exogenous level of resident utility available in alternative world locations. Our MSA contains one central city and one suburb (or many identical suburbs). City firms produce the world commodity using city land, city resident workers, corporate managers (who all live in the suburbs), and firm capital. The density of workers within the city provides an agglomeration advantage to city firms, specified here as a Hicks-neutral shift in firm productivity.[48] The elasticity of city firm output with respect to the density of city workers is set at a very modest value of .01 to reflect the fact that not all of city output benefits from agglomeration economies; for comparison, Ciccone and Hall and Ciccone find aggregate elasticities of output with respect to worker density of .05.[49] There are no agglomeration economies in city consumption in our model.

---

47. Haughwout and Inman (2001).
48. Ciccone and Hall (1996); Ciccone (2002); Beardsell and Henderson (1999).
49. Ciccone and Hall (1996); Ciccone (2002).

Suburban firms provide retailing services by combining the single consumption good with suburban land, suburban resident workers, and firm capital. There are no agglomeration economies in suburban retailing. Suburban residents buy all their private good consumption from suburban "retailers" even though they might actually consume the good, such as entertainment, hospital and legal services within the central city.[50] City firms may not be able to fill all of the suburban demand in equilibrium. In this case, suburban retailers import the consumption good from outside the MSA. Transportation costs are higher for these marginal units because city firms have a transportation cost advantage over non-MSA firms, set at $.15 for each dollar of suburban imports in our model in order to replicate actual Philadelphia suburban land values in our baseline simulations. City and suburban households have a common utility function defined over this single consumption good, housing structures, land, and the locally produced public good.

In our MSA, there is a common public good provided separately by the city for city residents and by the suburbs for suburban residents. There are no public good spillovers across jurisdictions. The public good is paid for by local taxes and consumed jointly by firms and households within the jurisdiction. The good is a pure Samuelsonian public good specified as a stock, such as roadways, tenured teachers, and schools, that provides an annual flow of benefits to firms and households within the local jurisdiction. Households pay the annual interest costs and depreciation needed to purchase and maintain this stock. For city producers and suburban retailers, the public good acts as a Hicks-neutral shift in output which improves the firm's total factor productivity.[51] The public good provides direct utility to each jurisdiction's residents.

There are poor and elderly families residing in both the central city and the suburbs of our MSA. Poor residents receive a federal and state-funded income transfer and elderly households receive social security benefits. Both the poor and the elderly purchase the private consumption good, housing, and residential land. They also benefit from the locally provided public good. Both the poor and the elderly receive mandated services from their local city or suburban government, paid for by local taxation. Poor and elderly families do not move between the city and the suburbs nor will they exit or enter the MSA.[52] Poor families pay taxes on their housing, land, and goods consumption but not

---

50. City residents receive their retailing services directly from city firms as a by-product of city firm production.

51. Haughwout (2002a).

52. Meyer (1998).

on their transfer income. To the extent there are mandated services for these households and the cost of these services exceeds the poor and elderly's tax payments, poor and elderly families are a net fiscal burden on city and suburban firms and working households. Residents do not care about the welfare of the poor and elderly, that is, there are no redistributive preferences within the MSA.

The model's private economy determines, for both the city and suburbs populations, employment including corporate managers needed to run city firms, firm capital, wages, land prices, production and sales, and finally, consumption, including the purchase of residential land and housing services. The MSA's private economy equilibrium defines the tax bases available to city and suburban governments. Governments can tax the property of firms and households, the wages and consumption of residents, and the sales of city firms. Tax revenues *plus* exogenous (lump-sum) state and federal intergovernmental transfers *minus* the mandated costs of services for poor and elderly residents are allocated to purchase a single public good that benefits both firms and households within the taxing jurisdiction. In the MSA's public economy, city and suburban tax rates and thus the level of the city's and the suburb's public goods are chosen by city and suburban politicians. City politicians are assumed to be revenue maximizers and therefore to always select those tax rates that maximize city aggregate revenues—that is, city politicians go to the top of their city's revenue hill.[53] We assume suburban politicians are responsive to the public goods demand of suburban residents and select the tax rate that gives the median resident household their preferred level of the suburban public good. We assume the suburban government uses only property taxes to pay for suburban public services.

Tax rates and public goods affect the after-tax rates of return for city and suburban firms and the final utilities received by city and suburban residents. After-tax rates of return and resident utilities, coupled with the assumption that our MSA is one of many competitive MSAs, define the location of firms and households in the MSA's city and suburbs and determine city and suburban population, employment, wages, land rents, and consumption. Together, these define the city and suburban tax bases. We solve for the joint equilibria of the MSA's private and public economies.

53. We adopt this specification of city politics based upon the results in Haughwout and others (2000), which estimates revenue hills for four large U.S. cities—Houston, Minneapolis, New York City, and Philadelphia—and finds that, with the possible exception of Minneapolis, each city has selected tax rates that almost maximize city revenues.

The model formalizes the intuitions of the mayor's argument and figure 1 for how weak city finances can jointly depress city and suburban economic activities. By construction, there are no direct public good spillovers from the city to the suburbs, all suburban residents except commuting city managers work in the suburbs, and suburban residents have no altruistic motives towards central city households. Weak city finances mean higher city taxes and lower city public goods, both of which encourage firms and households to leave the central city. Fewer city firms mean lower aggregate city output and less efficient city production because of lost agglomeration economies. Both effects raise the cost to suburban residents of buying the private consumption good.

The direct economic benefits to suburban residents from locating near the central city are measured by the income savings from living near an economically efficient central city: $Z_s = x_s^c \cdot [(k^o + t^o) - (k^c + t^c)]$. Weak city finances have the potential to lower these suburban economic gains by reducing the availability of low-cost output coming from the central city ($\Delta x_s^c < 0$), by raising the production costs of city output because of lost agglomeration economies ($\Delta k^c > 0$), or by raising the cost of shipping goods from the city to the suburbs ($\Delta t_c > 0$). Generally,

$$\Delta Z_s = \Delta x_s^c \cdot [(k^o + t^o) - (k^c + t^c)] + x_s^c \cdot [-(\Delta k^c + \Delta t^c)] \leq 0.$$

In our model, the most important of these effects is the loss in city output ($\Delta x_s^c < 0$) and the resulting need for suburbanites to purchase goods from other cities.[54]

We conduct four simulations. Each is designed to approximate adverse changes in the central city's fiscal institutions comparable to those experienced by the average central city during our sample decade, 1980 through 1990. To approximate the effects of an average increase in the central city's tax price ($\Delta City\ tax\ price = .01$), we increase the percent of the MSA population classified as elderly from 22.2 percent to 26.8 percent. Because elderly residents own smaller homes, this increases the tax price for firms and wealthier homeowners. To approximate the fiscal consequences of the decade's average increase in the rate of city poverty ($= .03$), we first increase the city's equilibrium poverty rate from .20 to .23. This increases the fiscal costs to the city

54. Our model assumes constant costs of shipping, so $\Delta t^c = 0$. Our model is an open economy model in which city firms not only ship output to the suburbs, but compete with other cities' firms in the world market. Thus city firms must be as efficient as other cities' firms and thus kc—the average cost of firm output—must be constant. This is achieved in the model by capitalizing all fiscal and production inefficiencies into an offsetting decline in the price of land or labor for city firms. Because of this specification $\Delta k^c = 0$ as well. Thus $\Delta Z_s = \Delta x_s^c \cdot [(k^o + t^o) - (k^c + t^c)]$.

of current poverty mandates and lowers city tax prices, but these effects alone have only modest adverse effects on city and suburban home values. To more closely approximate the empirically estimated changes following increases in city poverty reported in table 6, it is also necessary to double the mandated budgetary costs of poverty. This suggests the empirically observed adverse effects of poverty are likely due to more than simply the direct fiscal effects of having more poor families drawing city budget dollars. The fiscal consequences of having strong public employee unions are approximated by a decade-long increase in the production costs of city public goods of 15 percent, or equivalently by a 1.4 percent annual rate of increase in city workers' real wages. Finally, the fiscal consequences of weak budgetary institutions are approximated by a shift in the tax burden from residents to business by reducing the city's exemption of business capital (machines) from property taxation from a .25 percent to a .15 percent exemption. The resulting additional business taxes are allocated to provide more of the city's public good, which benefits both residents and firms.

Table 7 reports the effects of these four adverse city fiscal changes on city and suburban output, Z_c and Z_s, city and suburban land values, city and suburban resident wages and incomes, and city and suburban population for our model MSA. The first two lines show the baseline equilibrium of the city and suburban economies before changes in city fiscal institutions. The baseline is calibrated to correspond to the Philadelphia MSA and provides a reasonable approximation to the actual 1990 Philadelphia MSA economy, except that aggregate city output and city population are both somewhat smaller than actual 1990 city output and population.[55] The remaining rows report change from the baseline values; change as a percentage of the baseline is in parentheses. All the fiscal changes except for city tax price reduce the city population, and all four fiscal changes lower the output of city firms.[56] Since

55. We compute the baseline economy assuming city politicians set the city property tax rate to maximize city revenues. Actual 1990 Philadelphia property tax rates were below this revenue-maximizing rate (Haughwout and Inman 2001).

56. In the simulations of $\Delta City\ tax\ price = .01$, we exogenously increased the number of *immobile* elderly sufficient to reduce the ratio of b/B for the typical working city resident. The necessary increase in the elderly population means that total population in equilibrium rises ($\Delta N_c > 0$), though the number of worker residents does decline. The city economy is smaller, but not by very much because the increase in the elderly population sustains demand for city goods. But exports to the suburbs fall significantly and this has an associated large negative effect on the suburban economy. Thus suburban employment in the retail sector falls. However, because the city economy has declined only slightly, the number of corporate managers earning the fixed corporate wage of \$140,000 falls only slightly. Thus the distribution of income in the suburbs moves in favor of the wealthier residents. This fact explains the rise in average suburban income ($\Delta Y_s > 0$) seen in table 7.

Table 7. Weak City Finances and the Private Economy: Philadelphia MSA

	Output (X*, $ billions)	Z (Z*, $ per household)	Land value (R*, $ per household)	Wages (W*, $ per worker)	Earned income (Y*, $ per resident household)	Households (N*)
			Baseline			
City	$15.8	$2,754	$22,810	$33,120	$33,120	364,197
Suburbs	$28.3	$2,134	$19,517	$27,090	$45,000	635,576
			Changes from baseline			
City tax price, excluding poverty = .01[a]						
City	-$0.6 (-3.7%)	0 (...)	-$420 (-1.8%)	0 (...)	0 (...)	23,535 (6.5%)
Suburbs	-$2.2 (-7.8%)	-$162.26 (-7.6%)	-$2,264 (-11.6%)	-$90 (-0.3%)	$578 (1.3%)	-34,333 (-5.4%)
City percent poverty = .03[b]						
City	-$1.7 (-11.0%)	0 (...)	-$2,269 (-9.9%)	0 (...)	0 (...)	-19,997 (-5.5%)
Suburbs	-$1.9 (-6.8%)	-$275.5 (-12.9%)	-$2,312 (-11.8%)	-$90 (-0.3%)	-$763 (-1.7%)	-35,732 (-5.6%)
Strong city unions = 1[c]						
City	-$4.3 (-27.0%)	0 (...)	-$5,700 (-25.0%)	$5 (0.0%)	$5 (0.0%)	-58,917 (-16.2%)
Suburbs	-$1.3 (-4.5%)	-$664.1 (-31.1%)	-$2,410 (-12.3%)	-$90 (-0.3%)	-$3,770 (-8.4%)	-38,665 (-4.7%)

Weak City Governance = 1^d

Exhibit[e]

City	-$3.1 (-19.6%)	0 (. . .)	-$4,646 (-20.4%)	-$216 (-0.7%)	-$216 (-0.7%)	-104,157 (-11.0%)
Suburbs	-$1.5 (-5.5%)	-$486.9 (-22.8%)	-$2,375 (-12.2%)	-$90 (-1.2%)	-$3,746 (-8.3%)	-97,632 (-5.9%)

Full taxation of business property[e]

City	-$6.3 (-40.0%)	0 (. . .)	-$9,343 (-40.9%)	-$518 (-1.6%)	-$518 (-1.6%)	-83,391 (-22.9%)
Suburbs	-$7.0b (-24.9%)	-$995.7 (-46.6%)	-$7,619 (-39.0%)	-$315 (-1.2%)	-$3,746 (-8.3%)	-132,288 (-20.8%)

a. Approximated by raising Philadelphia's initial percent elderly from 22.2 percent to 26.8 percent, sufficient to raise the city's tax price from 0.40 to 0.41.

b. Approximated by increasing Philadelphia's initial percent poor from 20 percent sufficient to ensure an equilibrium percent poor equal to 23 percent, and increasing the mandated local share of transfer income costs from 0.095 to 0.2.

c. Approximated by increasing the production cost of the public good for Philadelphia from 1 to 1.15 to approximate the relative growth in public employee wages in strong union cities during the 1980s.

d. Approximated by increasing the share of the business property subject to the city's property tax from 75 percent to 85 percent, implying a balanced budget increase in public goods available for households and firms.

e. Approximated by increasing the share of the business property subject to the city's property tax from 75 percent to 100 percent, implying a balanced budget increase in public goods available for households and firms.

* Denotes equilibrium values.

enough city output remains to satisfy city residents' demands, there is no change in Z_c for the remaining city households and $\Delta Z_c = 0$. However, suburban residents see a fall in their value of Z_s under each fiscal change. Suburban wages, city and suburban land values, and the suburban population fall in all four scenarios. In each case, the equilibrium result is an economically smaller suburban economy and a fall in suburban land values, wages, and population. This structural model of an open economy MSA provides an economic foundation for the mayors' argument and the reduced form econometric results in tables 2 through 6. Weak city fiscal institutions can *cause* declining city and suburban economies.

In this setting, how much would Philadelphia suburbanites, as modeled here, be willing to pay to prevent the introduction of these weak city fiscal institutions? The values of $\Delta Z_s *$ reported in table 7 measure the initial burden on suburban resident incomes (fall in $V_s = V_0$ in figure 1) or suburban retailing profits (fall in $\Pi_s = 0$ in figure 1) from increases in city tax prices, rates of poverty, union wages, and business taxation. The final, equilibrium effect on suburban resident welfare is measured by the fall in suburban land values in table 7 ($\Delta R_s *$)—that is, a fall in what people will pay to live in the suburbs. The amortized cost of these land value losses gives a measure of suburbanites' annual willingness to pay (WTP_s) to remove or to offset the adverse fiscal effects of these weak city fiscal institutions in our simulated economy. At an annual interest rate of .04, these annual WTP_ss are \$91 for each current suburban household ($= .04 \cdot \Delta R_s * = .04 \cdot \$2,264$) for a .01 increase in Philadelphia's tax price, \$92 a household for the .03 increase in the equilibrium rate of city poverty, \$96 a household for the added labor costs from strong city unions, and \$95 for each household because weak governance shifts city property taxation from residents to firms. These simulated WTP_ss for the Philadelphia suburbanites fall within one standard deviation of the estimated results for the U.S. sample as a whole as reported in table 6.

The last panel of table 7 includes a final simulation as an exhibit to illustrate the importance of city business taxes for the economic performance of the MSA economy. The exhibit shows what happens in our simulated MSA economy when the city completely removes its exemption of business capital from property taxation. The effect is to increase the equilibrium tax rate on business property from 0.02175 to 0.029. This is a 33 percent increase in the effective rate of business property taxation, and it leads to a 40 percent decline in the equilibrium size of the city economy and a 25 percent decline in the equilibrium size of the suburban economy. City and suburban land values both decline by 40 percent, and city and suburban populations both decline by slightly more than 20 percent. The exhibit suggests that in a city with just a modest degree of agglomeration, taxing city business can have very large negative effects on MSA economic performance and on the welfare of current MSA residents as measured by changes in city and suburban land values. If suburban residents wish to give fiscal assistance to their central cities, then assistance should be targeted towards tax relief for central city businesses, particularly those businesses where production and consumption agglomeration economies are important.

A structural model of a MSA economy whose three key features are fully mobile firms and households, both inefficient and redistributive city fiscal institutions, and modest city-specific agglomeration economies can explain both the direction and magnitude of the city-suburban interdependencies found in our reduced-form econometric analysis for U.S. MSAs over the 1980s. The structural model clearly reveals the importance of business taxation to the overall economic performance of cities and suburbs. City business taxation that undermines the productive advantage of central city locations has large negative effects on the city economy and, because of the importance of city-to-suburban trade, nearly as large negative effects on the suburban economy. Protecting these center city production advantages from the consequences of redistributive local politics is in the interest of most city and suburban residents.

How Should Suburbs Aid Their Central Cities?

Because of natural competitive advantages or simply economic history, U.S. central cities are important production and consumption centers favored by significant agglomeration economies. Unfortunately, our current institutions of local public finance impose redistributive burdens on mobile city firms and middle- and upper-income households that undermine the efficiency advantages of city production. Unfunded poverty mandates, monopoly unions, redistributive local taxation, and weak city governance each strengthen the ability of lower income households, public employees, and neighborhoods to extract fiscal resources from productive but mobile firms and households. The exit of these firms and households undermines city agglomeration economies, resulting in economic losses for the average city and suburban resident.

Can we reorganize central city public finance so that all parties to the city's redistribution game—city and suburban landowners *and* the current winners from city redistribution—might be made better off? The answer is potentially yes. Comparing our earlier estimates of the average transfer paid per city resident by redistributive fiscal institutions to the maximal gain to suburbanites of removing those institutions as reported in table 6 suggests that sufficient compensation can be found to facilitate institutional reform. The above comparison suggests suburbanites will gain $2 to $4 annually for every $1 of suburban aid.[57] Suburban aid must be tied to successful institutional reforms, however. Four reforms seem particularly promising.

First, poverty mandates should be fully funded, and revenues lost through poverty's direct effect on the city tax base should be replaced by a residential tax base equalization grant. Second, efforts should be made to encourage the competitive provision of city services, either by relaxing strong duty-to-bargain rules or by passing laws that allow cities to contract out for the provision of city services. The state of Pennsylvania's recent takeover of city school management, requiring the city to accept bids from private providers to manage the city's worst schools, is an example of such reform. Third, cities losing tax base because of demographic shifts and structural declines in their manufacturing job base should be given transition aid tied to business tax relief to prevent further declines in the business tax base. Even more aggressive reforms would replace the city's general property tax by a resident-based property tax or a resident-based income tax and exempt business property, but would allow cities to impose user fees for city-provided business services. To the extent city businesses use city infrastructure that cannot be priced through

57. For example, in our sample, city households pay an average $2,500 a year in city taxes; a 5 percent increase in city taxation due to duty-to-bargain rules implies a $125 transfer from each city household to city public employees. Removing duty-to-bargain rules removes this transfer. If suburbanites were to compensate city public employees for their losses, then in our sample each suburban family would need to contribute $62.50. There are typically two suburban households for each city household in our sample. If this aid ensured the passage of duty-to-bargain reform and lower city taxes, suburban households would benefit by an annual value of $162 a year (see table 6). The implied benefit-to-cost ratio for suburban residents of paying compensation to ensure reform would be $162 to $62.50 or 2.6 to 1. Note that city residents (who also benefit) cannot pay this annual compensation through the current structure of city taxation since this would simply return the city to the original fiscal status quo. For full benefits, funding must come from outside the city—for example, from the suburbs or from the state. Similar calculations can be done for reform of each of the other weak city fiscal institutions. Calculations available upon request.

user fees—roads are the prime example—the city should be given matching infrastructure grants tying funding to new construction or maintenance. Fourth, ward-based city politics should be replaced by at-large politics and by requiring cities to elect an at-large mayor. The elected mayor should be given broad agenda setting and veto powers.

Each of these institutional reforms may require compensation of the reform's losers in order to achieve passage at the state or metropolitan level. This is where suburban-to-city aid plays a useful role. First, suburban or state aid should be given to fully fund all poverty mandates imposed upon the city budget. Further, a city-suburban tax base equalization aid program equalizing the residential component of local tax bases should be adopted to remove the adverse tax price effects of large poverty concentrations in central cities. Second, suburban aid can be made available to local governments that adopt competitive bidding for core city services. Such aid should be sufficient to compensate the current median-aged public employee, paid perhaps through targeted pensions or early retirement payments; once that worker retires with her fully funded pension, however, aid should stop. Third, suburban-funded transition aid should be given to cities for their loss of revenues from the reform of city business taxes, perhaps most easily done as part of a general reform of local property taxation. We recommend that local property taxation be restricted to the taxation of resident property. Alternatively, a resident-only income or wage tax could be used. Fourth, suburban aid should be given, as above for private contracting reforms, to current city workers released by cutbacks in neighborhood services because of the adoption of more efficient strong mayoral politics. Each of these four aid programs can be financed and administered at either the state or metropolitan level.

As economists, we stress the virtues of competition. Charles Tiebout first noted, and much recent evidence confirms, that those virtues are clearly present in large metropolitan public economies.[58] We also note the virtues of cooperation. As Paul Samuelson has argued, when there are significant economic spillovers or increasing returns to scale—of which city agglomeration economies is one important example—then cooperative behavior is appropriate.[59] This paper suggests that in city agglomeration economies there might be a compelling new reason for our cities and suburbs to work together to reform inefficient central city fiscal institutions.

58. Tiebout (1956).
59. Samuelson (1954).

Appendix A. Suburban Welfare Gain

Suburban households can purchase the consumption good x_s at a production plus transportation cost of $(k^c + t^c)$ from city firms or at production plus transportation cost from non-city firms of $(k^o + t^o)$, where $(k^c + t^c) < (k^o + t^o)$. Suburban households will first purchase all they can from city firms, denoted as x_s^c. The remainder of their demand for x_s, denoted as x_s^o, will be supplied by non-city firms. For suburban households, x_s^c is assumed to be exogenous and defined by the profit-maximizing decisions of city firms. If I equals the typical suburban household's after tax income, y is the consumption of nationally produced goods and services, and x_s $(= x_s^c + x_s^o)$ is the total consumption of goods and services for which the city's economy has a potential competitive advantage, then the suburban household's budget constraint is specified as:

$$I = y + x_s^c \cdot (k^c + t^c) + x_s^o \cdot (k^o + t^o), \text{ or,}$$

$$I = y + x_s \cdot (k^o + t^o) - x_s^c \cdot [(k^o + t^o) - (k^c + t^c)], \text{ which equals,}$$

$$I + x_s^c \cdot [(k^o + t^o) - (k^c + t^c)] = I + Z_s = y + x_s \cdot (k^o + t^o).$$

The expression on the left is often referred to as the household's "full income" which is allocated to goods and services generally (y) and to those goods and services where the central city has a competitive advantage (x_s). The gains to the typical suburban household from being close to an efficient central city will be the added income it enjoys from its ability to buy city-produced goods and services at prices lower than those available from either suburban firms or firms outside the region:

$$(A.1) \qquad Z_s = x_s^c \cdot [(k^o + t^o) - (k^c + t^c)].$$

This income gain from lower prices is an exact income equivalent measure of the welfare benefits of being close to a productive central city when at least some of x_s is purchased from non-city suppliers in equilibrium—that is, when $x_s^o > 0$. Z_s is no longer an exact measure of the welfare gain of being near a productive central city when $x_s^o = 0$, but it does provide a reasonable income equivalent approximation to this gain when the city cost advantage is not too large.[1]

---

1. Varian (1978, pp. 212–13).

Appendix B. Descriptive Statistics for Key Variables

	1980		1990		
	City	Suburbs	City	Suburbs	Source
Dependent variables					
Average house value	48,705.76	50,588.61	53,146.24	57,740.93	Voith (1998)
	(17,061.46)	(19,352.93)	(27,482.17)	(37,268.31)	
Population	216,033.80	380,820.80	226,504.40	440,103.90	Voith (1998)
	(540,339.60)	(584,602.00)	(561,303.10)	(678,963.70)	
Per capita income	8,350.57	8,777.52	9,694.51	10,694.30	Voith (1998)
	(1,233.39)	(1,363.02)	(1,691.45)	(2,338.34)	
City and suburban fiscal and economic environment					
Poverty (percent)	15.72	10.22	18.52	10.91	Decennial censuses, standard tape file 3,
	(5.55)	(4.50)	(6.42)	(5.95)	1980 and 1990
Employment in	18.79	...	14.50	...	County business patterns, 1980 and 1990
manufacturing (percent)	(9.06)		(6.98)		
Elderly (percent)	12.24	...	13.21	...	Decennial censuses, standard tape file 3,
	(3.15)		(3.20)		1980 and 1990
Strong city unions	0.13	...	0.13	...	Valetta and Freeman (1986)
	(0.33)		(0.33)		
Weak city governance	0.68	...	0.68	...	International City Managers Association,
	(0.47)		(0.47)		*Municipal Yearbook*, 1985
City tax price[a]	0.51	...	0.52	...	See below
	(0.02)		(0.02)		
City tax price,	0.48	...	0.49	...	See below
excluding city poverty	(0.02)		(0.02)		
Research university	0.22	0.03	0.22	0.03	*U.S. News and World Report* website:
	(0.51)	(0.16)	(0.51)	(0.16)	www.usnews.com/usnews/edu/college/
					rankings/natudoc/tier1/t1natudoc.htm

(continued)

Descriptive Statistics for Key Variables (continued)

Dependent variables	1980		1990		Source
	City	Suburbs	City	Suburbs	
Cultural rank	0.25	...	0.25	...	*Places Rated Almanac*, 1985 edition.
	(0.43)		(0.43)		
1980 population density	3,766.59	250.26	...	...	Voith (1998)
	(2,779.01)	(339.46)			

	1980		1990		Source
Metropolitan area fiscal and economic environment					
State aid	0.04		0.05		Census of Governments, 1982 and 1992
	(0.04)		(0.05)		
Suburban school districts	25.77		25.77		Census of Governments, 1982
	(39.96)		(39.96)		
Strong teacher unions	0.09		0.09		Valetta and Freeman (1986)
	(0.29)		(0.29)		
Suburban support	0.06		0.06		See text
	(0.23)		(0.23)		
Airline hubs	0.17		0.17		*Air Traveler's Handbook* website; www.faqs.org/faqs/travel/air/handbook/part2/section-13.html
	(0.48)		(0.48)		
Interstate highways	0.40		0.40		Authors' calculation (map inspection)
	(0.49)		(0.49)		
New England	0.06		0.06		Authors' calculation (map inspection)
	(0.24)		(0.24)		
Middle Atlantic	0.12		0.12		Authors' calculation (map inspection)
	(0.33)		(0.33)		
Midwest	0.21		0.21		Authors' calculation (map inspection)
	(0.41)		(0.41)		

Plains	0.21 (0.41)	Authors' calculation (map inspection)
Southeast	0.23 (0.42)	Authors' calculation (map inspection)
Mountain	0.06 (0.24)	Authors' calculation (map inspection)
West Coast	0.11 (0.31)	Authors' calculation (map inspection)
Large MSA	0.49 (0.50)	See text
Heating degree days	4,675 (2,160)	Census Bureau, *City-County Data Book*; National Weather Service
Cooling degree days	1,308 (896)	Census Bureau, *City-County Data Book*; National Weather Service

a. This specification of *tax price* is for a middle-class household and defined as b_m/B. The average tax base in the city is defined as:

$$B = b_m(1 - CPOV \cdot COLD) + b_{pov} \cdot CPOV + b_{old} \cdot COLD + CI,$$

where b_m, b_{pov}, and b_{old} are the tax bases of middle-class, poor households, and old households, respectively, and *CI* is the commercial-industrial tax base per household. Alternatively:

$$B = b_m[(1 - CPOV \cdot COLD) + (b_{pov}/b_m)CPOV + (b_{old}/b_m)COLD + (CI/b_m)].$$

Assuming poor households and older families live in older housing (Glaeser and Gyourko, (2001)), then the ratios (b_{pov}/b_m) and (b_{old}/b_m) can be approximated by $(1 - \delta)^{\Delta T}$, where δ is the rate of depreciation of housing and ΔT is the difference in the age of the housing stocks occupied by middle-class households and poor/elderly households. Following Katz and Herman (1997), we assume $\delta = .02$ and $\Delta T = 45$ years, so that $(b_{pov}/b_m) = (b_{old}/b_m) = .40$; that is, the elderly and the poor live in homes roughly 40 percent of the value of the homes occupied by the middle class. We specify *CI* as

$$CI = \kappa_{nman} \cdot (1 - CMAN) + \kappa_{man} \cdot CMAN = \kappa_{man} \cdot [(\kappa_{nman}/\kappa_{man}) + (1 - (\kappa_{nman}/\kappa_{man}) \cdot CMAN], \text{ and:}$$

$$CI/b_m = (\kappa_{man}/b_m) \cdot [(\kappa_{nman}/\kappa_{man}) + (1 - (\kappa_{nman}/\kappa_{man}) \cdot CMAN],$$

where κ_{nman} and κ_{man} are the capital-land to labor ratio's for the non-manufacturing and manufacturing sectors, respectively. (We assume here that city employment approximately equals city households.) If production is Cobb-Douglas and the capital plus land share is .4 in the manufacturing and .3 in the non-manufacturing sectors, then for profit-maximizing firms in the two sectors: $\kappa_{nman}/\kappa_{man} = .64$ (Varian 1978, p. 15). Haughwout and Inman (2001, table 3) estimate $(\kappa_{man}/b_m) \approx 1.6$. Thus $CI/b_m = [1.02 + .58 \cdot CMAN]$. Finally, since $(b_{pov}/b_m) = (b_{old}/b_m) = .40$, we have:

$$B = b_m[1 - .6(CPOV + COLD) + (1.02 + .58 \cdot CMAN)],$$

from which the specification of *tax price* as b_m/B follows. *Tax price* can be defined for businesses within the city simply by multiplying the middle class *tax price* as defined here by the ratio (b_{firm}/b_m), a constant for each firm. Thus, for any individual business property, we have the same positive covariance between $(CPOV + COLD)$ and the firm's *tax price* and the same negative covariance between *CMAN* and its *tax price*. Each individual firm within the city, even a manufacturing firm, will prefer to have more capital-intensive manufacturing firms in the city's tax base. Thus *tax price* as defined above carries the essential information regarding the city's fiscal structure as that structure impacts on the fiscal costs to mobile households and firms of remaining within the city.

Appendix C. "Open" City-Suburban Public Economy

Household Sector: The populations of the city and its suburbs consist of three groups:[1]

1. Resident workers ($N_{c,s}$), who work, live, and consume in the either the city (c) or the suburbs (s);

2. Dependent households ($D_{c,s}$), who do not work but live in either the central city (c) or the suburbs (s) and receive an exogenous transfer income of Y paid for in part by their city or suburban government; and,

3. Commuting managers (M_s) who manage city firms but live in the suburbs.

The number of resident workers living and working in the city and the suburbs and the wage paid to these workers ($W_{c,s}$) are both determined endogenously within the model. The number of dependent households is set exogenously; poor households do not relocate in response to changing city or suburban fiscal conditions. The number of commuting managers is determined endogenously within the model; managers receive an exogenously determined managerial wage of S.

All households share a common set of preferences for land (l), housing capital (h), a composite consumption good (x), and a pure public good provided by their city or suburban government ($G_{c,s}$).[2] There are no spillover benefits of the local public good from the city to suburb or in reverse. Household utility for residents of the city (c) or the suburbs (s) is specified as

(C.1) $$U_{c,s} = x_{c,s}^{.75} h_{c,s}^{.20} l_{c,s}^{.05} G_{c,s}^{.05}.$$

City households maximize U_c subject to a household budget constraint and a politically decided level of city public goods and tax rates (see *Government Sector* below). The typical city resident's budget constraint is specified as:

(C.2) $(1 - \tau_{w,c}) \cdot W_c = (1 + \tau_{s,c}) \cdot x_c + (r + \tau_{p,c}) \cdot h_c + (r + \tau_{p,c}) \cdot (R_c/r) \cdot l_c,$

where $\tau_{i,c}$ represents the local city tax rate on sales ($i = s$), property ($i = p$), or wage income ($i = w$); R_c is the price of land in the city; and r is the exogenous interest rate. City worker-residents are fully mobile across locations throughout the country, not just to their suburbs. Equilibrium requires city

---

1. All endogenous variables in the model are denoted in *italics*; all exogenous variables are denoted in standard type.

2. The parameter specifications are from Haughwout and Inman (2001).

worker-residents to receive an exogenously set country-wide level of utility represented by $V(\cdot) = V_0$ in figure 1.

Suburban households maximize U_s subject to a household budget constraint and politically decided level of suburban public goods and tax rates (see *Government Sector* below). The median voter in the suburbs—also the median income resident since preferences are identical—does a full optimization of U_s since for this household the level of local public goods is endogenous. The budget constraint for suburban residents is the same as in (C.2) except we constrain all $\tau_{w,s} = \tau_{s,s} = 0$; only property taxation is used by suburban governments. Equilibrium requires suburban worker-residents to also receive the exogenously set country-wide level of utility again represented by $V(\cdot) = V_0$ in figure 1.

Dependent households in the city and the suburbs also maximize their utility as specified by (C.1), but their budget constraint is defined by:

$$(C.3) \qquad Y = (1 + \tau_{s;c,s}) \cdot x_{c,s} + (r + \tau_{p;c,s}) \cdot h_{c,s} + (r + \tau_{p;c,s}) \cdot (R_{c,s}/r) \cdot l_{c,s},$$

where Y is a common level of exogenous transfer income. Suburban dependent households will pay only property taxation ($\tau_{w,s} = \tau_{s,s} = 0$). Since dependent households cannot relocate, their utility levels will be endogenous in model, and specified as a fraction of the V_0.[3] Dependent households participate in all markets except the local labor market.

Manager households also maximize their utility again as specified by (C.1). Their budget constraint is defined by:

$$(C.4) \qquad S = (1 + \tau_{s,s}) \cdot x_m + (r + \tau_{p,s}) \cdot h_m + (r + \tau_{p,s}) \cdot (R_s/r) \cdot l_m,$$

where S is the exogenous manager's wage. Since managers live in the suburbs, they pay only the local property tax ($\tau_{w,s} = \tau_{s,s} = 0$). The city's tax on managers' wages is shifted back onto firms under our assumption that the competitive managers' market requires managers to receive their national market wage of S. Managers are assigned by their "corporation" to work in the city with the corporations deciding how many managers to employ in city firms depending upon the profitability of those firms (see *Production Sector* below). Managers participate in all markets except the local labor market.

Production Sector: The production sector of the metropolitan economy consists of:

1. *City firms that produce a composite city good* (x_c) using land ($l_{f,c}$), a composite input combining firm capital (κ_c) and managers (m), city workers (n_c),

---

3. Haughwout and Inman (2001).

and the city provided public good (G_c). In addition, city firm productivity is enhanced by agglomeration economies specified by the equilibrium density of city employment (N_c/L_c):

(C.5) $x_c = l_{f,c}^{.05} \cdot [.5 \, n_c^{.4} + .5(.5 \cdot \kappa_c^{-.5} + .5 \cdot m^{-5})^{.4/(-.5)}]^{.95/.4} \cdot G_c^{.04} \cdot (N_c/L_c)^{.01}$.

The agglomeration elasticity (= .01) is a conservative estimate from Ciccone and Hall, while all other parameter specifications are from Haughwout and Inman.[4] City firms choose their inputs so as to minimize their gross of tax costs specified as

(C.6) $C_c = (r + \tau_{p,c}) \cdot (R_c/r) \cdot l_{f,c} + W_c \cdot n_c + (r + \tau_{p,c}) \cdot (\kappa_c/r) + (1 + \tau_{m,c}) \cdot S \cdot m,$

where $\tau_{m,c}$ is the city tax rate on managers' salaries and assumed shifted back onto the firm, at least initially.

2. *Suburban firms provide retailing services* ($\tilde{x}_s$) to suburban residents using "unfinished" output (x_s) purchased from either the central city (x_s^c) or from producers outside the metropolitan area (x_s^o), where $x_s = x_s^c + x_s^o$. Purchased inputs are combined with resident suburban labor (n_s), capital (κ_s), and land ($l_{f,s}$) using a nested Cobb Douglas-CES specification. Suburban retailing also benefits from suburban produced public infrastructure (G_s):

(C.7) $\tilde{x}_s = [.5x_s^{\rho} + .5(n_s^{.85} \cdot \kappa_s^{.10} \cdot l_{f,s}^{.05})^{\rho}]^{1/\rho} \cdot G_s^{.04}.$

The parameter ρ defines the elasticity of substitution, $\varepsilon = 1/(1 - \rho)$, between unfinished output and the labor-capital-land composite input. We set $\rho = -999$ ($\varepsilon = .001$) to reflect our assumption that the unfinished good is essential to suburban retailing. Suburban firms select inputs to minimize the costs of providing retailing services, where costs of retailing are defined as:

(C.8) $C_s = (r + \tau_{p,s}) \cdot (R_s/r) \cdot l_{f,s} + W_s \cdot n_s + (r + \tau_{p,s}) \cdot (\kappa_s/r)$
$+ x_s^c \cdot (k^c + t^c) + x_s^o \cdot (k^o + t^o),$

where we assign per unit costs $k^c = k^o \equiv 1$ as a normalization, per unit transportation costs from city to suburb as $t^c \equiv 0$ as a normalization, and per unit transportation costs from outside the metropolitan area to the suburbs as $t^o = .15$. The value $t^o = .15$ was chosen to ensure suburban land values in the simulation model equal actual Philadelphia area suburban land values.

---

4. Ciccone and Hall (1996) and Haughwout and Inman (2001).

Government Sector: City and suburban governments produce the pure public good $G_{c,s}$ from pre-existing public infrastructure stocks ($G^0_{c,s}$) net of the costs of remaining principal and interest ($r^0_{c,s}$) plus additional infrastructure stock that can be purchased from the aggregate revenues made available from locally generated tax revenues ($T_{c,s}$), aid from higher levels of government ($A_{c,s}$), revenues earned from existing local financial assets ($F_{c,s}$) less payments to city and suburban dependent populations (whose population share is $\delta_{c,s}$):

(C.9) $$G_{c,s} = [G^0_{c,s} \cdot (r - r^0_{c,s})]/(r + \sigma) \cdot c_g +$$
$$[T_{c,s} + A_{c,s} + F_{c,s} - \psi \cdot Y \cdot \delta_{c,s}](N_{c,s} + D_{c,s} + M_s)/(r + \sigma) \cdot c_g$$

where σ is the rate of depreciation of public infrastructures, and c_g is the production costs of local infrastructure, set equal to $c_g \equiv 1$ for the baseline simulations, and ψ is the local government's mandated share of contributions to support its dependent population.

Local tax revenues ($T_{c,s}$) are endogenous. In both the city and suburbs the only locally chosen tax rate is the local property tax. City property tax rates are chosen in order to maximize aggregate revenues, while the suburban median voter chooses the utility-maximizing level of G_s and then sets property tax rates in order to produce that level of public spending. If the city also uses a wage, sales, or commuter tax, then aggregate city revenues include revenues from those taxes as well.

Solution Procedure: Through the government budget constraint, $G_{c,s}$ is a function of local wages and rents, household consumption, and firm production, while wages and rents, household consumption, and firm production depend in turn on $G_{c,s}$. The model is solved by first specifying an initial value for local property tax rates $\tau_{p,c}$ and $\tau_{p,s}$. For those rates we then specify initial values of $G_{c,s}$. The algorithm then calculates the private economic outcomes and tax bases and local revenues resulting in new values for $G_{c,s}$. Still holding the initial property rate fixed, new values of $G_{c,s}$ imply new private market outcomes and thus new tax bases, new revenues, and another set of new value for $G_{c,s}$. We solve the model until convergence is achieved for $G_{c,s}$. Our convergence criterion requires the levels of $G_{c,s}$ to be within \$1 of their previous iteration's values. Convergence occurs typically within 20 iterations or less. This is the public sector and private market equilibrium for the initial values of $\tau_{p,c}$ and $\tau_{p,s}$. The political equilibrium then selects a value of $\tau_{p,c}$ which maximizes central city revenues and that value of $\tau_{p,s}$ which maximizes the median suburban income resident's welfare, iterating as above to calculate the equilibrium values of $G_{c,s}$ and the private economy for each property tax rate.

Calibration to Philadelphia MSA, 1990: Land available for firm and household locations is set to equal useable land area in Philadelphia and its suburbs. The city and suburbs are assigned exogenous poor and elderly populations equal to their 1990 census values of 112,000 poverty households and 65,000 (non-poor) elderly households for Philadelphia (CPOV = .20; COLD = .12) and 99,000 poor households and 282,000 (non-poor) elderly households for the surrounding suburbs (SPOV = .048; percent non-poor elderly = .13). Poor and elderly households are assumed to receive a transfer income of $13,500 each from the state and federal governments and an additional $1,340 each from their local government as the value of state and federal mandated services on their city and suburban governments.[5] Philadelphia receives $3,753 for each household in intergovernmental transfers, while the suburban government(s) are paid $3,777 for each household in transfers.[6] Both Philadelphia and its surrounding counties have inherited stocks of the public good acquired from past investments but not yet fully depreciated. We have estimated the replacement value of these stocks for Philadelphia and its suburbs at $33,840/household in the city and $6,221/household in the suburbs.[7] There is an annual cost to maintaining this stock equal to its rate of depreciation of .03 plus the residual interest and principal expenses due on the stock's initial debt. These costs of the inherited stock are paid before additions to the stock are purchased at a current interest rate of .04. In all equilibrium outcomes studied here, the final purchase of the public good by the city and the suburbs exceeds these initial stocks. Philadelphia has four taxes: a property tax, a resident wage tax, a non-resident (commuter) tax, and a tax on gross receipts on city firms. The suburban government can use a property tax or a resident wage tax. To make our simulations for the Philadelphia MSA as representative as possible, we restrict the city to use only the property tax to pay for the added costs of public services under each of the four weak city finance regimes. Similarly, we require the suburbs to use the property tax to buy their additional units of the public good. City tax rates other than the property tax rate are exogenous and set at their FY 1990 values.

5. Summers and Jakubowski (1997).
6. U.S. Census Bureau (1992).
7. Haughwout and Inman (1996).

Comment

J. Vernon Henderson: Andy Haughwout and Bob Inman have written a provocative and interesting paper, articulating, with empirical evidence, why suburbs might aid central cities. There are two parts to the argument. First is the idea that central city economic development strongly affects economic development of the suburbs. Drawing upon the relevant literature, the authors explain that a high level of central city employment is important to exploiting local scale externalities and offering efficient central city production. Efficient central city production is important to suburban firms, looking for low-cost and high-quality intermediate service or other inputs. The second part of the argument is that central city "fiscal institutions" affect the willingness of firms to locate there. Poor institutions make local production costly and drive firms from the city, reducing central city scale and efficiency. The authors are careful to point out that the evidence suggests, while there is some degree of competition between cities and suburbs, their joint fortunes are intertwined in the upstream-downstream production process. Driving economic activity out of the central city, in net, ultimately harms suburban development. This is an extremely important insight. My more critical comments on the details of the paper should be kept in perspective. This is an important paper.

The authors examine the relationships between central city and suburban outcomes and central city fiscal institutions. Better center city institutions should help both the central city and the suburbs. Outcomes have to do with income and population growth. As measures of fiscal institutions, the authors use the central city poverty rate; state rules on duty to bargain in the public sector; and weak versus strong governance, where strong means centralization of budget powers with a directly elected mayor or a city council elected-at-large; and finally, an "estimate" of the tax price facing middle-class voters. The last is a formula that is supposed to estimate the ratio of housing values for middle-class owners to average property values in the city. Average property value declines and the tax price rises in the formula as poverty rates and the proportion of elderly rise or the percent of manufacturing declines. There are several issues with these measures of institutions.

The most critical is that even if the measures are the right ones and they have big effects on outcomes, it is not clear how they relate to suburban aid to the city. That is, the missing link in the paper is an articulation of how suburban governments could act or could aid central cities to change these "institutions." For example, the second measure involves state policy. Another missing link: what can suburbs realistically do to change central city poverty or property values? Is this a recommendation that suburbs offer financial subsidies to firms to locate in the central city? If so, what is the political support for this? How do suburbs go about changing weak city governance in any realistic fashion? Would proposals for incentives by suburbs for their central city to adopt better governance structures simply be used as local political ammunition about "outside influences"? Perhaps more critically, how do the more than 100 suburban governments in a large metro area such as Chicago act as a collective to offer incentives to the central city? Is this really a paper more about state policies and rewriting state constitutions to ensure better local governance all round? That would seem to be more realistic.

On the institutional measures themselves, the poverty rate and the tax-price construct seem like outcome variables, not institutional variables. In particular, the outcome measures in the paper have to do with separate city and suburb housing value, population, and overall income growth from 1980 through 1990. Growth in the poverty rate and the components of change in the tax-price variable—changes in the poverty rate, in the elderly rate, and in the share of manufacturing—seem like other outcome measures, rather than explanatory variables. In particular, the average income growth rate looks at changes in mean income, while the poverty tax looks at how the size of the lower tail of the income distribution changes. Both are outcomes.

Turning to the specific formulation in equations 1 and 2, we find that 1980 through 1990 growth is related to changes in 1980 through 1990 "exogenous" covariates, to difference out any city fixed effect. The Glaeser, Scheinkman, and Shleifer formulation in their 1995 *Journal of Monetary Economics* paper would instead relate 1980 through 1990 growth to 1980 base period variables.[1] Glaeser and others have a model explaining their

---

1. See Glaeser, Scheinkman, and Shleifer (1995, pp. 117–43).

choice, but Haughwout and Inman do not really explain theirs. In fact, their growth formulation is an odd mixture of explanatory variables that are sometimes in level form and sometimes in change form, which makes interpretation difficult.

In the econometrics, on the issue of the validity of using changes in the poverty rate to explain causal change in income or property values, the authors attempt some instrumental variable estimation. Instruments seem weak (a first-stage F-statistic well under ten) and no specification tests are reported (for example, a Sargan test). But, to reiterate, it is hard to assert that a change in the size of the tail of the income distribution in an economic structure sense causes a change in the mean. The relationship might be interpreted as simply indicating that a first-order stochastic dominance improvement or deterioration in a distribution raises or lowers its mean. That is, the poverty rate and mean income are simply alternative outcome measures.

Haughwout and Inman have tackled an extremely difficult problem. By analyzing aggregate city data, they find that arguably almost all measures are endogenous and valid; strong instruments are almost nonexistent. I think the work would be improved by following the Glaeser and others' model and using base period variables to explain growth. But I also think it would be interesting to see a simpler formulation. If changes in the poverty and tax price are removed as covariates, what happens to the effect of just institutions— weak versus strong governance and labor laws? If these really matter, the conclusion is that state policy governing local institutions and local public sector bargaining have a big effect on MSA economic health. While that might not support direct suburb–central city "aid" per se, it supports reform at the state level.

References

Acemoglu, Daron, and Joshua Angrist. 1999. "How Large Are the Social Returns to Education? Evidence from Compulsory Schooling Laws." Working Paper 7444. Cambridge, Mass.: National Bureau of Economic Research (December).

Arnott, Richard, Andre de Palma, and Robin Lindsey. 1991. "A Temporal and Spatial Equilibrium Analysis of Commuter Parking." *Journal of Public Economics* 45 (August): 301–35.

Bartik, Timothy. 1991. *Who Benefits from State and Local Economic Development Policies?* Kalamazoo, Mich: Upjohn Institute.

Beardsell, Mark, and Vernon Henderson. 1999. "Spatial Evolution of the Computer Industry in the USA." *European Economic Review* 43 (June): 431–56.

Brooks, Nancy, and Anita Summers. "Does the Economic Health of America's Largest Cities Affect the Economic Health of Their Suburbs?" Wharton School, University of Pennsylvania. Mimeo, no date.

Brown, Charles, and James Medoff. 1988. "Employer Size, Pay, and the Ability to Pay in the Public Sector." In *When Public Sector Workers Unionize,* edited by Richard Freeman and Casey Ichniowski, 195–213. University of Chicago Press.

Ciccone, Antonio. 2002. "Agglomeration Effects in Europe." *European Economic Review* 46 (February): 213–27.

Ciccone, Antonio, and Robert Hall. 1996. "Productivity and the Density of Economic Activity." *American Economic Review* 86 (March): 54–70.

Cox, Gary, and Timothy Tutt. 1984. "Universalism and Allocative Decision-Making in the Los Angeles County Board of Supervisors." *Journal of Politics* 46 (May): 546–55.

Cullen, Julie Berry, and Steven D. Levitt. 1999. "Crime, Urban Flight, and the Consequences for Cities." *Review of Economics and Statistics* 81 (May): 159–69.

Cutler, David, Edward Glaeser, and Jacob Vigdor. 1999. "The Rise and Decline of the American Ghetto." *Journal of Political Economy* 107 (June): 445–506.

Downes, Thomas, and Thomas Pogue. 1994. "Adjusting School Aid Formulas for the Higher Costs of Educating Disadvantaged Students." *National Tax Journal* 47 (March): 89–110.

Freeman, Richard, and Robert Valletta. 1988. "The Effects of Public Sector Labor Laws on Labor Market Institutions and Outcomes." In *When Public Sector Workers Unionize*, edited by Richard Freeman and Casey Ichniowski. University of Chicago Press.

Gilligan, Thomas, and John Matsusaka. 1995. "Deviations from Constituent Interests: The Role of Legislative Structure and Political Parties in the States." *Economic Inquiry* 33 (July): 383–401.

Glaeser, Edward. 2000. "The Future of Urban Research: Non–Market Interactions." *Brookings-Wharton Papers on Urban Affairs* (1): 101–38.

Glaeser, Edward, and Joseph Gyourko. 2001. "Urban Decline and Durable Housing." Working Paper 8598. Cambridge, Mass.: National Bureau of Economic Research (November).

Glaeser, Edward, and Matthew Kahn. 2001. "Decentralized Employment and the Transformation of the American City." *Brookings-Wharton Papers on Urban Affairs* (2): 1–47.

Glaeser, Edward, and Bruce Sacerdote. 1999. "Why Is There More Crime in Cities?" *Journal of Political Economy* 107 (December): Supplement 225–58.

Glaeser, Edward L., José A. Scheinkman, and Andrei Shleifer. 1995. "Economic Growth in a Cross-Section of Cities." *Journal of Monetary Economics* 36 (1): 117–43.

Glaeser, Edward, and others. 1992. "Growth in Cities." *Journal of Political Economy* 100 (December): 1126–52.

Gyourko, Joseph, and Joseph Tracy. 1991a. "Public Sector Budgeting and the Local Budgetary Process." *Research in Labor Economics* 12: 117–36.

———. 1991b. "The Structure of Local Public Finance and the Quality of Life." *Journal of Political Economy* 99 (August): 774–806.

Haughwout, Andrew. 2002a. "Public Infrastructure Investments, Productivity, and Welfare in Fixed Geographic Areas." *Journal of Public Economics* 83 (March): 405–28.

———. 2002b. "Local Public Sector Efficiency with Mobile Households and Firms." Federal Reserve Bank of New York. Privately circulated mimeo.

Haughwout, Andrew, and Robert P. Inman. 2001. "Fiscal Policies in Open Cities with Firms and Households." *Regional Science and Urban Economics* 31 (April): 147–80.

Haughwout, Andrew, and others. 2000. "Local Revenue Hills: A General Equilibrium Specification with Evidence from Four U.S. Cities." Working Paper 7603. Cambridge, Mass.: National Bureau of Economic Research.

Hellman, Daryl, and Joel Naroff. 1979. "The Impact of Crime on Urban Residential Property Values." *Urban Studies* 16 (February): 105–12.

Henderson, Vernon, Ari Kuncoro, and Matt Turner. 1995. "Industrial Development in Cities." *Journal of Political Economy* 103 (October): 1067–90.

Ichniowski, Casey. 1988. "Public Sector Union Growth and Bargaining Laws: A Proportional Hazards Approach with Time-Varying Treatments." In *When Public Sector Workers Unionize,* edited by Richard Freeman and Casey Ichniowski, 19–38. University of Chicago Press.

Inman, Robert P. 1979. "Fiscal Performance of Local Governments." In *Current Issues in Urban Economics*, edited by Peter Mieszkowski and Mahlon Straszheim, 270–321. Johns Hopkins University Press.

———. 1989. "Local Decision to Tax: Evidence from Large U.S. Cities." *Regional Science and Urban Economics* 19 (August): 455–91.

———. 1995. "How to Have a Fiscal Crisis: Lessons from Philadelphia." *American Economic Review* 85 (May): 378–83.

Inman, Robert P., and Michael A. Fitts. 1990. "Political Institutions and Fiscal Policy: Evidence from U.S. Historical Record." *Journal of Law, Economics, and Organization* 6 (Special Issue): 79–132.

Inman, Robert P., and Daniel L. Rubinfeld. 1979. "The Judicial Pursuit of Local Fiscal Equity." *Harvard Law Review* 92 (June): 1662–1750.

Jacobs, Jane. 1969. *The Economy of Cities*. Random House.

Ladd, Helen. 1975. "Local Education Expenditures, Fiscal Capacity, and the Composition of the Property Tax Base." *National Tax Journal* 28 (June): 145–58.

Marshall, Alfred. 1890. *Principles of Economics*. Macmillan.

Meyer, Bruce. 1998. "Do the Poor Move to Receive Higher Welfare Benefits?" Working Paper 58. Joint Center for Poverty Research.

Pauly, Mark. 1973. "Income Redistribution as a Local Public Good." *Journal of Public Economics* 2 (February): 35–58.

Rauch, James. 1993. "Productivity Gains from Geographic Concentration of Human Capital: Evidence from Cities." *Journal of Urban Economics* 34 (November): 380–400.

Roback, Jennifer. 1982. "Wages, Rents, and the Quality of Life." *Journal of Political Economy* 90 (December): 1257–78.

Rosen, Sherwin. 1979. "Wage-Based Indexes of the Quality of Urban Life." In *Current Issues in Urban Economics,* edited by Peter Mieszkowski, and Mahlon Straszheim, 270–321. Johns Hopkins University Press.

Rosenthal, Stuart, and William Strange. 2002. "Geography, Industrial Organization, and Agglomeration." *Review of Economics and Statistics* (forthcoming).

Samuelson, Paul. 1954. "The Pure Theory of Public Expenditures." *Review of Economics and Statistics* 36 (November): 387–89.

Small, Kenneth. 1992. *Urban Transportation Economics*. New York: Harwood Academic Publishers.

Summers, Anita, and Lara Jakubowski. 1997. "The Fiscal Burden of Unreimbursed Poverty Expenditures." *Greater Philadelphia Regional Review*: 10–12.

Thaler, Richard. 1978. "A Note on the Value of Crime Control: Evidence from the Property Markets." *Journal of Urban Economics* 5 (January): 137–45.

Tiebout, Charles. 1956. "A Pure Theory of Local Government Expenditures." *Journal of Political Economy* 60 (October): 416–24.

U.S. Census Bureau. 1992. *Census of Governments*. U.S. Government Printing Office.

Varian, Hal. 1978. *Microeconomic Analysis*. W. W. Norton and Company.

Voith, Richard. 1993. "Changing Capitalization of CBD–Oriented Transportation Systems: Evidence from Philadelphia: 1970–88. *Journal of Urban Economics* 33 (May): 361–76.

———. 1998. "Do Suburbs Need Cities?" *Journal of Regional Science* 38 (August): 445–64.

TERESA GARCIA-MILÀ
Universitat Pompeu Fabra (Barcelona)

THERESE J. MCGUIRE
Northwestern University

Tax Incentives and the City

> The General Assembly has determined that the relocation of the international head-
> quarters of large, multinational corporations from outside of Illinois to a location
> within Illinois creates a substantial public benefit and will foster economic growth
> and development within the State.
>
> *State of Illinois Public Act 92-0207, May 2001*

ON MAY 10, 2001, the Boeing Corporation announced its selection of Chicago as the new home for its corporate headquarters. The city of Chicago and the state of Illinois had teamed up to offer Boeing a generous package of tax incentives and other subsidies. The high-profile competition for Boeing was reminiscent of many others before in which city and state governments had opened their purses to lure or retain businesses. Why would Chicago be willing to offer tax breaks to attract Boeing? After all, there are plenty of other deserving businesses already located in Chicago or potentially interested in locating in Chicago. Moreover, is this sort of competition among cities not just a zero-sum game? In this paper we maintain that in some cases—arguably in the Boeing case—tax competition in the form of firm-specific tax breaks to lure or retain businesses can be welfare improving for the city and a positive-sum game.

Within the existing theoretical tax competition literature, it is difficult to justify tax incentives. As we interpret the literature, tax competition either

We received useful comments and suggestions from our two discussants, Ed Glaeser and Todd Sinai, and the editors, Bill Gale and Janet Pack. We are particularly grateful to Julie Cullen, Andy Haughwout, Vernon Henderson, and Bob Inman for their encouraging sugges-tions. We are indebted to Hongbin Cai, Antonio Ciccone, and Bill Zame for stimulating and productive conversations. We are grateful to Diane McCarthy and Rebecca Hanson for excel-lent research assistance. Garcia-Milà gratefully acknowledges support from DGICYT, Ministerio de Ciencia y Tecnologia, Spain.

95

results in benefit taxes being imposed on mobile capital or in inefficiently low taxes on mobile capital. Neither strand of the theoretical literature would seem to support tax incentives. We expand upon this argument below.

In addition, there appears to be very little empirical evidence to support the notion that tax incentives are effective, let alone efficient. We are unaware of any direct systematic evidence on the effect of firm-specific tax incentives. Then again, there is a large empirical literature that asks whether differences in general tax burdens are a significant factor in explaining differences in various measures of aggregate economic activity, including firm locations. The evidence is inconclusive, although some recent surveys and at least one recent paper conclude that taxes are, in some instances, statistically significant determinants of state and local economic growth.[1] Whether it is appropriate to infer from these studies of the effect of overall tax burdens that firm-specific tax breaks are effective is debatable.

Most empirical studies of the effect of taxes on aggregate economic activity measure economic growth as an increase in employment or investment. Courant argues that increases in employment do not necessarily translate into increases in welfare.[2] In the present study we ask a different question, but we argue, too, that cities might be interested in attracting firms for reasons other than jobs. From this perspective, the focus of the existing empirical literature may reveal little about the desirability of tax incentives.

Still, tax breaks in the form of property tax abatements, sales and income tax breaks, and other subsidies from state and local governments to attract or retain firms are pervasive. Why? The answer may simply be politics. No mayor or governor who seeks electoral success will risk being seen as the one responsible for losing the big automobile plant or high-technology firm. In Wolman's survey of the recent literature on the politics of local economic activity, he suggests that protection of tax base is a primary reason for economic development activities.[3] Pagano and Bowman argue that even fiscally healthy cities may offer tax breaks and subsidies for symbolic reasons to maintain a city's image.[4] Another possibility is that the theory may need to be modified to accommodate more realistic assumptions. Within the existing theoretical economics literature, one can find arguments that real world taxes may be higher than the efficient level because, for example, governments

1. For recent surveys, see Bartik (1991) and Wasylenko (1997); for a recent paper, see Mark, McGuire, and Papke (2000).
2. Courant (1994).
3. Wolman (1996).
4. Pagano and Bowman (1995).

maximize an objective function other than social welfare. Thus tax breaks may be needed to pull tax levels closer to the efficient level.[5]

Within a simple model of tax competition we ask whether tax incentives, defined as a tax rate lower than the marginal benefit of the public goods and services provided to firms, can be justified. Starting from a base case in which communities impose benefit taxes on firms in equilibrium, we add one new assumption: new capital investment is assumed to generate a form of agglomeration economies, which we call concentration externalities.[6] In this case, in contrast to the usual reason given for tax competition and tax breaks (protection of tax base), we argue that tax breaks may be justified because they can be welfare improving.

The remainder of the paper is structured as follows: In the next section we provide a review and our interpretation of a limited selection from the theoretical tax competition literature. We present our theoretical model in the subsequent section and describe in the penultimate section the Boeing case, which seems to fit well with our theory. We provide conclusions and possible directions for future research in the final section.

Can Tax Incentives Be Justified under Existing Models of Tax Competition?

The theoretical treatment of tax competition has two rather distinct strands. Each is concerned with the question of whether tax competition results in efficient outcomes, but the two come to opposite conclusions. Our interest in these theories is to explore whether firm-specific tax incentives (or tax breaks) can be justified. In our interpretation, for different reasons, neither model argues for tax breaks to lure firms to communities.

One strand of the literature, dating back at least to Oates and continuing with several papers in the mid-1980s, finds that tax competition results in inefficiently low taxes and public services.[7] Oates argues that tax competition designed to attract firms that seek to maximize profits by freely choosing among localities will lead local officials to reduce taxes on capital.[8] When deciding the level of public goods to be financed by taxes, communities will take into account the cost of losing potential firms. This will result in an

---

5. Oates (1996).
6. See Oates and Schwab (1991).
7. See Oates (1972); Zodrow and Mieszkowski (1986); Wilson (1986); Wildasin (1989). These papers and many others referenced herein are summarized in Wilson (1999).
8. Oates (1972).

underprovision of public goods and services, especially if communities do not offer services of direct benefit to the firms. If all jurisdictions follow the same pattern, none gain a competitive advantage, but they all will have lower revenues and will provide lower levels of public goods than if they were not competing.

Authors using formal models of tax competition reached similar conclusions. Two of the earliest and most influential papers are by Zodrow and Mieszkowski and by Wilson.[9] These authors analyze tax competition within a framework where the provision of a consumption public good is financed by a local tax on capital. No other forms of taxation are available in an unrestricted form. There is a fixed total amount of capital in society, which is perfectly mobile across jurisdictions and for which jurisdictions compete. Jurisdictions are all alike and small so that their decisions do not influence the going interest rate. In equilibrium, a community will choose a level of public good provision at which the marginal benefit equals the marginal cost. Because the community finances the unit increase in the public good with an increase in the tax on capital, capital will flow out of the jurisdiction at hand into other jurisdictions in response to the tax increase. Thus the marginal cost of a unit increase in the public good includes not only the resource cost, but also the loss in tax revenues associated with the loss of capital. The latter is a local loss but not a social cost because other jurisdictions realize a fiscal benefit from the inflow of capital. The cost of local public goods is therefore overestimated by the jurisdiction, which will choose an inefficiently low level of public good and capital tax rate. As Wildasin shows, this inefficiency could be corrected by a central government subsidy to local governments that internalizes the externality.[10]

In another instance of competition leading to inefficiently low taxes, McGuire examines a case of mobile residents in which the residents-consumers have preferences for redistribution.[11] To accomplish the redistribution, local governments rely on ability-to-pay taxes. The residents-consumers are heterogeneous in terms of income (or wealth) and mobility. In this setting, a local jurisdiction has an incentive to offer tax breaks to relatively mobile and wealthy people to try to induce them to move in. In equilibrium, all jurisdictions would offer tax breaks to the relatively mobile and wealthy and thus there would be no movement of wealthy people across jurisdictions. The

9. Zodrow and Mieszkowski (1986); Wilson (1986).
10. Wildasin (1989).
11. McGuire (1991).

result is an inefficiently low level of public good provision (in this case, redistribution).

To summarize and interpret this strand of the literature, in a world where tax competition results in inefficiently low taxes on mobile factors, tax breaks that offer even lower tax rates to specific firms are in the wrong direction and enhance the distortions generated by competition.

Another strand of the literature, dating back to Tiebout and continuing with papers by Oates and Schwab, reaches very different conclusions.[12] Under these models, tax competition among local governments results in an efficient allocation of resources with mobile residents and firms facing nondistortionary benefit taxes.

Oates and Schwab analyze the allocation of capital across jurisdictions in a model where local governments provide public inputs to firms as well as public consumption goods for residents.[13] What distinguishes Oates and Schwab's model from the Zodrow-Mieszkowski-Wilson models is that regions have access to other forms of taxation in addition to taxes on mobile capital. Under these assumptions, tax competition yields efficient outcomes: local taxes become benefit taxes and the allocation of capital across jurisdictions is socially efficient. The tax on capital equals the value of the increased production attributable to a marginal increase in the public input, while a head tax on workers pays for the consumption good. As in Zodrow-Mieszkowski-Wilson, if jurisdictions can rely only on capital taxes, then the equilibrium is inefficient, and an underprovision of public goods results.[14]

Although the Oates-Schwab conclusions about the desirability of tax competition are very different from those reached by Zodrow-Mieszkowski-Wilson, the implications for tax incentives are similar. The Oates-Schwab model results in taxes on mobile capital that are benefit taxes; thus tax breaks to firms would move the economy away from the efficient point and would reduce the utility of consumers.

For very different reasons, tax competition is also beneficial in a world where the local government is not a benevolent social planner that aims to maximize the welfare of its constituents, but rather wishes to maximize the public budget.[15] Brennan and Buchanan argue that, in this case, interjurisdic-

12. Tiebout (1956); Oates and Schwab (1988, 1991).
13. Oates and Schwab (1991).
14. Zodrow and Mieszkowski (1986); Wilson (1986). In a related paper, Oates and Schwab examine the case where local authorities set environmental regulations (Oates and Schwab,1988). Again, under certain assumptions, they find that competition results in efficient outcomes.
15. Niskanen (1977).

tional competition prevents officials from excessively taxing constituents and firms.[16] Across-the-board tax reductions, rather than selective tax breaks, would appear to be the appropriate policy response under this model.

None of these theories seems to support the idea that tax breaks are beneficial and can be a key factor in improving the economies of the localities that offer them.[17] Tax breaks either move the economy away from the efficient allocation, or worsen an already inefficient outcome. Our departure from the existing literature considers the possibility that new capital investment brings benefits to the community in addition to the increase in production and wages associated with the new capital. These benefits are concentration externalities, a form of agglomeration economies associated with increased capital investment. In our model, a reduction in capital taxes below the level of a benefit tax will induce firms to make optimal decisions and will result in an efficient allocation of both public and private resources.

A Model of Tax Competition with Agglomeration Economies

The models of Zodrow-Mieszkowski-Wilson assume that communities are restricted to one tax instrument, a tax on mobile capital.[18] This assumption has some basis in fact as local governments in the United States rely heavily on property taxes. The tax on capital must finance all of the locally provided public goods. In their models, competition for mobile capital leads to an underprovision of public goods—the tax imposed on capital is too low from an efficiency perspective. Oates and Schwab assume that communities have access to a head tax on residents, thus allowing for more degrees of freedom in setting the tax on capital.[19] Competition for mobile capital under their assumptions results in an efficient allocation of resources with benefit taxes being imposed on capital as well as residents. These assumptions and results also have some basis in fact. Local governments do have access to multiple tax sources, and many of them have the potential, at least at the margin, to be designed as benefit taxes.

We choose to use the Oates and Schwab framework as our starting point for two reasons. First, while both the Zodrow-Mieszkowski-Wilson and the Oates-Schwab tax assumptions are inherently unrealistic, we are comfortable

16. Brennan and Buchanan (1980).
17. Black and Hoyt (1989), under the assumption that public good provision is characterized by decreasing average cost, find that if taxes are set according to average cost, selective subsidies to firms may improve welfare.
18. Zodrow and Mieszkowski (1986); Wilson (1986).
19. Oates and Schwab (1991).

with Oates and Schwab's assumption that communities have access to at least some form of benefit taxes. Arguably, even the local property tax, when coupled with local zoning laws, can be viewed as a benefit tax.[20] The second and more compelling reason for choosing the Oates and Schwab framework is that we are fundamentally interested in a different question. Both Zodrow-Mieszkowski-Wilson and Oates-Schwab explore whether tax competition leads to efficiency. We are interested in exploring whether it can ever be optimal to offer tax incentives. It thus seems natural to start with a framework in which tax competition leads to an efficient allocation of resources, and in which firms face benefit taxes in equilibrium. From this nice state of affairs, we ask whether it can be in the interests of consumers to offer tax breaks to firms.

The basic Oates and Schwab model has several elements. Many jurisdictions compete for a mobile capital stock by offering low taxes on capital and providing a productive input to firms. The benefit of attracting firms and their capital is higher wages for the resident workers (consumers). This benefit must be weighed against the loss of tax revenues and the cost of providing the public input. Oates and Schwab find that the optimal tax charged by each community is a benefit tax; in other words, the tax rate is equal to the marginal benefit of the public input to the firm. The tax on capital does not generate any fiscal surplus or deficit to apply against a second public good, which communities provide to consumers. Instead, consumers pay a head tax that just covers the costs of providing the consumption public good. The allocation of resources under this model is efficient.

Clearly, tax incentives, which we define as a tax rate lower than the marginal benefit of the public goods and services provided to firms, are not offered by communities in the Oates and Schwab world because they are not in their best interest. One justification often given by cities that offer tax breaks to new firms is that the new firms will improve the business environment for existing and future business. One form this could take is agglomeration economies wherein all firms experience productivity increases as the number or size of geographically concentrated firms increases. Such externalities and their impact on cities are explored by several authors including Rauch, Henderson and others, and Henderson.[21] Many of these authors stress information spillovers as a source of interfirm externalities, and their focus is almost exclusively on manufacturing.

20. Hamilton (1975).
21. Rauch (1993a); Henderson, Kuncoro, and Turner (1995); Henderson (2001).

If the location of new firms generates agglomeration economies, effective tax incentives may improve the welfare of the winning community. To explore this idea we adapt Oates and Schwab's model by adding what we call concentration externalities. Our idea is that a greater concentration of externality-producing firms (capital) results in increased productivity through, for example, an easier exchange of ideas, particularly among business services firms. Specifically, we write the production function for a particular jurisdiction as

$$(1) \qquad\qquad Q = F(K, L, X)\left(\frac{K}{L}\right)^{\delta},$$

where K is private capital, L is labor, and X is a publicly provided input distributed to firms in proportion to their capital stocks.[22] It is assumed that society has a fixed stock of capital, perfectly mobile among the jurisdictions, and that labor is immobile and fixed for each community. The term $(K/L)^{\delta}$ represents the augmentation to productivity associated with greater concentrations of private capital, our representation of agglomeration economies. This representation is related to the density measure explored by Ciccone and Hall.[23] Assuming that the function F is homogeneous of degree one, equation 1 can be rewritten as

$$(2) \qquad\qquad q = f(k, x)k^{\delta},$$

where q is the output to labor ratio, k is the capital to labor ratio, and x is the public input to labor ratio.

We assume that firms in the jurisdiction are identical and that each individual firm takes the aggregate amount of private capital as given when making its choices of capital and labor.[24] Thus a representative firm maximizes profits subject to the production function in equation 2 taking k^{δ} as a constant. That is, the firm does not take into account that an increase in its capital has a productivity effect on all firms in the region, including its own. The firm will choose levels of private capital and labor such that their marginal returns equal their respective per unit costs. Assuming a per unit tax on capital of t,

22. X is not a pure public good; it is subject to congestion to the same extent as a private good.

23. Ciccone and Hall (1996).

24. As all firms are identical, per capita capital and public input are the same for each firm and for the regional aggregate. Therefore, equation 2 can also be viewed as representing the production function of a firm, where k and x are the firm's inputs per unit of labor.

and an interest rate of r, this implies the following condition for the optimal choice of private capital for the firm:[25]

(3)
$$\left(f_k + \frac{x}{k}f_x\right)k^\delta - t = r,$$

where subscripts represent partial derivatives.

The wage in each community is set competitively and according to

(4)
$$w = f(k,x)k^\delta - kf_k k^\delta - xf_x k^\delta.$$

Assume that, unlike the firm, the social planner (or mayor) recognizes that an increase in aggregate private capital makes all firms more productive. Essentially, there is a spillover benefit to all firms if any one firm increases its level of private capital or if a new firm enters the jurisdiction thereby expanding the existing level of private capital. The local government's objective is to maximize the welfare of its constituents, taking into account the competitive conditions for the capital and labor markets and the private and public budget constraints. The local government's problem is

$$\max_{c,g,k,x,t,z} u(c,g)$$

(5)
$$\text{s.t.} \quad y + w = c + z$$
$$w = f(k,x)k^\delta - kf_k k^\delta - xf_k k^\delta$$
$$r = f_k k^\delta + \frac{x}{k}f_x k^\delta - t$$
$$z + kt = p_g g + p_x x,$$

where c is a private consumption good and the numeraire, g is a publicly provided good that can be purchased at price p_g, p_x is the price per unit of the publicly provided input, and y is nonwage income. The local government can impose a head tax z on its residents. The first order conditions can be rearranged to yield the following conditions:

(6)
$$\frac{u_g}{u_c} = p_g$$

(7)
$$f_x k^\delta = p_x$$

(8)
$$f_k k^\delta + f(k,x)\delta k^{\delta-1} = r$$

---

25. We assume that all jurisdictions are small and take the interest rate as a parameter.

$$(9) \qquad t = \frac{x}{k} f_x k^\delta - f(k,x) \delta k^{\delta - 1}$$

To induce the firm to choose the socially optimal level of capital according to equation 8, the tax rate faced by the firm in equation 3 must be set according to equation 9. The optimal tax rate on capital when agglomeration economies are taken into account, what we refer to as t^*, is equal to the marginal benefit to the firm of the public input minus the marginal agglomeration benefit of additional capital. The latter term is the subsidy needed to induce each firm to choose the socially optimal amount of private capital.

If instead k^δ is taken as a constant, that is, if the local government overlooks the concentration externalities when it maximizes utility subject to the constraints in equation 5, the optimal tax rate $\hat{t}$ is

$$(10) \qquad \hat{t} = \frac{x}{k} f_x k^\delta.$$

As in Oates and Schwab, the optimal tax rate when agglomeration economies are ignored is a benefit tax equal to the marginal benefit to the firm of the public input.[26]

Clearly, for any pair of x and k, t^* is less than $\hat{t}$. Thus we obtain the result that when agglomeration economies are taken into account, the optimal tax rate is lower than the tax rate that results when agglomeration economies are present but not accounted for. A tax incentive, defined here as a tax rate less than the marginal benefit to the firm from the public input, is justified to induce firms to choose the optimal amount of private capital.

The optimal amount of private capital when agglomeration economies are recognized, k^*, is greater than the amount of private capital chosen by the firm when they are not, $\hat{k}$. To see this, note that when the tax rate is equal to $\hat{t}$, that is, when it is a benefit tax, equation 3 becomes

$$(11) \qquad f_k k^\delta = r.$$

Comparing this equation, which determines $\hat{k}$, to equation 8, which determines k^*, it is clear that $\hat{k}$ will be less than k^* as long as $f_k k^\delta$ is decreasing in k (because the second term of equation 8 is positive). This will be the case if as k increases the decline in the derivative of f with respect to k dominates the increase in the agglomeration effect, which seems a reasonable assumption.

---

26. Oates and Schwab (1991, pp. 130–31).

Figure 1.

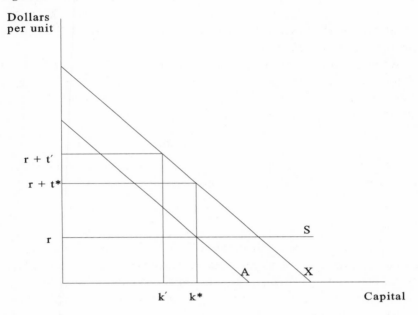

In figure 1, we compare the optimal solution with the one that would occur if firms did not receive a tax incentive. Line *A* represents the local government's demand for capital when agglomeration economies are taken into account. It is the lefthand side of equation 8 or $f_k k^\delta + f(k,x)\delta k^{\delta-1}$. Line *X* represents the firm's demand for capital. If we rewrite equation 3 slightly, we see the firm's choice of capital is the amount that equates $f_k k^\delta + x/k f_x k^\delta$ to $r + t$. The functions represented by line *A* and line *X* differ only in the second terms. The second term of the equation defining line *A* reflects the increase in output due to agglomeration economies associated with an increase in *k*, whereas the second term of the equation defining line *X* reflects the additional output due to the increase in the public input associated with an increase in k.[27]

The perfectly elastic supply of capital is represented by line *S* at the going interest rate *r*. The intersection of *A* with *S* determines the optimal amount of capital k^* as given by the solution to the maximization problem (5) when the

27. If *X* were below *A*, that is, if the agglomeration effect were stronger than the productivity benefit attributable to the public input, the optimal tax would be a negative tax, that is, a subsidy to capital. Our best guess, although it is not necessary to our results, is that the productivity benefit of the public input exceeds the agglomeration effect and that *X* is above *A*, as has been illustrated in the figure.

agglomeration externality is taken into account. To induce the firm to choose k^*, we must set the tax equal to t^*. If agglomeration economies are not recognized and the tax is set at a higher level, say t', the firm will choose a sub-optimal level of capital k'.

When the tax rate is set at the socially optimal level according to equation 9, the tax revenues raised do not cover the costs of providing the public input. To see this, multiply the tax on capital times the number of units of capital to obtain tax revenues per capita T equal to

(12) $$T = xf_x k^\delta - f(k,x)\delta k^\delta.$$

Dividing by p_x to convert into units of x, and noting that by equation 7 p_x is equal to $f_x k^\delta$ in equilibrium, this reduces to

(13) $$T = x - \frac{f(k,x)\delta}{f_x}.$$

Thus t^* does not raise enough revenue to finance the public input x. This is in contrast to the case where agglomeration economies are not recognized and the tax rate is set equal to $\hat{t}$ (equation 10). In this case the tax rate is a benefit tax and taxes on capital (just) cover the cost of providing the public input x.

When the tax rate is set optimally, in order to obtain enough public revenues to cover the cost of providing x, the local government will have to set the head tax, z, above the value that would correspond if it were a benefit tax (as a benefit tax $z = p_g g$). The additional amount will be equal to $f(k,x)\delta k^\delta$, the subsidy to firms attributable to the concentration externality, and therefore $z = p_g g + f(k,x)\delta k$.

That welfare is higher in the case when agglomeration economies are taken into account can be seen from the derivation of the equilibrium under the two cases. When the agglomeration effect is not taken into account, the equilibrium is a restricted solution to the more general problem that takes the externality into account and allows for a solution that internalizes its effects. Although consumers pay a head tax above the benefit tax, their utility is maximized when firms are given a tax incentive to induce them to choose k^*, and therefore they benefit by being partly responsible for financing the provision of the public input. The tax break offered to firms benefits consumers as it induces firms to invest a higher, optimal level of capital in the jurisdiction.

This theory is developed from the perspective of one jurisdiction and one firm or several identical firms, assuming there are numerous jurisdictions competing with one another for the firms, and it implies that tax incentives are offered across the board to all firms. If each jurisdiction benefits from agglomeration economies in a similar fashion, and if each firm presents similar agglomeration economies to each jurisdiction, it will be socially optimal for each jurisdiction to offer similar tax incentives to all firms. More realistically, jurisdictions and firms will differ in terms of the agglomeration economies received and offered. These differences may justify selective, as opposed to across-the-board, tax breaks. We explore these ideas next.

It is quite plausible that different cities present different potentials for agglomeration economies because of the number and character of existing firms. Glaeser and others find that knowledge spillovers might occur between rather than within industries, so a diversified economy is more likely to present agglomeration effects of the type described in our model and, therefore, is more likely to offer and benefit from tax breaks.[28] Industrial mix can also be an important factor in determining the potential growth of a region.[29] Existing business services firms are likely to benefit more than existing manufacturing firms from the spillovers of human capital and knowledge associated with a newly locating corporate headquarters firm. Thus it may be optimal for a city with a base of business services firms to offer a tax incentive to a relocating headquarters firm, whereas it may not be in the best interests of a city with a base of traditional manufacturing firms to do so. Therefore, we might find different cities offering different levels of tax incentives to try to attract the same firm.

We formalize these ideas in our model by allowing the concentration externality to differ across cities through different values of δ. The second term of the righthand side of equation 9 is the tax incentive. Taking the derivative of that term with respect to δ, yields

$$(14) \qquad f(k,x)\delta k^{\delta-1}\ln(k) + f(k,x)k^{\delta-1}.$$

This expression is positive for positive values of k, so the larger δ is, the larger will be the tax break. Cities that are more receptive to concentration externalities, represented here by larger δ, will find it in their interest to offer larger tax breaks.

Another interesting extension of our model is to allow firms to differ in terms of the concentration externalities they generate. Our idea is that the headquarters of a large, global company, or a product development center for a high-technology firm, or the production plant of a very innovative firm,

28. Glaeser and others (1992).
29. See Garcia-Milà and McGuire (1993, 1998).

might generate positive externalities for existing business services firms. Because the externality-generating firm presents challenging and innovative problems and contracts, and its employees are highly educated and experienced, the skills, knowledge, and capabilities of the services-providing firms might improve by virtue of doing business with the externality-generating firm. On the other hand, traditional manufacturing plants may not generate such externalities. Under these circumstances, it would be optimal for local officials to offer selective tax incentives, according to their beliefs about the different agglomeration impacts of the different firms. Thus not all city-firm pairings are likely to be fruitful, and we would expect local officials to act accordingly by offering tax incentives selectively to those newly locating or relocating firms with the potential to improve the productivity of existing firms.

We illustrate this possibility formally through an extension of our model. Consider that the economy of the city is formed by two sectors. Sectors differ by the type of capital they use, with one sector, say sector 1, using capital H that produces concentration spillovers, and the other sector 2 using capital K that does not generate spillovers.

The production function for a particular jurisdiction in each sector can be represented by

$$(15) \qquad Q_1 = F_1(H, L_1, X_1) \left(\frac{H}{L_1} \right)^\delta$$

$$(16) \qquad Q_2 = F_2(K, L_2, X_2) \left(\frac{H}{L_1} \right)^\delta.$$

Assume that the aggregate society has a fixed stock of capital of type H and a fixed stock of capital of type K, both perfectly mobile across jurisdictions. Labor is assumed immobile and fixed for each community and for each sector within the community.[30] Assuming that functions F_1 and F_2 are homogeneous of degree 1, equations 15 and 16 can be rewritten as

$$(17) \qquad q_1 = f_1(h, x_1) h^\delta$$

$$(18) \qquad q_2 = f_2(k, x_2) h^\delta,$$

---

30. Although this assumption is unrealistic, it greatly simplifies the analysis and allows us to obtain a closed-form solution comparable to the solution in the one-sector case.

where q_1 and q_2 are the output per worker of each sector, h is capital per worker in sector 1, k is capital per worker in sector 2, and x_1 and x_2 are units of public input per worker provided to each sector. The output of sector 1 is taken as the numeraire, and p_2 is the relative price of q_2 in units of q_1.

In each sector all firms are identical and take the total amount of private capital in use in the sector as given when making individual choices of capital and labor. Thus a representative firm in sector 1 (sector 2) maximizes profits subject to the production function in equation 17 (equation 18), taking h^δ as a constant.

Let $t_1(t_2)$ be the per unit tax on capital in sector 1 (sector 2), then the conditions for the private maximizing choice of private capital in each sector are given by the following conditions:

$$(19) \qquad \left(f_{1h} + \frac{x_1}{h} f_{1x} \right) h^\delta - t_1 = r$$

$$(20) \qquad p_2 \left(f_{2k} + \frac{x_2}{k} f_{2x} \right) h^\delta - t_2 = r.$$

The wage in each sector of a community is set competitively and according to

$$(21) \qquad w_1 = f_1(h, x_1)h^\delta - hf_{1h}h^\delta - x_1 f_{1x_1} h^\delta$$

$$(22) \qquad w_2 = p_2 f_2(k, x_2)h^\delta - p_2 kf_{2k}h^\delta - p_2 x_2 f_{2x_2} h^\delta.$$

We assume, as before, that the social planner, unlike the firm, recognizes the concentration spillover effect of capital in sector 1 and maximizes the welfare of its constituents, taking into account the competitive conditions for the capital and labor markets of both sectors, and the private and public budget constraints. The local government problem is

$$\max_{c_1^1, c_1^2, c_2^1, c_2^2, g, h, k, x_1, x_2 t_1, t_2, z_1, z_2} \quad 1_1 u_1(c_1^1, c_1^2, g) + 1_2 u_2(c_2^1, c_2^2, g)$$

$$\text{s.t.} \quad y + w_1 = c_1^1 + p_2 c_1^2 + z_1$$

$$(23) \qquad\qquad y + w_2 = c_2^1 + p_2 c_2^2 + z_2$$

$$\qquad\qquad w_1 = f_1(h, x_1)h^\delta - hf_{1h}h^\delta - x_1 f_{1x_1} h^\delta$$

$$w_2 = p_2 f_2(k, x_2)h^\delta - p_2 k f_{2k} h^\delta - p_2 x_2 f_{2x_2} h^\delta$$

$$r = \left(f_{1h} + \frac{x_1}{h} f_{1x} \right) h^\delta - t_1$$

$$r = p_2 \left(f_{2k} + \frac{x_2}{k} f_{2x} \right) h^\delta - t_2$$

$$l_1 z_1 + l_2 z_2 + l_1 h t_1 + l_2 k t_2 = p_g g + l_1 p_{x_1} x_1 + l_2 p_{x_2} x_2,$$

where c_i^j is consumption per worker in sector i of goods produced by sector j; z_1 and z_2 are lump sum head taxes for each sector's workers; p_{x_1} and p_{x_2} are prices per unit of the publicly provided inputs in the two sectors; l_1 and l_2 are the share of workers of the jurisdiction in sectors 1 and 2 respectively, such that $l_1 + l_2 = 1$.

Solving the maximization problem, we obtain the optimal taxes for each type of capital:

(24) $$t_1 = \frac{x_1}{h} f_{1x_1} h^\delta - \delta h^{\delta-1} f_1(h, x_1) - \frac{l_2}{l_1} p_2 \delta h^{\delta-1} f_2(k, x_2)$$

(25) $$t_2 = p_2 \frac{x_2}{k} f_{2x_2} h^\delta.$$

The tax on capital in the sector that does not generate concentration externalities (sector 2) is a benefit tax equal to the marginal benefit to the firm of the public input. But the capital tax in the sector that produces concentration externalities, sector 1, is below the benefit tax. Its tax equals the marginal benefit of the public input to the firm minus the marginal concentration benefit to both sectors of additional capital in sector 1.[31]

We thus find that a city will find it optimal to offer selective tax breaks in equilibrium. Firms that generate concentration spillovers will face a lower tax rate than firms that do not. Before we can use the model to assess tax incentives in the real world, we must come to grips with two of our simplifying assumptions. First, we assume that jurisdictions have access to taxes other than capital taxes so that, absent concentration externalities, firms would face benefit taxes in equilibrium. Given the myriad of taxes and varying tax structures imposed on firms by different cities, it is difficult even to speculate about

31. Note that the last term in equation 24 is the externality benefit to sector 2 of additional amounts of capital of type h, expressed in terms of units of output of sector 1 per unit of labor of that same sector.

whether the resulting tax burdens approximate benefit taxes. On the other hand, if we believe that firms are essentially mobile and that cities have access to at least some forms of benefit taxation, then it is not implausible that the taxes imposed on firms are close to benefit taxes. This assumption is important to our analysis because we assume that benefit taxation is the benchmark from which selective tax breaks may be offered. Second, we model the concentration externality as total capital per unit of labor. Clearly, this variable increases if either the number of externality-generating firms increases through relocations or existing externality-generating firms increase their investment in capital. Strictly speaking, we would expect to see tax breaks offered under both scenarios. However, the phenomenon we want to explain is the granting of tax breaks to relocating firms. We can appeal, perhaps, to the idea that existing firms are less mobile and therefore less able to extract tax breaks from the city (even if they are as deserving as relocating firms according to our model). We also note that virtually all studies in the tax competition literature and many in the agglomeration economies literature make similar assumptions: new capital (new employment in some cases) is beneficial whether it results from a new or newly relocating firm or expansion on the part of existing firms. With these two simplifications in mind, we turn next to a case study of a firm that recently relocated its corporate headquarters.

The Courtship of Boeing

On March 21, 2001, the Boeing Corporation announced that it was moving its headquarters out of Seattle, its birthplace and home for eighty-five years, to one of three cities: Chicago, Dallas, or Denver. Several factors made this high-profile relocation unusual. First, the company was moving its headquarters rather than a manufacturing plant. Indeed, the bulk of its manufacturing concerns would remain in Seattle. Second, and related, the traditional concerns of wages, utility costs, and other input costs did not seem paramount in the decision. The company argued that they were seeking a new location that could better accommodate a restructuring of the firm from one focused almost exclusively on the production of domestic and military aircraft to a global, diversified aerospace company. The company wanted to distance its headquarters from its traditional manufacturing in Seattle at the same time that it sought a more central location.[32] Third, the number of jobs—a tradi-

32. Duranton and Puga (2001) provide evidence that firms are increasingly separating their management operations (headquarters) from their manufacturing concerns and locating these different functions in different types of cities.

tional focus of economic development officials—was small: Boeing estimated that it would relocate 400 to 500 employees, pared down from approximately 1,000 headquarters employees in Seattle. The company made no promises to hire locally and the focus was on bringing employees to the new location rather than creating jobs for local residents.[33]

An entertaining competition among the three cities ensued with Boeing orchestrating stealth visits to each city. The idea was to experience firsthand the fixed attributes of the three cities and to compare them to Seattle's. All three cities offered central locations and hub airports. Denver offered nearby recreation and scenic beauty. Dallas offered the home state of President Bush and a low cost of living, while Chicago played up its cultural institutions and Lake Michigan location—much was made of the fact that Boeing CEO Phil Condit is a sailor and an opera fan.

While insisting that incentives were not the major factor, Boeing sought favorable relocation deals from each city. Denver refused to play the incentives game and offered only minimal tax incentives. City Councilman Ed Thomas stressed the high quality of life in Denver saying, "I don't know if we even need to compete on financial incentives."[34] Dallas offered property tax abatements of $10 million plus millions more in infrastructure and relocation costs. The city of Chicago and the state of Illinois teamed up to offer upwards of $50 million in property and income tax abatements and other incentives.[35]

In the end, Chicago won the competition, and on May 10, 2001, Boeing CEO Phil Condit announced the company's decision to move its corporate headquarters to Chicago, to a building across the river from the Lyric Opera of Chicago, near both Metra and Amtrak train stations, and a ten-minute walk to the LaSalle Street financial district. We may never know the real reasons for Boeing's decision or how important the tax incentive package was in that decision. Indeed, some commentators speculated that Chicago was the choice all along and that Boeing's strategy of pitting three cities against one another was just an attempt to get the best deal from Chicago.[36]

Moreover, a good deal was negotiated for Boeing. Why was Chicago so eager to land Boeing? Are the $50 million in tax incentives justified? Is there

33. In mid-July Boeing hosted a three-day job fair in Chicago with the intention of hiring 100 local support staff employees. Approximately 7,000 people submitted resumes.

34. "More Boeing for the Buck." In *Denver Post*, April 29, 2001, pp. K-01.

35. The state of Illinois promised fifteen years of corporate income tax credits worth approximately $22 million plus reimbursement of relocation costs of $4 million to $5 million. The city of Chicago promised twenty years of property tax abatements worth approximately $20 million. Other miscellaneous city and state grants totaled approximately $8 million.

36. See James Wallace, reporter for *The Seattle Post Intelligencer*. Interview by Steve Edwards, *Eight Forty-Eight*, WBEZ Chicago Public Radio, May 10, 2001.

any evidence that residents and existing firms in Chicago will benefit? Local, state, and national politicians touted the so-called signaling effect of attracting a global headquarters to Chicago. U.S. Senator Dick Durbin was quoted on the day Boeing announced its move saying, "This is an investment to bring the leading aerospace company in the world to Chicago, Illinois. That certainly says a lot about Chicago, and it also sends a signal to other companies that we're open to do business."[37] Chicago Mayor Richard Daley stated that "Boeing's decision reinforces what most of us already know: Chicago has a quality of life that is unmatched by any major city in the country. Chicago, like Boeing, is world class."[38] CEOs of other large companies supported the efforts to woo Boeing through their active participation in a blue ribbon committee formed in April by the governor of Illinois and the mayor of Chicago. Further, just as the red carpet was being laid for Boeing, the city dropped its efforts to prevent a long-term Chicago manufacturing concern (Brach's candies) from closing a large plant with 1,000 employees on the city's west side. The Brach's case is further evidence that jobs may not be the main concern of politicians, at least not in every instance. The wooing of Boeing and the simultaneous spurning of Brach's are consistent with the notion that some firms, but not others, provide valuable spillovers to existing workers and firms in Chicago.[39]

Why did Chicago offer Boeing a more lucrative tax incentives package than Dallas did? Perhaps Chicago, given its concentration of financial, advertising, and other business services firms, felt that its potential to reap concentration externalities from Boeing was greater.

Conclusions

Two major strands of the tax competition literature reach opposite conclusions about whether tax competition is efficiency enhancing. Under either model, firm-specific tax breaks are not justified. In the strand of the literature that formalizes Tiebout's original conjecture that competition among local governments would lead to efficient provision of public goods, the resulting taxes on mobile factors are benefit taxes. Communities hope to attract firms (mobile capital) in order to increase local wages or jobs. They do so by pro-

37. *All Things Considered*. On National Public Radio, May 10, 2001. Boeing would be the only Dow Jones Industrial Average company with its headquarters in Chicago and one of only two Dow Jones companies (McDonald's Corporation is the other) in the metropolitan area.

38. "Chicago Snags Boeing." In *Chicago Tribune*, May 11, 2001, p. 1.

39. In their study of Tennessee's successful efforts to attract the Saturn plant after a fierce competition with several other states, Bartik and others (1987) argue that the particular match between Tennessee (a low-wage state) and Saturn (a high-wage automobile plant) justified the tax incentives offered by Tennessee.

viding firms with a public input that is financed by benefit taxes on capital. In our model, it is desirable to attract firms for similar reasons, such as higher wages, but also because firms provide a type of public good to the community—when a firm locates in a community, the productivity of the existing firms increases, resulting in even higher wages. A community's optimal policy is to impose a tax on capital that is lower than a benefit tax in order to attract new capital and experience this positive externality. Tax breaks are a means of internalizing the positive externality of agglomeration economies.

Thus in our theoretical model tax breaks are economically justified. In the real world, if our model is to be believed, it would seem to be good policy for cities to offer selective tax breaks to firms that they have identified as providing the benefit of concentration externalities.

Not all cities would necessarily offer the same incentives to a given firm, as the benefit of new capital would depend on the potential externalities that a specific firm could offer to each location. At the same time, a given locality may offer tax breaks to some firms and not to others, depending on the type of business they would bring, and, in general, whether the match with the location would enhance agglomeration economies.

If our theoretical model is capturing reality, or bits of it, then selective tax incentives can be justified in some instances. The question is whether our model can be used to assess actual tax incentive deals.

The case study of Boeing presents some interesting facts. The three cities that bid for Boeing's headquarters differ remarkably in terms of location, specialization, and amenities. In addition, they offered quite different tax breaks and incentives to attract the firm. Also, at the same time that Chicago was wooing Boeing, it was neglecting efforts to retain a Brach's manufacturing plant. Not only are Boeing and Brach's very different types of firms, but the former offers the potential for knowledge spillovers through incoming headquarters activity, while the latter, with traditional manufacturing activity, is likely to generate few concentration externalities. One could read this case as evidence that cities do not offer indiscriminate tax breaks to firms, but rather offer them when there is a potential benefit to the locality in addition to the jobs that the company brings in.

The lack of systematic data on and empirical studies of tax incentives leaves us with inconclusive evidence to explain the reasons for and benefits of tax breaks. Our work could provide a new prism through which to assess tax breaks and some guidance for future empirical studies.

Comments

Edward Glaeser: Why did Chicago offer Boeing $50 million in tax abatements to locate in that city? Are tax deals like this welfare enhancing or socially damaging? Garcia-Milà and McGuire's "Tax Incentives and the City" presents a new approach to this question, taking into account the possibility that there are significant agglomeration economies. This is a fine paper with a new idea. In this comment, instead of responding directly to the paper, I will give an overview of locational tax incentives and suggest how I think that empirical work should proceed in this area.

What are tax incentives conceptually? There are two rival definitions of tax incentives. First, they can be seen as tax rates that are chosen on a firm-by-firm basis. As such, the interesting thing about tax incentives is their heterogeneity among firms. Needless to say, they also represent a great increase in the discretionary nature of taxation. Second, the tax breaks may also represent a reduction in the total tax rate. Indeed, Garcia-Milà and McGuire define tax incentives as "a tax rate lower than the marginal benefit of the public goods and services provided to the firm." Garcia-Milà and McGuire's model focuses on the level of taxes in a single jurisdiction. It provides both a justification for why tax incentives should be below the cost of public goods and services and a possible framework for understanding interfirm heterogeneity in tax rates.

When a company like Boeing—the topic of Garcia-Milà and McGuire's case study—receives a $50 million dollar tax package, this is both an increase in the degree of heterogeneity of tax rates and a decrease in the main level of taxes. However, I think that the most striking thing about the Boeing example is its firm-specific nature, and it is this aspect of tax incentives I will focus on here. Moreover, it is hard to know whether Boeing is actually covering the costs of the public services it consumes. I am not sure if tax incentives ever

115

exist using the author's definition. As such, I think the heterogeneity of tax rates, and the fact that these tax rates are handled on a firm-by-firm basis, are much more important than the effect of these tax incentives on the overall tax rate. The rest of this note will focus on two linked but fundamentally different questions: why do tax incentives occur (the positive question), and what are the welfare effects of tax incentives (the normative question)?

Why do cities offer tax incentives? In this section, I review five theories about why tax incentives occur. Some of these theories (such as the agglomeration view) suggest a benign side of tax incentives, and other theories (such as influence and corruption) suggest that tax incentives are pernicious. However, almost all of these theories are fundamentally positive and leave the normative question—should tax incentives be banned?—unanswered. The first two theories start with the view that governments maximize the consumer welfare of their current residents. Theories three and four are based on the assumption that local governments maximize total tax revenues. Theory five assumes that corrupt officials maximize their own well-being and pay little attention to the needs or demands of their community.

—Positive Theory 1: Consumer and Producer Surplus. The simplest theory of tax incentives is that they represent bids by communities to attract firms that will generate either consumer or producer surplus for the current residents of the community. According to this theory, when the firm moves in, it will be involved in local markets for inputs (mainly labor) and perhaps also local markets for outputs. In both these cases, conventional welfare and analysis suggest that there will be welfare triangles gained by the city. Even if the firm acts as a local monopolist or monopsonist, there will be inframarginal workers or consumers who strictly benefit from the firm's presence. Upward-sloping labor demand curves mean that some workers will be strictly better off by the presence of the firm. Downward-sloping consumer demand curves mean that some customers are made better off by the new producer.

According to this theory, when cities bid for firms, their bids reflect the different levels of welfare gain they expect their residents to get from the presence of the firm. As such, this bidding presence is essentially benign (since, after all, Pareto optimality requires that the firm takes this surplus into account when making its location decision). This force seems to matter mostly for firms that are hiring large numbers of workers, or firms that are supplying to the local market. One positive explanation for the subsidization of local sports teams is that these teams generate consumer surplus they are not directly able to capture.

What are the implications of this theory? In general, the size of the subsidy that the government will pay should be equal to the level of consumer and producer surplus that will be generated. This implies that when labor supply is elastic (that is, workers and jobs are homogeneous), there will be little local surplus. When labor supply to this firm is more inelastic, then workers will get rents from this new source of labor demand and the city should be willing to offer tax incentives to the firm. Obviously, if (as is the case of Boeing) there will be few local employees from the move, then this theory predicts that Chicago should not be willing to pay for the firm's location.

The same simple price theoretic arguments apply when thinking about consumer products. If demand is highly elastic, and the price is close to willingness-to-pay for all of the consumers, then this product generates little consumer surplus. However, more inelastic demand yields higher surpluses. Naturally, cities with bigger local demand for the firm's product will generally be willing to offer most in terms of tax incentives. A further important factor in this case is returns-to-scale technology on the part of the firm. If the product has large fixed costs and the firm prices at close to marginal cost, then the consumers will get almost all of the surplus. This may be the case for some sports teams that have large fixed costs and in either the cases of stadiums or television coverage, marginal costs are small. Of course, Boeing does not supply any local products.

A final implication of this theory is that the level of tax incentives may be higher than the net present value of the taxes (minus cost of public services) that the firm will pay to the city. As the tax incentive is meant to pay for the surplus that the firm will bring to the city, then this tax incentive should represent a net transfer to the firm.

—Positive Theory 2: Agglomeration Economies. This theory represents the contribution of Garcia-Milà and McGuire to the literature. Their work argues that if there are agglomeration economies, then cities will bid to capture firms that generate these agglomeration economies. They have modeled this case in some detail so it makes little sense for me to review it here. Instead, I will stress two aspects of the model that limit its ability to generate testable implications. These comments should not be seen as a slight on their work, but rather an attempt to stress just the full extent to which this theory can be useful.

My first point is that the primary empirical implications of this model will come from the agglomeration production function. Firms that offer higher spillovers will get bigger tax incentives. Cities that stand to benefit most from these spillovers will pay most for these firms and offer higher incentives. This type of cross-city, cross-industry variation will stand to be the primary testable implication of this model. Since we aren't so sure about the factors that lead to greater spillovers, probably the most sensible modeling approach would be to put together a very flexible function that includes both firm and location characteristics as determinants of the level of spillovers.

Garcia-Milà and McGuire assume that agglomeration economies are a function of "k"—the capital to labor ratio of the jurisdiction. This is certainly one plausible assumption, but the agglomeration economy literature has generally focused on skill levels rather than capital or labor ratios as the source of agglomeration economies. Rauch documents that wages and rents both rise in skilled cities.[1] Glaeser and others show that skilled cities grow more quickly than unskilled cities.[2] As such, it is at least as reasonable to assume that the magnitude of spillovers generated by a new firm is a function of the number of skilled workers it brings to the city. This different specification of agglomeration economies would yield the prediction that tax incentives will be larger toward firms that have more skilled workers.

Another stylized fact from the urban growth literature is that cities with lots of small firms grow faster than cities with a few large firms. This work suggests that externalities are more likely to be associated with small start-ups than with large established companies. If this is true, then it becomes much harder to rationalize tax incentives for big firms as sensible responses to agglomeration economies. Indeed, if agglomeration economies are a function of the number of small firms, then Chicago's subsidy for Boeing can be best understood if the Boeing employees are likely to start their own start-ups after they leave Boeing.

A third fact from the agglomeration literature relates to the connection between cities and firms—Glaeser and others find that growth is associated with urban diversity and interpret this as evidence for the important of cross-industry intellectual spillovers.[3] If this is correct, then cities would be expected to offer tax incentives for firms that greatly broaden the scope of the activities in that particular city. If new ideas are formed by combining old ideas, then bringing in new industries that add diversity will have particular value. This theory predicts that firms which add industrial diversity to the city are particularly likely to receive tax incentives.

1. Rauch (1993b).
2. Glaeser, Scheinkman, and Shleifer (1995).
3. Glaeser and others (1992).

A second sensible extension of the theory would be to consider more dynamic concerns—in particular the location of other firms. Agglomeration-based tax incentives become more and more attractive when they induce other firms to come to the city. In that case, the optimal tax incentive includes both the direct effect of the first firm plus the indirect effects that work through the location of other firms. This is one way to understand the massive subsidies paid to railroads in the nineteenth century. Railroads were thought to be attractive because they would induce other firms to locate in the town.

This type of argument suggests that spillover-based tax incentives are likely to be used when other firms, ready to follow the first mover, are in large supply. For example, two locations might engage in a dynamic battle to attract a particular firm. The location that wins the firm will prove extremely attractive to a large number of other firms, which will then consider relocating there. In that case, the two locations should be willing to pay a great deal to attract the first firm. This can be thought of as a case where the elasticity of future migration to the city with respect to the location of the firm is extremely high.

A final implication of this theory is, as Garcia-Milà and McGuire prove, that tax incentives will be sufficiently high so that tax payments net of public services costs will be negative. As such, this aspect of the theory predicts the same thing as the consumer surplus theory.

—Positive Theory 3: Ex post Appropriation. A third theory of tax incentives is that these large up-front payments exist to compensate firms for future tax payments. According to this view, once firms move to a particular location, they will be easy for the local government to exploit. The firm's fixed resources create an immobility that means that it is easy prey for a taxing authority. Forward-looking firms recognize this fact and demand up-front tax breaks to compensate for *ex post* appropriation.

This type of theory also has some clear implications for the firms that will be given particularly generous tax breaks. In particular, more immobile firms will be more likely to receive up-front payments than less mobile firms. Furthermore, firms that have highly inelastic demand for land and local labor will be the most attractive prey for *ex post* appropriation. As such, they will be most likely to receive large up-front payments. Generally, the firms that will end up paying the most *ex post* will receive the largest tax breaks *ex ante*.

This theory also predicts that tax incentives will never be so high that the total net present value of future tax payments minus the tax break are less than the total net present value of providing the firm with public services. As such, this is a theory that can explain the tax incentives that we see in practice, including the Boeing deal. However, this theory cannot explain tax incentives as they are defined by Garcia-Milà and McGuire.

—Positive Theory 4: "Tax" Discrimination. A fourth related theory is tax discrimination. According to this theory, there are firms with different levels of demand for different locations. As such, local governments face a supply of potential resident firms. Just as monopoly providers of any goods ideally charge different prices for the product to consumers with different reservation values, this theory predicts that locations will charge different tax rates to different firms depending on how much they want to locate in the city. If the city is to extract maximum revenues (while attracting as many firms as possible), it needs to tax inframarginal firms more and marginal firms less.

This theory predicts that the recipients of tax incentives will be those firms that are on the locational margin. Thus firms that really need to be in Chicago will receive no tax incentives. Firms like Boeing, which are on the margin, will receive these breaks. In principle, empirical work could test this hypothesis by calculating the extent to which some firms are differentially drawn to any given location on the basis of that location's assets (including its labor force). Firms that are strongly attracted to the location should receive lower tax incentives.

Like the previous theory, this theory cannot predict tax incentives as defined by Garcia-Milà and McGuire. In this case, tax incentives will never be so high that the net present value of taxes minus the cost of public services is negative. At the most extreme, tax incentives will mean that for the firm on the margin, the flow of tax revenues minus public costs will equal zero.

—Positive Theory 5: Corruption and Influence. The fifth theory of why tax incentives occur is corruption and influence. According to this theory, these incentives do not represent maximization of tax revenue or maximization of the welfare of current residents of the city. Instead, tax incentives reflect the ability of the firm to bribe or coerce the leaders of the government. The nineteenth century tax incentives for railroads were often motivated by this force as railroads regularly bribed politicians to get generous tax treatment.[4] In the nineteenth century, explicit bribes were often the norm. In the twentieth century, contributions to election campaigns or skillful use of the revolving door were presumably more common.

This theory predicts that the level of tax incentives is determined by the ability of the firm to get away with this bribery. Situations where detection is difficult will be more likely to lead to tax incentives. This predicts that tax

4. See Glaeser (2000) for details.

incentives will be linked to the appearance of spillovers or large consumer surplus. Tax incentives will be more likely to be granted to firms that are politically influential. Furthermore, when it is difficult to monitor public officials, we will expect to see higher levels of tax incentives. This theory predicts that tax incentives should be more common in countries with weaker rule of law, and that tax incentives should have been more common in the nineteenth century when detection was difficult.

Naturally, this theory predicts little about the overall tax level. Tax incentives may be so generous that the overall net tax revenue may even be negative. On the other hand, tax incentives may be much less, depending on what the firm and politicians can get away with.

Should cities offer tax incentives? There are two separate normative questions related to tax incentives. First, do these incentives distort the location decisions of firms? Second, do these tax incentives lead to tax burdens that are too low and correspondingly low levels of public services? A question that is related to the second question is whether these incentives lead to an undesirable level of transfer to mobile firms.

—Normative Question 1: Will tax incentives lead firms to make the wrong location decisions? From an urban economics perspective, this is perhaps the central normative question. Does the behavior of local government lead to spatial distortions where tax incentives distort the decisions of firms? Some of the positive theories of tax incentives predict that these incentives create spatial distortions. Other theories predict that tax incentives are necessary corrections to existing distortions.

What does efficient location actually mean? In principle, it means that firms choose locations that maximize total social surplus. The benefits of a firm moving to a particular location should include the profits the firm earns from the location, any external effects, and the consumer and producer surplus created by the locational choice. The costs include the cost of providing public services. For the purposes of this question, I will avoid discussion of so-called fiscal externalities that lead to transfers of funds from one location to another. These fiscal externalities can, of course, always be undone at the central government level and will be addressed in the subsequent section.

The way I have framed the question makes it clear that if either agglomeration economies or these consumer surplus type issues exist, then tax incentives are almost surely necessary to get the efficient location of firms. The misallocation of firms will depend on the extent to which agglomeration effects differ across space. In principle, if firms generate agglomeration economies, but these are constant, then there is no need for tax incentives. However, this will generally be unusual. More likely, tax incentives will lead to efficient, not inefficient, location of firms if there are heterogeneous agglomeration effects across space.

If there are no agglomeration effects and no spatial impacts of consumer or producer surplus effects, and if tax incentives address tax issues, then there is also no malign effect of tax incentives. For example, if locations maximize tax revenues and are not allowed to offer tax incentives, then locations will act like local monopolies. Taxes will be too high, and too few firms will come to the location. Just as price discrimination creates an efficient level of consumption of a monopolist's product, tax discrimination creates a more efficient allocation of firms across space. Likewise, in the *ex post* appropriate case, tax incentives are needed to undo the distortions that are created by governmental expropriation. In these cases, tax incentives would help to eliminate distortions that would otherwise be created by local taxing.

The only theory that suggests that tax incentives would create spatial distortions is the corruption and influence theory. If this theory is correct, firms will move to locations that offer the most generous packages, and the magnitude of these packages will be based exclusively on the venality of the local government. Obviously, choosing a location on the basis of which area is most susceptible to bribery will probably not lead to efficient outcomes. As such, this theory predicts that tax incentives will probably lead firms to locate in the wrong places.

Overall, this analysis suggests that almost all of the theories predict that location decisions will be better with tax incentives than without these incentives. Local taxes often distort locations (unless they are perfectly tied to the cost of local services). Agglomeration economies mean that private firms' decisionmaking will not internalize important spillovers. The existence of tax incentives can, in principle, remedy these problems and banning these incentives will make things worse. The only exception occurs if tax incentives are based primarily on corruption and influence.

—Normative Question 2: Will tax incentives lead mobile firms to get too many rents and will this lead to underprovision of other public goods? The bulk of the public finance literature on tax competition has focused more on the "race to the bottom" of tax levels than on any other impact. The models that argue that tax competition does bad things suggest that locations will cater to mobile residents and deprive their less mobile residents of needed public services.[5] As such, the reduction in income associated with tax incentives will produce underprovision of socially productive public goods.

Alternatively, followers of Tiebout stress that local tax competition disciplines the leviathan aspects of local government.[6] According to this literature, local government expenditures naturally tend toward inefficiency and waste. Tax competition eliminates this waste.

I think tax competition can be considered an income transfer where funds are transferred from the local government to mobile firms. This is clearly a boon for the shareholders of these firms. The question is what the losses are from depriving the localities of income. If local governments act as oligopolies rather than as separate competing entities, they could charge higher taxes and this would increase their funds. Would this be better?

There is no question that, in principle, this can be worse. The mobility of firms certainly stops some localities from redistributing to the poor. However, the mobility of the rich also stems the ability of localities to redistribute. More to the point, I think that mobility generally means that local redistribution is almost always a bad idea. Tax incentives may certainly limit the ability to engage in local redistribution, but probably that local redistribution should never have gone on in the first place.

More generally, will reducing the income available to local governments cause a loss in social welfare? This question can certainly not be answered in the abstract. Economists need to estimate what happens when localities are deprived of the marginal dollar. Does this loss lead to eliminating very valuable services or are fairly marginal services cut off? In principle, anything local competition does can be offset by transfers from the central government. My suspicion is that optimal policy always involves allowing localities to compete with tax incentives (unless we are sure that those transfers are motivated by corruption). Then if localities are thought to make highly efficient use of the marginal dollar, money can be transferred to those localities.

Of course, tax incentives will have redistributional effects, even beyond their negative impact on local redistribution. Taxes will lead to a transfer in rents from less mobile firms to more mobile firms. It's not clear why this type of redistribution between one type of shareholder to another is a particularly pressing subject for government action. However, if this type of redistribution is thought to be highly undesirable, it can always be cut off by

5. See, for example, Wilson (1986); Zodrow and Mieszkowski (1986).
6. See, for example, Brennan and Buchanan (1980).

central government action. I cannot help thinking that the best way to handle the redistributional impacts of redistribution is not to eliminate competition, but to have a separate redistribution policy.

Conclusion. Tax incentives seem to be a permanent part of the urban economic landscape. However, economists do not yet know why these incentives occur and whether they are desirable. These two questions are intrinsically linked. It is hoped that Garcia-Milà and McGuire's paper will lead to further investigation of these questions. In ten years, I hope we may be able to conclusively reject some of the theories discussed above and be closer to knowing what is really going on with these incentives.

My discussion suggests that tax incentives will almost surely improve the efficiency of the locational decisions of firms. The only case where this is not true occurs when tax incentives are driven by corruption and influence. Tax incentives may lead to a redistribution from local governments to mobile firms. However, the efficient response to this redistribution should be a central government redistribution policy, not eliminating local government competition.

Todd Sinai: The issue of tax competition between cities, states, and even countries is pervasive and appears in many contexts. From U.S. states trying to attract manufacturing, to cities subsidizing sports stadiums, to countries trying to attract foreign investment, all levels of government attempt to influence economic decisions by providing tax incentives. Indeed, there is plenty of evidence that tax incentives affect firms' choices, whether the incentives are intentional or not. To name just a few examples, work by Hines as well as work by Hines and Desai find that taxes affect the location of firm investment.[1] Goolsbee and Cummins, Hassett, and Hubbard address whether tax incentives affect firm investment and the prices of capital goods.[2]

But the fact that tax incentives influence firms does not mean they are a justifiable policy. Herein lies the contribution of this fine paper by Teresa Garcia-Milà and Therese McGuire. The authors provide an example of how cities providing tax breaks to firms can be justifiable *ex ante*. They do not claim that any particular tax break is justified *ex post*, but instead outline conditions under which tax incentives may increase economic efficiency. They then turn to the very interesting case of Boeing Corporation's relocation

---

1. Hines (1996); Hines and Desai (2001).
2. Goolsbee (1998); Cummins, Hassett, and Hubbard (1994).

of its headquarters to Chicago to see if their theory could apply to that particular instance.

Chicago's courtship of Boeing is especially fascinating because it does not seem to conform to the usual stories about why cities give tax breaks. One common argument is that politicians buy jobs with taxpayer dollars by giving subsidies to firms to situate themselves locally. However, that was not the case with Boeing, which brought nearly all its 500 headquarters' employees with it from Seattle. Chicago Mayor Richard Daley argued that the $50 million in subsidies to Boeing was good advertising for the city as other companies might then view Chicago as a good place to establish their businesses. However, that explanation seems particularly unlikely since the same companies would also be aware of the lucrative tax deal that was awarded to Boeing.

Garcia-Milà and McGuire propose an alternative hypothesis: the relocation by Boeing may create a positive externality for Chicago. The authors label the externality "benefits from agglomeration," but it really could be anything productivity-enhancing: from greater civic pride to honest-to-goodness knowledge spillovers. Since externalities constitute a market failure, government intervention is called for. The typical pricing solution is a Pigouvian tax (subsidy) and that, in essence, is what this paper shows should happen. If Boeing would provide spillovers for other firms and workers in Chicago but not realize all those benefits itself, the firm should be induced to locate in Chicago via a subsidy.

This alternative is an attractive one that has received little attention in the literature. Of course, it may not be the only reason cities provide tax incentives, but that's not the point. Rather, it may explain the existence of some tax breaks when other theories break down.

The paper proceeds along two paths. One is to augment a model of tax competition to allow for agglomeration effects. The second is to relate the model to the Boeing case. I like both these parts independently. The model conveys an insight in an intuitive way. It probably can explain many tax incentives, and it certainly provides guidance to policymakers on how to target their subsidies. The Boeing case is a fascinating example of how these tax deals evolve. However, I would like to see each part developed on its own. In particular, I'm not sure the model describes the Boeing case as well as the authors would have us believe. On the one hand, I believe the argument in the model is correct, but Boeing may not be the best illustration of it. On the other hand, there are features of the Boeing case that would be interesting to try to explain, but which cannot be addressed using the framework in the paper.

In the basic model, every firm is identical and has operations in every (identical) market. Labor is immobile, but productivity increases in the capital-to-labor ratio not only for a firm's own workers but for other firms' workers as well, increasing wages. The spillovers in productivity reflect agglomeration benefits. Since firms choose the capital-to-labor ratio in each market and are not compensated by their peers for the benefits of the spillovers they provide, the natural solution for a social planner is to subsidize firm investment.

Garcia-Milà and McGuire augment this approach by considering two extensions. First, what if cities differ in their benefits from agglomeration? Then cities with larger spillovers would provide greater subsidies to firms. Second, what if there are two sectors: one that produces spillovers and one that does not? Then, naturally, investment in the former sector would be subsidized relative to the latter.

Overall, I think this model makes a fundamental point in an elegant, clear, and efficient manner: that with concentration externalities, investment incentives are justifiable. But there are fascinating features of tax incentives, and especially of the Boeing case, that are not predicted by the model in this paper, and I think they are worth pondering in future work:

Spillovers are due to high-value labor. In this model, a greater investment of private capital in a city is expected to generate positive externalities. Since labor is immobile, the pool of workers does not change. How does the additional capital create greater productivity? A typical example of investment in private capital is when a company purchases better machines for its workers so their productivity increases. But the externalities in the Garcia-Milà and McGuire model derive from when a company buys machines for its workers, and all the other workers in the economy have greater productivity as well. How does that happen? Does the capital investment reflect the firm investing in worker training and that knowledge diffusing through the economy? Is it simply that morale in a city, and thus workers' effort, is higher when a big company erects a showcase building? Understanding the channel through which the capital investment leads to spillovers will have important implications for city government. Since mayors get to choose which investments to subsidize, recognizing which ones generate the greatest externalities is crucial for accurate social planning in this model.

In addition, in the example in the paper, Boeing invested little capital in Chicago. Instead, it simply moved its headquarters' staff to an existing building there. That had little effect on the capital-to-labor ratio and, if anything, may have lowered it. But it is consistent with what may be a more intuitive model of spillovers: knowledge diffusion due to highly skilled labor entering the market.

The model in the paper does not allow for this channel for spillovers since labor is not mobile. If it were, however, it seems that the predictions would be different. Rather than subsidizing firms, cities may prefer to subsidize high-skill labor. A subsidy to capital may only lead to labor migration without any overall increase in wages.

Tax breaks affect firm location. It seems that investment subsidies for firms that are already located in a city rarely are trumpeted on the front pages of local newspapers. Instead, stories about tax giveaways to entice corporations to come to town—or not to leave—get all the ink. Boeing is no exception. The corporation received a tax incentive to locate in Chicago, not to increase their capital investment on the margin. The discrete decision of whether to locate in a city or not seems to be as important, if not more important, than how much to invest.

As the authors note, the base model in the paper does not consider location decisions. Rather, it uses tax subsidies to increase the amount of investment spillover-creating firms undertake in their current locations (which is everywhere, since all cities are identical). Since firms don't locate everywhere in reality, firm location would be an interesting, and relevant, avenue to explore. If there is a minimum efficient investment for firms, then the optimal tax rate reduction may rise and then decline in the size of the investment. Some firms may simply be too large for some cities and would increase the capital-to-labor ratio more than would be optimal, so cities would not compensate them for the extra investment. If there are moving costs, subsidies may need an up-front lump-sum component in order to induce firms to relocate. That would raise the average cost of attracting investment, reducing the number of firms a mayor would want to try to entice to her town. If moving costs were sufficiently high, one might try to attract a firm that provided fewer spillovers but had lower moving costs. In the extreme, it may be preferable to distribute the $50 million among local firms that provide spillovers since they have no moving costs. Perhaps paying firms not to leave your city is more efficient than paying firms to move to it.

Jurisdictional competition plays a role. Boeing entertained offers from several cities and the competition between them seemed to be an important aspect of the process. Would Chicago have offered $50 million if Dallas had not bid? There is no jurisdictional competition in the Garcia-Milà and McGuire model, except implicitly in the extension where cities are allowed to have different agglomeration benefits. But this competition can have real welfare implications. For example, in this paper, cities offer firms the package of tax incentives that lead them to invest the social welfare-maximizing amount of capital. However, with perfect competition between cities, it seems Chicago should be willing to offer Boeing tax incentives up to the point where Chicago was indifferent if the firm invested in it or not. In such a world, the spillover-producing firm would capture all the economic surplus. Even with a distribution of spillover benefits among cities, the best "match" city would have to pay enough to beat out the city that was the second best match, which could still leave it on the wrong side of the optimal amount of investment in the capital investment case and with little increase in welfare in the firm location case.

This could also be an argument for why high fixed-amenity cities will continue to grow: They do not need to pay as much cash to attract firms. If this advantage is not fully capitalized into land rents, such cities could retain more of the surplus from attracting spillover-producing firms.

Few firms receive subsidies. In the base model in the paper, every company is eligible for a subsidy. In the extension of the model, the authors argue that a matching process between cities and companies, where spillovers flow downstream and some companies provide more effective spillovers in certain cities, implies that cities would be willing to pay more for firms that are particularly good matches. Still, every company that produced spillovers would, and should, be eligible for some subsidy, somewhere.

However, Chicago offered only Boeing $50 million. It did not make Raytheon, for example, an offer to move (that we know about). Why just Boeing? Why does Chicago not have a standing offer to General Motors or General Electric? It seems unlikely that Boeing is the only firm that could provide a nonzero level of spillovers for Chicago.

Optimal outcomes do not arise endogenously. In the Boeing example, Chicago appears to have believed that Boeing was more socially efficient there than in Seattle. But Boeing was not necessarily going to move its headquarters to Chicago on its own volition. It needed an incentive to do so.

The base model in the paper predicts the opposite. Firms in that model would naturally agglomerate where there were other spillover-producing firms. (They would underinvest, but they would locate in the right place.) In the extension, Boeing would not have moved since it is a provider of spillovers and does not receive any agglomeration benefits from other firms. The downstream firms, on the other hand, should have moved to Seattle and clustered around Boeing in order to receive some spillovers. (Still, Boeing would have

Figure 1. Corporate Tax Share of Revenues versus Agglomeration

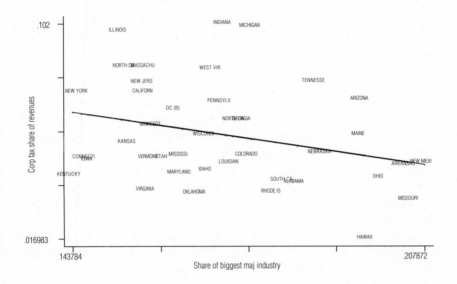

been providing too little capital since it did not receive any benefit from the positive externality it provided.)

This line of reasoning provides an alternative rationale for the kind of subsidies Boeing received. Boeing may have been a "loss leader" for Chicago, not intended to make existing firms more productive, but to act as a magnet for additional firms. There, the agglomeration benefits come from proximity— firms that work together want to cluster near each other—rather than knowledge spillovers. This pattern is similar to the one that has followed some auto plants: once the plant is established, suppliers build facilities nearby even though they do not receive subsidies themselves

While these features of the Boeing example may be best addressed in future work with a two-city model, two types of firms, and an endogenous firm location, the inability of the existing model to explain them does not diminish its real value: it provides a defensible justification for the presence of tax subsidies for firms.

The model also has the virtue of providing some empirically testable implications. For one, the size of the tax break should be increasing in the level of agglomeration of the city since the value of the spillovers would be greatest there. Since the externalities are nonrival, a little spillover over a large base of firms is just as valuable as a big spillover over a small base. (The alternative hypothesis proposed in the previous section would have the opposite effect.) Big cities should thus give larger breaks than small cities. Finally, good "matches" between cities and firms (however defined) should lead to larger spillovers.

I think such empirical analysis would be quite valuable. In the spirit of illustrating that it can be done, I constructed a measure of agglomeration by state, which is the employment share of the largest industry. I then regressed the state's share of tax revenues due to the corporate tax on the agglomeration measure. A graph of the corporate tax share of revenues versus agglomeration is plotted as figure 1, with the regression line drawn as well. The crude results here are at least consistent with the authors' story, namely that in more agglomerated places the corporate tax is less burdensome. (A reduced corporate tax rate, in the authors' model, is a subsidy.)

To be sure, there are a number of econometric problems with this crude regression—for example, it does not control for variation in the tax base across states—but it is intended to be merely suggestive and a call for future work. Given the illuminating insight in the Garcia-Milà and McGuire paper, it would be very interesting to see if their view held true generally, beyond Boeing.

References

Bartik, Timothy J. 1991. *Who Benefits from State and Local Economic Development Policies*. Kalamazoo, Mich.: W. E. Upjohn Institute for Employment Research.

Bartik, Timothy J., and others. 1987. "Saturn and State Economic Development." *Forum for Applied Research and Public Policy* 2 (1): 29–40.

Black, Dan, and William Hoyt. 1989. "Bidding for Firms." *American Economic Review* 79: 1249–56.

Brennan, Geoffrey, and James M. Buchanan. 1980. *The Power to Tax: Analytical Foundations of a Fiscal Constitution*. Cambridge University Press.

Ciccone, Antonio, and Robert E. Hall. 1996. "Productivity and the Density of Economic Activity." *American Economic Review* 86 (1): 54–70.

Courant, Paul N. 1994. "How Would You Know a Good Economic Policy If You Tripped Over One? Hint: Don't Just Count Jobs." *National Tax Journal* XLVII (4): 863–81.

Cummins, Jason, Kevin Hassett, and R. Glenn Hubbard. 1994. "A Reconsideration of Investment Behavior Using Tax Reforms as Natural Experiments." Brookings Papers on Economic Activity 2: 1–59. Brookings.

Duranton, Gilles, and Diego Puga. 2001. "From Sectoral to Functional Urban Specialization." Discussion Paper 2971. Washington: Center for Economic Policy Research (September).

Garcia-Milà, Teresa, and Therese J. McGuire. 1993. "Industrial Mix as a Factor in the Growth and Variability of States' Economies." *Regional Science and Urban Economics* 23 (6): 731–48.

———. 1998. "A Note on the Shift to a Service-Based Economy and the Consequences for Regional Growth." *Journal of Regional Science* (38): 353–63.

Glaeser, Edward. 2000. "The Future of Urban Research: Non–Market Interactions." *Brookings-Wharton Papers on Urban Affairs* (1): 101–38. Brookings.

Glaeser, Edward L., and others. 1992. "Growth in Cities." *Journal of Political Economy* 100 (6): 1126–52.

Glaeser, Edward, Jose Scheinkman, and Andrei Shleifer. 1995. "Economic Growth in a Cross-Section of Cities." *Journal of Monetary Economics* 36 (1): 117–43.

Goolsbee, Austan. 1998. "Investment Tax Incentives, Prices, and the Supply of Capital Goods." *Quarterly Journal of Economics* 113 (1): 121–48.

Hamilton, Bruce W. 1975. "Zoning and Property Taxation in a System of Local Governments." *Urban Studies* 12: 205–11.

Henderson, Vernon. 2001. "Marshall's Scale Economies." Brown University. Mimeo.

Henderson, Vernon, Ari Kuncoro, and Matt Turner. 1995. "Industrial Development in Cities." *Journal of Political Economy* 103 (5): 1067–90.

Hines, James R., Jr. 1996. "Altered States: Taxes and the Location of Foreign Direct Investment in America." *American Economic Review* 86 (5):1076–94.

Hines, James R., Jr., and Mihir Desai. 2001. "Foreign Direct Investment in a World of Multiple Taxes." Working Paper 8440. Cambridge, Mass.: National Bureau of Economic Research (August).

Mark, Stephen T., Therese J. McGuire, and Leslie E. Papke. 2000. "The Influence of Taxes on Employment and Population Growth: Evidence from the Washington, D.C. Metropolitan Area." *National Tax Journal* LIII (1): 105–23.

McGuire, Therese J. 1991. "Federal Aid to States and Localities and the Appropriate Competitive Framework." In *Competition among States and Local Governments: Efficiency and Equity in American Federalism*, edited by Daphne A. Kenyon and John Kincaid, 153–66. Washington: Urban Institute Press.

Niskanen, William, Jr. 1977. *Bureaucracy and Representative Government*. Chicago: Aldine.

Oates, Wallace E. 1972. *Fiscal Federalism*. Harcourt Brace Jovanovich.

———. 1996. "The Invisible Hand in the Public Sector: Interjurisdictional Competition in Theory and Practice." Unpublished paper. University of Maryland.

Oates, Wallace E., and Robert M. Schwab. 1988. "Economic Competition among Jurisdictions: Efficiency Enhancing or Distortion Inducing?" *Journal of Public Economics* 35: 333–54.

———. 1991. "The Allocative and Distributive Implications of Local Fiscal Competititon." In *Competition among States and Local Governments: Efficiency and Equity in American Federalism*, edited by Daphne A. Kenyon and John Kincaid, 127–45. Washington: Urban Institute Press.

Pagano, Michael A., and Ann O. Bowman.1995. *Cityscapes and Capital: The Politics of Urban Development*. Johns Hopkins University.

Rauch, James E. 1993a. "Does History Matter Only When It Matters Little? The Case of City-Industry Location." *Quarterly Journal of Economics* 108 (3): 843–67.

———. 1993b. "Productivity Gains from Geographic Concentration of Human Capital: Evidence from the Cities." *Journal of Urban Economics* 34 (3): 380–400.

Tiebout, Charles. 1956. "A Pure Theory of Local Expenditures." *Journal of Political Economy* 64 (5): 416-24.

Wasylenko, Michael. 1997. "Taxation and Economic Development: The State of the Economic Literature." *New England Economic Review* (March-April): 37–52.

Wildasin, David E. 1989. "Interjurisdictional Capital Mobility: Fiscal Externality and a Corrective Subsidy." *Journal of Urban Economics* 25: 193–212.

Wilson, John D.1986. "A Theory of Interregional Tax Competition." *Journal of Urban Economics* 19 (3): 296–315.

———.1999. "Theories of Tax Competition." *National Tax Journal* LII: 269–304.

Wolman, Harold, with David Spitzley. 1996. "The Politics of Local Economic Development." *Economic Development Quarterly* 10 (2): 115–50.

Zodrow, George R., and Peter Mieszkowski. 1986. "Pigou, Tiebout, Property Taxation, and the Underprovision of Local Public Goods." *Journal of Urban Economics* 19: 356–70.

JACOB L. VIGDOR

Duke University

Does Gentrification Harm the Poor?

FOR SEVERAL DECADES, social scientists have tracked the fiscal health of American central cities with some degree of concern. Suburbanization, spawned by technological innovations, consumer preferences, and at least to some extent by government policy, has selectively pulled affluent households out of urban jurisdictions.[1] The leaders of these jurisdictions are left with the prospect of satisfying more concentrated demands for services with a dwindling tax base, realizing that further increasing the burden they place on residents will simply drive more of them away. In the process, cities have become concentrated centers of poverty, joblessness, crime, and other social pathologies.[2]

A detached observer of this cycle might conclude that its reversal—the return of affluent households to the central city, associated increases in property values and the government's tax base—would be welcomed by city leaders. In fact, the response to such a turnaround, if labeled as "gentrification," is quite likely to be negative. In San Francisco, for example, a mayoral candidate in 1999 pledged to declare "war on any and all gentrification" if elected.[3] Though usually associated with larger and faster-growing cities, gentrification and its associated tensions have been noted in cities from Milwaukee to Baton Rouge.[4] Scholarly interest in gentrification peaked in the

The author wishes to thank William Gale, Janet Pack, Alice Rivlin, Douglas Massey, Charles Clotfelter, and Phil Cook for helpful comments on earlier drafts, as well as Melanie Kadlic and Tyler Will for exceptional research assistance.

1. Jackson (1985).
2. Wilson (1987).
3. Edward Epstein and John Wildermuth, "Neighborhood Issues Topic A in 2nd Debate," *San Francisco Chronicle*, November 18, 1999, p. A1.
4. Greg J. Borowski, "Rejuvenation Resentment: Prosperity in Brewers Hill Area Has Some People Feeling Left Out," *Milwaukee Journal-Sentinel*," May 27, 2001, p. 1A; Lanny Keller, "Gentrification Benefits Residents, Baton Rouge," *The Advocate* (Baton Rouge), April 5, 2001, p. 9B.

first half of the 1980s, as neighborhood revitalization occurred in a number of U.S. cities. In recent years, as reports of gentrification across the country have accelerated, there are signs of renewed scholarly interest in the process. A number of studies, past and present, have debated whether the process is significant and/or sustainable.[5] Still others have addressed the issues that most frequently concern political observers of gentrification: that the process imposes costs on disadvantaged households.[6] Does gentrification cause a reduction in well-being among disadvantaged households? This paper examines the question and finds it extraordinarily difficult to answer, for reasons that few previous authors have considered.

The first section begins the examination by illustrating the demographic shifts most commonly associated with gentrification, and then offers two competing explanations for them. The competing explanations motivate two very different views of the distributional effects of gentrification. In the first view, revitalization of urban neighborhoods *causes* changes in well-being among disadvantaged households. In the second view, gentrification is merely a *side effect* of other broad economic trends that affect the poor. The analysis also makes clear that residential displacement—the primary focus of most existing literature on the consequences of gentrification—is neither a necessary nor sufficient condition for declines in the living standards of poor households.

The following section considers the general equilibrium effects of gentrification beyond the housing market. Increases in the local tax base might improve the quality of local public goods and services. Employment opportunities in certain industries might improve with the arrival of a more affluent clientele; that is to say, gentrification might partially solve the urban "spatial mismatch" problem.[7] Finally, gentrification might decrease the urban concentration of poverty, ameliorating the ills associated with it.[8] The subsequent section reviews the literature on the distributional impact of gentrification, and concludes that previous studies are too narrowly focused to fully address the question of whether gentrification harms the poor.

The literature review is followed by a broader analysis of the question, using data from the American Housing Survey (AHS) to consider gentrification in the Boston area between 1970 and 1998. Overall, the data point to no

5. Berry (1985); Bourne (1993); Wyly and Hammel (1999); Berry (1999).
6. Schill and Nathan (1983); Marcuse (1986); LeGates and Hartman (1986); Atkinson (2000); Kennedy and Leonard (2001).
7. Kain (1968).
8. Wilson (1987).

obvious conclusion, which is not surprising considering the difficulty of the task. The greatest empirical difficulty in assessing gentrification is determining what would have happened to individuals had gentrification not occurred. Notwithstanding these difficulties, the empirical work here presents some striking patterns. There is no evidence to suggest that gentrification increases the probability that low-status households exit their housing unit. Poor households are more likely to exit poverty themselves than to be replaced by a nonpoor household. Nonetheless, low-status households have experienced increased housing costs without sufficient compensation in terms of increased income, and without discernible changes in self-assessed housing unit quality, public service quality, or neighborhood quality. Census tract demographic data do suggest, however, that gentrification promotes the socioeconomic integration of metropolitan areas.

The final section presents concluding remarks, as well as comments on appropriate policy responses should future research more definitively establish a link between gentrification and the well-being of disadvantaged households.

What Is Gentrification?

Existing literature on gentrification has failed to arrive at a consensus definition of what the process entails.[9] Some authors define gentrification as private sector–initiated residential and commercial investment in urban neighborhoods accompanied by inflows of households with higher socioeconomic status than the neighborhood's initial residents.[10] Other authors impose an additional necessary condition that initial residents must be displaced in the process.[11] Kennedy and Leonard impose the additional condition that gentrification must change "the essential character and flavor of the neighborhood."[12] An impartial observer's opinion of gentrification might easily be determined by the number of necessary conditions incorporated into the definition.

This section briefly reviews the demographic trends most commonly associated with gentrification and analyzes the economic forces underlying the process. Reinvestment and demographic transitions in urban neighborhoods

9. Palen and London (1984); Kennedy and Leonard (2001, p. 6).

10. Nelson (1988).

11. "Displacement" is itself a term defined in various ways in the literature. The question of what constitutes displacement is considered in the literature review.

12. See Kennedy and Leonard (2001, p. 6).

might result from changes in preferences among high socioeconomic status households, or from increases in income inequality within a metropolitan area. This distinction is an important one from a policy perspective—the former explanation implies that gentrification can be a root cause of harm; the latter suggests that gentrification is one side effect of a broader societal trend. While either of these forces will generally lead to land price appreciation in certain neighborhoods, they will not lead to demographic transitions, nor will they necessarily cause displacement of a neighborhood's initial residents, if moving costs among these residents are sufficiently high. This implies that displacement is neither a necessary nor a sufficient condition for the forces underlying neighborhood reinvestment and demographic transition to lower the living standards of initial residents. Thus when considering the question of whether gentrification harms the poor, it is not necessary to restrict the term "gentrification" to include only cases where displacement of initial residents results.

Demographic Trends in a Gentrifying Neighborhood

To illustrate the population and demographic trends associated with gentrification, table 1 reports simple statistics for a single census tract in Boston at seven points in time, beginning in 1940 and ending with preliminary information from the 2000 Census. Wyly and Hammel identify this tract, number 708 in the city's South End, as a "core" gentrifying tract, based on statistical analysis and fieldwork undertaken in 1998.[13] Nelson groups this tract with others exhibiting gentrifying trends between 1970 and 1980.[14]

Tract 708, a collection of thirteen city blocks just over one mile from the central business district, reached a local population maximum—nearly six thousand residents—in 1950. During the subsequent twenty years, the tract depopulated rapidly, shrinking by more than 50 percent. This population trend appears consistent with "white flight," as the share of white residents declined from over 40 percent to under 10 percent between 1940 and 1960. The depopulation of tract 708 is also associated with a marked increase in housing vacancy: nearly one-fourth of all housing units in the tract were vacant in 1970. Throughout this period of decline, the tract maintained a relatively small share of college graduates in the population, a small share of workers in professional occupations, and a median income thirty to forty percentage points below the city's.

13. Wyly and Hammel (1999).
14. Nelson (1988).

Table 1. Long-run Demographic Trends in Census Tract 708, Boston[a]

Percent unless otherwise indicated

Demographic characteristic	1940	1950	1960	1970	1980	1990	2000
Population (N)	5,177	5,624	3,728	2,305	2,742	3,274	3,600
Vacancy rate	7.9	0.9	13.6	22.9	16.6	13.2	1.8
Adults with college degree	2.8	3.7	3.5	10.5	26.5	54.0	n.a.
Workers in professional or managerial occupations	9.1	7.6	5.6	10.6	30.3	55.3	n.a.
Ratio of tract median income to city median income	n.a.	0.603	0.618	0.667	0.832	1.037	n.a.
White (non-Hispanic) residents	43.1	24.7	7.9	13.4	29.6	58.6	58.2
Black residents	56.5	74.8	89.8	83.7	63.3	34.9	26.6

Source: U.S. Decennial Census reports.

n.a. Not available.

a. Before 1970, tract was designated "L-2."

Sometime between 1960 and 1970, the first indications of a new demographic transition begin to appear. The outflow of white households stopped during this decade, and the share of the population with a college degree or a professional occupation increased substantially. Between 1970 and 2000, this upswing continued. The tract's population increased by more than 50 percent during this time period, though the population in 2000 was still more than a third lower than the peak in 1950. Non-Hispanic whites reclaimed the racial majority in the tract in 1990, while blacks declined from five-sixths to roughly one-quarter of the population between 1970 and 2000. As of 1990, the majority of adults in this tract held college degrees, and the majority of workers in the tract held professional or managerial occupations. The tract's median income surpassed the citywide average in 1990, and vacancy rates in the 2000 census approached the all-time low observed in 1950.

This simple example illustrates the basic stylized facts associated with gentrification. The process occurs in urban neighborhoods that have experienced decline, as witnessed by population losses and high vacancy rates in recent years. Gentrification brings renewed population growth, accompanied by an inflow of households with high educational attainment, professional jobs, and few children. Corresponding outflows of low socioeconomic-status households are tempered to the extent that the neighborhood begins the process with high vacancy rates or the potential for more intensive development. Finally, gentrification often implies racial transition. Tract 708, on the fringe of the predominantly black Roxbury section of Boston, experienced offsetting racial transitions in consecutive generations. Racial tension has been an important subtext of gentrification in many revitalizing neighborhoods, such as Harlem, in New York, and Columbia Heights, in Washington.

Gentrification as Cause: Changes in Preferences

A simple model can illustrate the potential causes and implications of gentrification in urban areas. Consider the case where land in two neighborhoods, denoted 1 and 2, must be allocated between two types of households, labeled rich and poor. For each type, land is valued solely as an input in the production of housing services. While the supply of land is inelastic, the intensity of its use in the production of housing will vary according to its value.

Land is allocated to the highest bidder. Each household's willingness to pay for land in a given neighborhood is based on its valuation of a bundle of amenities associated with that neighborhood, and the set of amenities varies between neighborhoods 1 and 2. Rather than live in either neighborhood, each household has the option, at least initially, of selecting a residence outside the urban area, where they are guaranteed a reservation level of utility. This reservation level is presumed to be unaffected by the outcome of land allocation in the urban area. The amount each household is willing to pay in either neighborhood, then, is that which makes it indifferent between locating in that neighborhood and living outside the urban area. Households may either purchase land or rent it from a landlord.

One possible outcome of this allocation process is illustrated in figure 1. In this case, the bundle of amenities available in neighborhood 1 is considered superior by households of all types, as evidenced by their greater willingness to pay. Poor households submit the highest bids for land in neighborhood 1, and consequently occupy the neighborhood. Rich households submit the highest bids for land in neighborhood 2. The set of amenities in neighborhood 1 might include availability of public goods and services or other amenities that are differentially attractive to the poor.[15] Poor households respond to the relatively high price of land in their neighborhood by consuming less of it.

Starting with the baseline scenario as shown in figure 1, suppose that rich households' valuation of the bundle of amenities available in neighborhood 1 increases.[16]

Figure 2 shows one possible result of such a preference shift.[17] Rich households' willingness to pay to live in neighborhood 1 increases by a sufficient amount to change the rank order of bids in that location. Poor owner households experience a capital gain from this shift in preferences. Households choosing not to realize this gain, however, may face higher user costs if ad valorem property taxes are in place.[18]

---

15. Closer proximity to the city center might be one important amenity associated with neighborhood 1. Wheaton (1977); Glaeser and others (2000). Disamenities such as high crime rates might differentially repel the rich from neighborhood 1 as well. Cullen and Levitt (1999).

16. Such a change could be induced by a number of factors. If neighborhood 1 is closer to the city center, a shift to two-earner households within the wealthy group might increase the total household disutility associated with commuting time. Later and less frequent childbearing might change wealthy households' demand for certain location-specific amenities, such as public schools, or for land itself. Neighborhood 1 might also feature housing stock or neighborhood characteristics that come into fashion among the wealthy.

17. The new bid level shown in figure 2 can be considered what rich households would be willing to pay for land in neighborhood 1 net of any moving costs they face.

18. Households that respond to increased valuation of neighborhood 1 by purchasing land may end up worse off if land values subsequently decline. As table 4 below illustrates, some owner-occupiers in the Boston area appear to have locked in high housing costs at the peak of the 1980s real estate boom, leading to substantial losses in income-after-housing costs during the subsequent bust.

Figure 1. Two-Neighborhood, Two-Type Model: Initial Equilibrium

Type's bid for land in

Household type	Neighborhood 1	Neighborhood 2
Rich	125	100
Poor	150	50

Figure 2. Preference-Driven Gentrification

Type's bid for land in

Household type	Neighborhood 1	Neighborhood 2
Rich	175	100
Poor	150	50

Poor renter households could react to changing land values in one of several ways, depending on the magnitude of costs associated with moving. Potential responses are illustrated in figure 3, which depicts the trade-offs faced by poor households in allocating income between land and all other goods. This figure ignores potentially important effects of the change depicted in figure 2 that occur outside the market for land. These general equilibrium effects, which could potentially offset or reverse any changes in utility experienced by the poor, are considered more carefully below. The initial bundle of land and goods consumed by poor households is point A, determined by the point of tangency of the budget constraint B_0 and the indifference curve I_0, which represents the reservation utility initially available outside the urban area. An increase in the price of land shifts the budget constraint to B_1, making I_0 unattainable.

If poor renter households can move costlessly, they will exit this neighborhood and obtain their reservation utility outside the urban area. If moving between urban areas is sufficiently costly, but the costs of moving within the urban area are negligible, poor renter households will remain in this neighborhood and reoptimize their land consumption, selecting point B. This point reflects a clear decrease in utility for poor households. Finally, if moving costs are sufficiently high both between and within urban areas, poor renter households will continue to consume their initial amount of land. This choice, marked as point C in figure 3, once again implies a clear utility loss for poor renters, as their consumption of other goods must decline in order to com-

Figure 3. Poor Household's Consumption Decision in the Wake of Gentrification

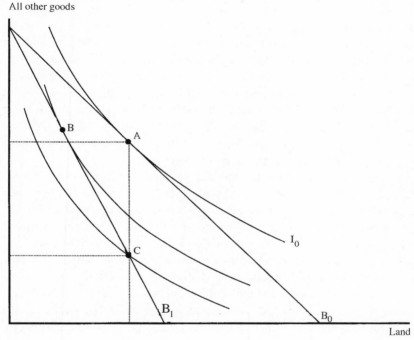

All other goods

pensate for the higher cost of land. Theoretically, if all initial residents of neighborhood 1 chose point *C*, the demographic transitions associated with gentrification might not occur in the first place.

This scenario shows that gentrification, spurred by an increase in the value that rich households place on amenities in poor neighborhoods, can result in lower levels of utility for some poor households if moving costs are not negligible and any countervailing benefits outside the housing market are small. It is also clear from this illustration that displacement is neither a necessary nor sufficient condition for gentrification to harm the poor. If moving costs are zero, displacement may occur without any loss in utility among the initial residents of neighborhood 1. If moving costs are prohibitively high, poor households may absorb any increase in housing costs, avoiding displacement but experiencing a decline in utility nonetheless.

Underlying the discussion to this point has been the presumption that an effectively unlimited supply of rich households is available to occupy neighborhood 1 once the shift in preferences occurs. A more realistic model would consider the preference modification driving gentrification to be selective, involving only a fraction of the population of rich households. A second modification to the model would incorporate one important feature visible in Boston's tract 708 and other gentrifying neighborhoods: high initial vacancy rates. Underutilization of existing land, whether due to poor maintenance of the structures found on it, environmental considerations, or other factors, introduces the possibility that neighborhoods might be able to absorb some additional residents without creating significant upward pressure on land values. To the extent that these supply adjustments take time, the harm associated with gentrification may be temporary in nature.

Figure 4 illustrates a second potential outcome of preference-driven gentrification, starting from the initial conditions portrayed in figure 1. Here, rich households' land bids increase to the point where they exactly equal those of poor households. In this case, neither group outbids the other; thus poor and rich households may cohabit neighborhood 1. If voluntary residential turnover in neighborhood 1 mirrors that in the typical urban community—where approximately half of all residents move over a five-year period—the demographic transitions associated with gentrification might very well take place without any adverse impact on poor residents whatsoever. In addition to non-negligible moving costs, then, actual land value escalation is a necessary condition for gentrification to cause a reduction in the well-being of poor households.

This model of gentrification conforms most readily to the visions of those who rally against it. Rich households, that as a group have access to many other residential options within the urban area, price existing residents out of poorer neighborhoods. Gentrification might, however, be a symptom of broader societal trends rather than an outcome of changing preferences among rich households.

Gentrification as Side Effect: Changes in Income

Suppose a technological innovation increases the productivity of highly skilled workers in the urban area depicted in figure 1, while leaving the productivity of low-skill workers unchanged. Identifying the former group with rich households and the latter with poor, figure 4 shows the change in land markets that might result. The increase in productivity will lead to an increase in the wages of high-skill workers, so long as labor markets are competitive.

Figure 4. Another Form of Preference-Driven Gentrification

	Type's bid for land in	
Household type	*Neighborhood 1*	*Neighborhood 2*
Rich	150	100
Poor	150	50

Figure 5. Income-Driven Gentrification

	Type's bid for land in	
Household type	*Neighborhood 1*	*Neighborhood 2*
Rich	175	150
Poor	150	50

If the increase in wages of the highly skilled is unique to this area, skilled workers in other areas will have an incentive to migrate toward it.[19] The presence of lucrative wage opportunities increases skilled workers' willingness to pay to live in this area. One potential outcome of this process is depicted in figure 5. Here, rich households' bids increase in both neighborhoods. Income-driven gentrification corresponds to the traditional "supply-side" view, which identifies the process as a quest for reasonably priced housing on the part of individuals who face high and escalating prices in other parts of the urban area.[20] From the perspective of poor households, this situation resembles the one portrayed in the previous section. Facing an increase in land values, owners experience a capital gain coupled with a potential increase in ownership costs. Renters face the same set of choices illustrated in figure 3. They can be expected to relocate if moving costs are low, adjust their land and housing con-

19. Morrill (2000) presents evidence that changes in income inequality varied significantly across U.S. metropolitan areas between 1970 and 1990. This evidence suggests that geographically selective technological innovations are widespread. As more informal evidence, consider that many of the metropolitan areas most commonly associated with gentrification, such as San Francisco, Boston, Washington, and Seattle, are also associated with technologically advanced industries. If skill acquisition takes place through personal interaction, as in Glaeser (1999), productivity may grow differentially in cities that are initial centers of human capital.

20. Berry (1985).

sumption if within-neighborhood moving costs are low, and remain in place if moving costs are prohibitively high.

From a policy perspective, linking gentrification to changes in the income distribution opens a new set of potential instruments. Policy responses outside the housing market, such as employment training programs or education subsidies, would be potential remedies for any harm caused by gentrification. On the other hand, policies aimed at altering the preferences of rich households, which could ameliorate upward pressure on housing prices in the preference-based model, would be less effective in an environment where land values are escalating universally.

Any discussion of policy responses to gentrification is premature at this point, since potentially important effects exist outside the housing market. This discussion simply describes two sets of economic forces that have the potential to adversely impact renter households of low socioeconomic status through escalating land values. These forces may or may not cause displacement—indeed, they may not even cause the neighborhood demographic changes associated with gentrification—depending on the distribution of moving costs within the subject population.

Gentrification in General Equilibrium

Low socioeconomic-status households suffer a decrease in utility any time they are forced to increase their bids for housing without receiving any countervailing local benefit. Gentrification might create these countervailing benefits in three ways. One channel is the labor market. Gentrification might create job opportunities for low-status households, or relocate existing opportunities into areas more accessible to them.[21] Second, increases in land values present property tax–dependent local governments with additional resources, which might translate into improved services or lower effective tax burdens for poor residents. Finally, the process of gentrification might improve neigh-

21. A second labor market channel opens up if some low-status households exit the urban area. This may lead to an increase in wages for low-skilled workers that remain, depending on the net effect on labor demand. The availability of higher wages in the local labor market will tend to increase poor households' willingness to pay for housing in the area. This mechanism enables households with high moving costs to benefit from the presence of other households with low moving costs. In some situations, this labor market effect, combined with the reduced pressure on housing prices caused by outmigration, will be sufficient to preclude any negative impact on the poor.

borhood quality for poor residents, offsetting the hypothesized negative effects of middle-class and upper-class abandonment of the central city.[22] In the context of the simple model of a poor household's choices shown in figure 3, the first countervailing benefit increases the household's income, shifting the budget constraint B_1 out and increasing the maximum attainable utility level. Changes in public service or neighborhood quality shift a household's indifference curves, so that a higher level of utility is associated with each given combination of land and other market-based goods.

The Labor Market

The spatial mismatch hypothesis, first advanced by John Kain, posits that labor market outcomes for central-city dwellers have suffered as a result of the continued decentralization of employment in metropolitan areas.[23] An extensive empirical literature remains divided on whether spatial mismatch effects are important.[24] As a centralizing force, gentrification could potentially improve labor market outcomes for central city residents by offsetting spatial mismatch. Residential gentrification might cause a relocation of jobs in personal service industries and retail trade towards central cities. Centralization of other types of employment, if truly induced by changing residential patterns, could produce gains for central city dwellers as well.[25] Improved employment prospects for central city residents translate into some combination of lower unemployment, higher wages, or better workplace amenities. These in turn make the city a more attractive place to live for low socioeconomic-status households, implying an increase in willingness to pay for land in or near the city.

The realization that household income might be endogenous to the process of gentrification introduces an important question: what constitutes a "poor" household? The fact that poverty status itself might be a function of gentrification suggests the use of an alternative measure of low socioeconomic status. Poverty itself is rather transitory in nature: about half of all households entering poverty in a given year will escape poverty within a year.[26] For these

22. Wilson (1987).
23. Kain (1968).
24. For reviews, see Kain (1992); Ihlanfeldt and Sjoquist (1998).
25. The question of whether centralization of households causes centralization of firms or vice versa parallels the equally difficult question of whether employment decentralization causes residential decentralization. On the latter question, see Margo (1992); Mieszkowski and Mills (1993); and Thurston and Yezer (1994).
26. Stevens (1994); Bane and Ellwood (1986).

reasons, the empirical evidence presented below will focus primarily on educational attainment, rather than income, as a socioeconomic indicator.[27] Stevens presents evidence that poverty spells tend to be more persistent for individuals with low educational attainment.[28]

Local Taxes and Public Services

Increasing land values, along with more intensive development, are positive developments for property-tax dependent local governments. The potential for additional revenue with no increase in the underlying property tax rate is offset somewhat to the extent that households entering a jurisdiction bring additional service demands along with them. Since the archetypal gentrifying household is one without children, demand for public education—the largest local government responsibility in the United States—should be relatively unaffected.[29] Empirical evidence suggests that reductions in the concentration of poverty within a jurisdiction reduce per capita expenditures on a number of other services, including police and fire protection.[30] On net, jurisdictions experiencing gentrification have the opportunity to either lower the effective property tax rate without compromising service quality, or increase service quality without increasing the tax rate. Either change has the potential to improve living standards for low-status households, especially in situations where selective property value increases allow local governments to shift the property tax burden away from them.

Two factors might mitigate or negate this positive impact. First, rising property values without a countervailing decrease in effective property tax rates could significantly increase housing costs for some households, especially the elderly and others who own their homes free and clear. These increased costs might lead to better public services, but the valuation that homeowners attach to these services might not compensate for increased tax

27. Neighborhood transitions that come about as the result of changes in the characteristics of existing households rather than mobility are referred to as "incumbent upgrading" in the literature.

28. Stevens (1999).

29. Evidence from the 1990, 5 percent Integrated Public Use Microdata Sample (IPUMS) confirms that few highly educated migrants into the city of Boston had children. In the sample of college-educated individuals who moved into central Boston between 1985 and 1990, approximately 7 percent shared a household with a child under the age of 18 ($N = 1,095$). In over half of these households with children, the eldest child was no more than 5 years old. Statewide, 37 percent of college-educated individuals shared a household with a child under the age of 18 ($N = 31,796$). Ruggles and others (1997).

30. Pack (1998).

bills. Second, extensive displacement of low-status households could prevent them from reaping the benefits of better public services in a gentrifying jurisdiction.

Neighborhood Quality

If gentrification harms the poor by pricing them out of the local housing market, then abandonment of central cities by high-status households would bring countervailing benefits, by lowering land values. Abandonment of central cities, by contrast, is usually portrayed in a negative light, largely because of hypothesized negative effects on those individuals left behind.[31] Two causal channels used to explain these effects are Kain's spatial mismatch hypothesis and increased strain on local governments. A third set of hypothesized causal channels involves peer and role model interactions within neighborhoods. Several studies have demonstrated correlations between neighborhood characteristics and child or adolescent outcomes.[32] Household mobility initiatives, such as the Gautreaux program in Chicago and the federal Moving to Opportunity program, have provided additional evidence that residence in a high-poverty neighborhood influences outcomes including juvenile crime, safety and health, student test scores, and economic self-sufficiency.[33] By increasing the amount of neighborhood interaction between households of varying socioeconomic status, gentrification might lead to long-term improvements in the living standards of poor households, for the same reason that central city abandonment might lead to long-term reductions. For this causal channel to operate, gentrification must actually lead to greater socioeconomic integration in metropolitan areas, which might not occur if extensive displacement of the poor results.

A possible negative consequence of land value increases and demographic shifts is the loss of "character," as perceived by a neighborhood's initial residents. For an incumbent household, character might be determined by the demographic composition of the neighborhood or the amenities, commercial establishments, and local institutions present. While character itself is subjective and difficult to quantify, the net effect of a decrease in neighborhood

31. Wilson (1987).

32. Case and Katz (1991); Brooks-Gunn, Duncan, and Aber (1997); for a review of the literature, see Ellen and Turner (1997).

33. For outcomes related to juvenile crime, see Ludwig, Duncan, and Hirschfeld (2001); safety and health, see Katz and others (2001); student test scores, see Ludwig, Ladd, and Duncan (2001); and economic self-sufficiency, see Ludwig, Duncan, and Pinkston (2000).

character should be a reduction in a household's willingness to pay to live in a particular area. A householder's assessment of neighborhood quality, as recorded in the American Housing Survey, should capture these character effects.

Assessing gentrification's complete impact on the poor is not an easy task. The following section evaluates prior attempts to measure this impact. The subsequent section offers new analysis, using data from the American Housing Survey and other sources, focusing on gentrification in the Boston metropolitan area.

Existing Literature

Previous attempts to identify gentrification's distributional consequences focus almost exclusively on residential displacement.[34] The definition of the term "displacement" varies from study to study.[35] Some researchers consider displacement to occur only when a household is involuntarily required to relocate—when a property is demolished, for example, or when a rental property becomes occupied by its owner.[36] Some researchers consider household movement in the wake of rent increases to be involuntary displacement; others do not. The definition of involuntary displacement used here includes both forced and cost-driven moves, under the presumption that most individuals forced from their housing unit would have been able to stay if they had offered a large enough sum of money.[37]

Studies of gentrification and displacement overlook an important means by which escalating land values might adversely affect poor households: by increasing their housing costs without providing sufficient countervailing ben-

34. Atkinson (2000); Nelson (1988); LeGates and Hartman (1986); Marcuse (1986); Lee and Hodge (1984); Schill and Nathan (1983); U.S. Department of Housing and Urban Development (1981); Henig (1980).

35. Lee and Hodge (1984).

36. The American Housing Survey asks respondents who have moved in the past year to identify the "main" reason they left their previous residence. One response option, "A private company or person wanted to use it for some purpose," is equated with involuntary displacement by most researchers. See Lee and Hodge (1984).

37. This definition excludes some housing transitions that other authors have termed displacement. These include situations where a poor household moves out of a housing unit for reasons other than cost—changes in family structure or job location, for example—and is replaced by a nonpoor household. "Exclusionary" displacement, as defined by Marcuse (1986), is also excluded, since it effectively refers to all occupation of housing units by nonpoor individuals as displacement.

efits. Moreover, as illustrated above, the demographic transitions associated with gentrification can possibly occur entirely through voluntary housing turnover, in which case it is unclear that any original residents suffer harm. One challenge that any study of displacement faces, then, is distinguishing voluntary from involuntary moves.

So long as moving costs are not negligible, studies that correctly identify involuntary displacement show evidence of harm to incumbent residents. A second challenge for these studies, however, is to distinguish the involuntary displacement that can be directly attributed to gentrification. Displacement occurs for a number of underlying reasons, and even in gentrifying neighborhoods, some incidents might have taken place despite the absence of demographic transitions.

Most existing studies fail to meet one or both of the challenges outlined above. Many track movement of households across space, or changes in occupancy, without determining whether the underlying moves are involuntary.[38] Some investigators survey households known to have moved out of housing units in gentrifying areas to determine their reasons for relocating.[39] While most studies find that a considerable fraction of movers claim to have been involuntarily displaced, in all cases except one, they fail to address the question of how many involuntary moves would have taken place in the absence of gentrification. American Housing Survey data show that about 4 to 5 percent of moves nationwide can be categorized as involuntary. While many studies estimate higher rates among households that leave gentrifying neighborhoods—as high as 23 percent—they do not attempt to control for potentially important differences between gentrifying neighborhoods and other areas.[40]

The lone exception to this latter criticism is a 1981 study of conversions of rental housing to owner-occupancy by the U.S. Department of Housing and Urban Development (HUD), which singled out "revitalization" and "comparison" neighborhoods in four cities. In two of the sampled cities, conversion rates were nearly identical in the revitalization and comparison areas. In a third sample city, conversions actually occurred more frequently in the comparison neighborhood. In only one of the four studied cities was there a significantly higher rate of conversion in the revitalizing neighborhood. Overall, existing literature has failed to convincingly demonstrate that rates of involuntary displacement are higher in gentrifying neighborhoods.

38. Atkinson (2000); Nelson (1988); Marcuse (1986); Henig (1980).
39. Schill and Nathan (1983); U.S. Department of Housing and Urban Development (1981).
40. Schill and Nathan (1983, p. 109).

In some cases, researchers have broadened the scope of their work to consider the housing market outcomes of gentrification-displaced households. These studies find surprisingly little evidence of declines in living standards. The 1981 HUD report, in a separate analysis, tracks displacees from San Francisco's Hayes Valley neighborhood, comparing their housing market outcomes with those of voluntary movers out of the neighborhood as well as households moving into the neighborhood.[41] The report states that displacees "have not experienced severe negative changes in housing characteristics either absolutely or in comparison with other groups."[42] Those displaced were less cost-burdened than voluntary movers, experienced a decrease in crowding, and only a minority reported decreased satisfaction with neighborhood quality, public services, or housing characteristics. Displacees were actually more likely to make the transition to home ownership than voluntary movers.

Schill and Nathan report similar findings in their survey of displacement in five cities, and conclude that "displaced households do not appear to live in worse conditions following their move."[43] Most of those displaced reported increased satisfaction with their home and neighborhood. Relative to voluntary movers, displacees experienced smaller rent increases on average, with no associated increase in crowding. Their commute times were more likely to decrease than increase. Schill and Nathan proceed to compare their sample of displacees to a sample of voluntary movers, and conclude that displacees were worse off by comparison. It should be noted, however, that the sample of those who moved voluntarily differs from those who were displaced in many important respects.[44]

In summary, existing literature has failed to demonstrate convincingly that gentrification harms the poor. Most studies have erroneously focused on displacement as an indicator of harm and have failed to demonstrate that gentrification causes displacement. Studies tracking the outcomes of those dis-

41. U.S. Department of Housing and Urban Development (1981).

42. In a separate analysis, the HUD report uses the Panel Study of Income Dynamics to examine the outcomes of displaced households. While the results of this study are generally less positive than the Hayes Valley study, the report does not explicitly link displacement with gentrification in the PSID (1981, p. 49).

43. Schill and Nathan (1983, p. 112).

44. Schill and Nathan (1983) show that in their study those displaced are significantly more likely to be unmarried, unemployed, less educated, and poor relative to their sample of those who move voluntarily. The HUD study of displacement in Hayes Valley does not disclose characteristics of those displaced and comparison groups. The sample selection process differs substantially between those displaced and those who move voluntarily; hence any differences between their outcomes should be interpreted cautiously.

placed have generally found absolute increases in well-being, and mixed evidence on changes in well-being relative to comparison groups. By focusing on those displaced, however, these studies may fail to recognize negative consequences for households that choose not to exit gentrifying areas, or for residents of other neighborhoods who accept those displaced.

Given the insufficiencies of existing literature, one might ask whether it is empirically possible to demonstrate that gentrification harms the poor. Absent a true social scientific experiment, in which one of an otherwise identical pair of cities would be subject to the "treatment" of gentrification in core neighborhoods, the question is at best extremely difficult. A comprehensive study must consider:

1. Whether "poor" households, defined in varying ways, are involuntarily subjected to the costs of moving through displacement at higher rates than would exist without gentrification.

2. Whether gentrification causes poor households to spend more on housing.

3. Whether these increased housing costs are offset by increases in household income.

4. Whether the poor receive more or better quality housing in exchange for higher payments.

5. Whether the poor become more satisfied with public services or neighborhoods in urban areas marked by gentrification.

6. Whether the forces underlying gentrification can be attributed to changes in the preferences of wealthy households or to shifts in the income distribution. This question is of great importance for determining the set of policy tools that might be used to counteract any harm accruing to disadvantaged households.

The following empirical exercise, though flawed in certain critical respects, presents a template for future research on the distributional consequences of housing market changes in urban areas.

A Case Study: Boston 1970–98

As table 1 demonstrates, the process of neighborhood revitalization and gentrification began in some Boston neighborhoods between 1960 and 1970.[45]

45. U.S. Department of Housing and Urban Development (1981).

Trends in demographic composition and housing market conditions have continued in areas such as tract 708 through the 2000 Census.[46] An important component of revitalization in many Boston neighborhoods has been racial transition, though tension is somewhat muted by the historically low black share of the population in the city and metropolitan area. Generalizing one city's experience to make broad statements on the effects of gentrification is a tenuous exercise at best. The reader should therefore bear in mind that the purpose of this case study is to present a methodology and a baseline set of findings for use by future researchers.

This study makes use of several data sources to examine the trajectory of outcomes for low-socioeconomic-status households in the Boston area between 1970 and 1998. Foremost among these sources is the American Housing Survey (AHS), which collected detailed information on several thousand dwelling units in the metropolitan area in 1974, quadrennially between 1977 and 1993, and in 1998. One aspect of the AHS makes it particularly attractive for this study: it samples a roughly constant set of housing units between 1974 and 1981, and between 1985 and 1993. This makes it possible to observe housing units in transition from a low-status occupant to a high-status occupant, to the extent that these transitions actually occur. This methodology stands in contrast with most previous empirical work, which tracks households rather than housing units.

Geographic detail in the AHS varies over time. Between 1974 and 1981, housing units are identified as located either within the city of Boston or outside of it. Starting with the 1985 sample, units are associated with a "zone," a unit of area containing between 100,000 and 200,000 individuals. Figure 6 shows the arrangement of zones in the 1985–93 samples. The AHS covers a broad area, extending to the base of Cape Cod in the south, to southern New Hampshire in the north, and to the edge of Worcester County in the west. The city of Boston is divided into five zones, shown in detail in the inset map. In addition to Boston, the sample includes the smaller central city areas of Brockton, Lawrence, Lowell, and Nashua, New Hampshire.

46. In recent years, two discrete events have been associated with major changes in Boston's demographic composition. In 1980, Massachusetts voters approved Proposition 2 1/2, which forced the city to reduce its property tax levy dramatically over a four-year period. Vigdor (2001) shows that community composition changed significantly in cities and towns most affected by the Proposition, which made former high-tax jurisdictions more attractive to households with a relatively low demand for local public services. Second, municipal rent control regulations in Boston and in two nearby communities were overturned in another statewide vote in 1994. Many observers feared that the rent control repeal would displace disadvantaged households in the city.

Figure 6. AHS Zones, 1985–93

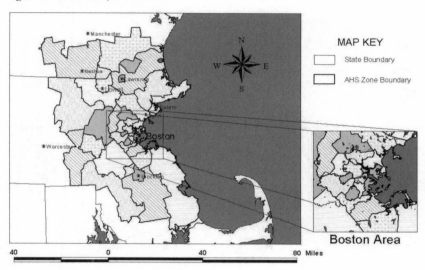

Where has gentrification taken place in the Boston metropolitan area? Figures 7, 8, and 9 provide some evidence along these lines. Figure 7 shows the collection of census tracts identified as "core" and "fringe" gentrifying tracts by Wyly and Hammel.[47] These authors use a combination of techniques, including extensive fieldwork undertaken in 1998, to categorize tracts. The gentrified core includes sections of Charlestown, the North End, Beacon Hill, the entire Back Bay, and parts of the South End—including tract 708, profiled in table 1. Fringe areas include parts of the South End, the entire Fenway and Kenmore district, parts of Allston and Charlestown, and two scattered tracts in South Boston and Dorchester. As the map shows, the vast majority of these gentrifying tracts are located within a single AHS zone. Two other zones have small numbers of gentrifying tracts, and two zones within the city—one of which is not visible in figure 7—have no gentrifying tracts at all.

Evidence taken from the Public Use Microdata Sample of the 1990 Census document the nature of demographic changes in these areas during the late 1980s. The PUMS identifies geographic areas similar to, but not coterminous with, AHS zones. Two of these Public Use Microdata Areas, or PUMAs, together encompass most of Wyly and Hammel's gentrified tracts, plus some

47. Wyly and Hammel (1999).

Figure 7. Gentrified Census Tracts in Boston, 1970–90

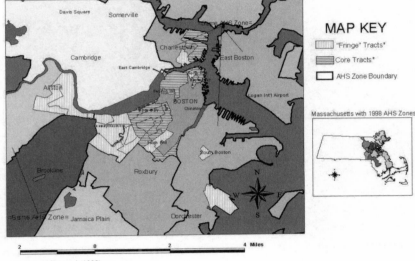

a. Wyly and Hammel (1999).

additional parts of Charlestown and East Boston.[48] Within these PUMAs, nearly 30 percent of all persons over 25—both movers and nonmovers— were college-educated individuals who lived outside the city of Boston in 1985.[49] This flow of high-socioeconomic-status individuals into certain Boston neighborhoods is a telling indicator of gentrification.

Wyly and Hammel did not extend their fieldwork to jurisdictions outside of Boston. As figure 8 shows, demographic patterns in several cities and towns near the central city mirror those observed in Boston's gentrifying areas. The map shows the change in the share of a zone's population having a four-year college degree, as reported in the decennial census, between 1970 and 1990. The zone encompassing central Boston records the highest change, from 24 percent in 1970 to 54 percent in 1990. Similarly large increases occur in one neighboring zone in Boston and in three close-in suburban zones. These residential areas, including the cities of Cambridge, Somerville, and Newton, plus the towns of Brookline, Arlington, Belmont, and Watertown, post college-educated share increases of greater than 24 percentage points between 1970

48. In the 1990, 5 percent IPUMS sample, these are Massachusetts PUMAs 2001 and 2002.

49. The sample of college-educated movers into these two PUMAs exceeds the sample of college-educated persons over 25 who reported living anywhere in the city of Boston in 1985 but outside the city in 1990 by a factor of three. Statewide, about 14 percent of all persons over 25 were college-educated individuals who lived in a different PUMA in 1985.

Figure 8. Change in Percent College Educated, 1970–90

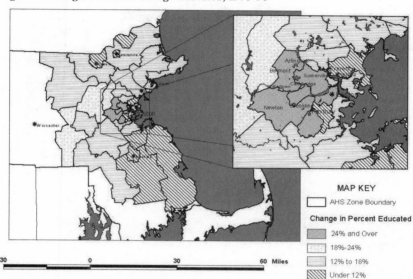

MAP KEY

☐ AHS Zone Boundary

Change in Percent Educated

24% and Over

18%–24%

12% to 18%

Under 12%

30   0   30   60   Miles

Source: Urban Institute, Urban Underclass Database.

and 1990. The next largest increases are found among more suburban areas. In most zones, the share of college-educated individuals increases between 12 and 18 percentage points—values close to the area-wide average of 16 percentage points.[50] Eight zones post increases below 12 percentage points; these include the zones encompassing Boston's Roxbury neighborhood, the poor inner-ring suburbs of Everett and Chelsea, and the satellite cities of Brockton, Lawrence, and Lowell.

Figures 7 and 8 suggest two different classifications of gentrifying areas around Boston. The first, an exclusive classification, consists of one zone, in central Boston, where most of Wyly and Hammel's gentrifying tracts can be found. The second, an inclusive classification, expands the area to include more of Boston, plus seven closer-in suburbs of the city that together experienced college-educated share increases more than 50 percent higher than the metropolitan average. Both definitions doubtlessly commit errors of inclusion and omission, but the limitations of AHS geography necessitate a coarse division of areas.

Is gentrification in Boston a symptom of shifts in the metropolitan income distribution, or the result of changing preferences on the part of certain house-

50. From the Urban Institute's Urban Underclass Database.

Figure 9. Real Annualized Growth in Mean Owner-Occupied Housing Value, 1970–90

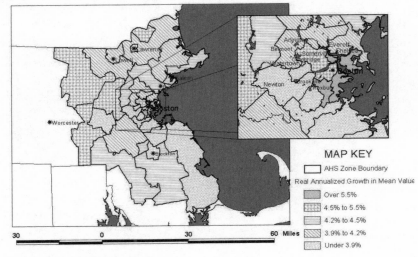

Source: Urban Institute, Urban Underclass Database.

holds? Figures 2 and 5 above suggest that the two underlying causes of gentrification can be distinguished based on area-wide shifts in land values. Preference-driven gentrification is associated with a selective increase in land values, affecting the target neighborhood alone. Income-driven gentrification occurs when increased demand creates upward price pressure in all parts of a metropolitan area. To investigate this matter, figure 9 graphs changes in mean owner-occupied housing values for AHS zones between 1970 and 1990.[51]

Consistent with the preference-driven model, the central Boston zone exhibits an above-average increase—4.8 percent in annualized real terms—over this time. Taken in context, however, the picture is decidedly more mixed. The zones with the highest value increases over this time period are two central city zones where only a limited amount of gentrification took place over this time. At the same time, two zones classified as gentrifying under the inclusive definition exhibit below-average value increases.

This evidence suggests that gentrification in Boston is part of a metropolitan area-wide pattern of escalating land values, which is, in turn, consistent

51. Mean housing values are an imperfect proxy for land values, as differences in construction patterns across zones may obscure trends in the value of underlying land. Since long-term increases in the intensity of land use are likely to be negatively correlated with proximity to the city center, figure 9 may understate relative growth in land value in the central areas of the Boston metropolitan area.

with the income-driven model of gentrification. Income data from the AHS samples provide additional support for this view. In 1974, the ratio of the 90th percentile to the 10th percentile in the unweighted family income distribution was 8.24. By 1998, the 90–10 ratio had nearly doubled, to 16.29. Any policy response to land value appreciation and neighborhood demographic transition should therefore consider these trends as a symptom of increased income inequality, rather than a unique problem rooted in the housing preferences of the wealthy.

Displacement

Most existing literature on the distributional consequences of gentrification has focused on residential displacement. For reasons explained above, this form of analysis provides little guidance as to whether low-status households are harmed by gentrification. Nonetheless, the question of displacement is of substantial interest and provides a useful starting point for the broader analysis to be undertaken below. In contrast to most previous studies of displacement, which track the exit of individual households without considering the fate of the housing unit they leave behind, the AHS data make it possible to focus on the changes occurring within individual housing units over time.

Table 2 presents a set of transition probabilities for housing units in the AHS Boston sample in various years. These probabilities track individual housing units enumerated at two points in time, and inhabited by a household with income below the poverty line at the time of the first sample. Three sample intervals are considered here: the periods between 1974 and 1977, between 1985 and 1989, and between 1989 and 1993.[52]

In all three intervals, certain patterns stand out. A housing unit containing a household in poverty in one year is relatively unlikely to retain a household in poverty three or four years later. Between 24 and 30 percent of the housing units sampled continue to shelter a poor family in the subsequent survey. Most of the remaining units have nonpoor occupants by the end of the sample interval. Intriguingly, this is not an indicator of dramatic displacement. Rather, this is an indicator of substantial mobility in the income distribution. In each time interval, a poor household is actually more likely to exit poverty than to be replaced by a nonpoor household.

52. The 1977 to 1981 interval is excluded from this analysis because coding of certain variables in the 1981 AHS make it impossible to determine whether some housing units contain the same households as in 1977.

Income mobility and household mobility together imply that a poor household in one AHS sample faces only a one-in-six chance of being enumerated as a poor household in the same unit in the subsequent sample. Initially poor households that vacate their housing unit are replaced by nonpoor households in about half of all cases. In the other half, either a second poor household moves in, the unit is recorded as vacant, or the unit becomes uninhabitable. Finally, the AHS fails to secure a follow-up response in 4 to 5 percent of all cases.

Table 2 underscores some of the difficulties in measuring residential displacement. Given that poor households themselves are more likely to exit poverty than remain, should the transition of a housing unit from a poor household to a nonpoor household be considered displacement? Also it is unclear how many of these residential transitions should be attributed to gentrification—that is to say, how many would not have occurred had gentrification not taken place.

To address these issues, table 3 presents the results of a probit analysis of household transitions. There are two central innovations in this table. First, rather than focus on "poor" households, the analysis uses a more permanent indicator of low socioeconomic status, educational attainment. Households headed by an individual with no postsecondary education are defined as low-status.[53] Second, household transitions are differentiated by their geographic location. The probit regression results displayed here seek to determine whether low-status households are more likely to exit housing units in gentrifying zones relative to other parts of the Boston metropolitan area. The dependent variable in each regression model is set equal to one if a household observed in the initial year of the period, in this case 1985, continues to reside in the same housing unit in the final year, in this case 1989.[54] If the housing unit is vacant, occupied by a different household, or has ceased to be habitable, the dependent variable is set equal to zero.[55]

Models 1 and 2 estimate the same equation using the "exclusive" and "inclusive" definitions of gentrifying areas described above. The estimated coefficients reveal a similar pattern in both models. The negative and significant gentrified zone effect indicates that housing turnover is more likely in

53. Alternative specifications, using income in the initial sample and whether the householder was over 65 years of age as indicators of low status, produce similar results in all cases.

54. Similar patterns of results were found when examining the 1989–93 and 1985–93 periods. It is not possible to perform this analysis with the 1974 through 1977 samples because the 1974 survey does not identify respondents' educational attainment.

55. Units were dropped from the sample if the AHS failed to conduct an interview with the occupant in 1989. There were ninety-seven such units. Each regression makes use of 1985 AHS sample weights.

Table 2. Transition Probabilities in the American Housing Survey Boston Sample[a]

Percent unless otherwise indicated

Period	Poor households in base year (N)	Transitioning to a nonpoor household		Retaining a poor household		Becoming vacant	Becoming uninhabitable	Probability of noninterview in follow-up survey
		Same occupant	Different occupant	Same occupant	Different occupant			
1974–77	1,330	29	24	17	10	11	6	4
1985–89	291	31	25	16	8	11	4	5
1989–93	258	30	20	16	14	13	2	5

Source: Transition probabilities based on observations in consecutive AHS samples.

a. Unit of observation is a housing unit. Columns may not sum to 100 percent due to rounding.

Table 3. Probit Estimates of Household Retention, 1985–89[a]

Independent variable	Dependent variables: same household in unit, 1985 and 1989			
	Model 1	Model 2	Model 3	Model 4
Gentrified zone (exclusive definition)	-0.541**	...	-0.138	...
	(0.167)		(0.172)	
Gentrified zone (inclusive definition)	...	-0.157**	...	0.151*
		(0.078)		(0.085)
Head had high school diploma	0.054	0.038	0.065	0.086
or less	(0.046)	(0.050)	(0.051)	(0.055)
Head had high school diploma	0.683**	0.205*	0.629**	0.086
or less gentrified zone*	(0.263)	(0.119)	(0.272)	(0.125)
Householder below 1st quartile	...	...	-0.163**	-0.165**
in income			(0.066)	(0.066)
Householder age	...	...	0.014**	0.014**
			(0.002)	(0.002)
Householder over 65	...	..	-0.249**	-0.255**
			(0.093)	(0.093)
Owner-occupied unit	...	...	0.754**	0.778**
			(0.056)	(0.056)
Subsidized unit	...	...	0.169	0.217
			(0.141)	(0.139)
Public housing unit	...	...	0.279**	0.283**
			(0.126)	(0.127)
Rent controlled unit	...	...	0.350*	0.240
			(0.181)	(0.185)
Householder's neighborhood rating	...	...	0.032**	0.033**
			(0.013)	(0.013)
Householder's housing unit rating	...	...	0.025*	0.025
			(0.016)	(0.016)
Log likelihood	-2173	-2177	-1953	-1952
N (unweighted)	3,195	3,195	3,195	3,195

a. Standard errors in parentheses. Sample consists of all housing units where an American Housing Survey interview took place in 1985 and remained in the AHS sample in 1989. Observations are weighted using 1985 AHS sample weights. The sample contains 163 units that were vacant in 1989, as well as 33 units that were either demolished or otherwise not inhabitable in 1989. Excluded from the sample are 97 units that were occupied in 1989 but where the household was not interviewed. *significance at the 10 percent level; ** at the 5 percent level.

revitalizing areas. The insignificant less-educated householder effect indicates that the probability of moving does not vary much by education level in nongentrifying areas. The significant positive interaction term indicates that less educated householders are considerably more likely to stay in their housing unit within gentrifying areas. Summing the main gentrified zone effect and the interaction term reveals that less educated householders are no more likely to vacate their housing units in revitalizing zones than in other parts of the metropolitan area.

Households and housing units in gentrifying areas need not be representative of the entire metropolitan area. To control for some potentially important differences between gentrified neighborhoods and the rest of the region, models 3 and 4 include additional control variables: measures of a household's income and age, and whether a housing unit is owner-occupied, subsidized, rent controlled, or part of a public housing complex. To control for general differences in housing unit or neighborhood quality, the regressions include controls for the householder's assessment of each, measured on a scale from one to ten, in the initial year. The results in table 3 show that several of these factors are important predictors of residential stability, especially owner-occupancy and residence in public housing. Householder age displays a nonlinear relationship with exit: older householders are more likely to stay in their units until retirement age. Low-income households are more likely to exit, and those who rate their neighborhoods more highly are more likely to stay. Interestingly, the importance of a high-quality neighborhood appears to outweigh that of a high-quality housing unit.

Controlling for these attributes, there is still no evidence to suggest that low-status households are more likely to move out of units in revitalizing areas. Using the exclusive definition of gentrified zones, less educated householders are actually significantly *more* likely to remain in their housing unit than they are elsewhere in the metropolitan area.[56] The inclusive definition suggests a more muted effect, but still supplies no evidence that low-status households face a higher probability of exit than either higher status households in the same neighborhood or low-status households in other parts of the Boston metropolitan area.

Does gentrification displace low-status households? While anecdotal evidence suggests that displacement does indeed occur, these results place the magnitude of the phenomenon in context. The exit of less educated households from units in gentrifying areas occurs no more frequently—and may indeed occur less frequently—than in other areas. While this finding does not directly address the counterfactual of what exit rates would have been in the absence of gentrification, it provides compelling evidence of the importance of considering baseline exit rates in any study of residential displacement.

56. While this result indicates that gentrification does not displace poor households, it should not be interpreted as evidence that gentrification does not harm poor households. Less educated householders living in gentrifying areas may face high moving costs. On the other hand, these households may remain in revitalizing neighborhoods because their quality of life has improved. An analysis of changes in quality of life for "stayer" households appears in table 7 below.

The absence of elevated exit rates in this sample does not imply that the gentrifying processes illustrated in figures 2 and 5 are absent. These processes might still operate if departing low-status households are more likely to be replaced by high-status households in gentrifying neighborhoods. Moreover, the absence of elevated exit rates does not imply that the poor have escaped harm in the case of Boston. As discussed above, the presence of high moving costs could lead such households to remain in place, pay more for the housing they occupy, and suffer a decrease in living standards as a consequence. However, these decreases might be reduced or reversed if gentrification brings increases in the quality of neighborhoods, public services, and employment opportunities. The following sections further examine these broader potential consequences of gentrification.

Housing Costs, Quality and Income

Table 4 examines the characteristics of households headed by an individual with no more than a high school diploma across six samples of the American Housing Survey in Boston, spanning the years 1977 to 1998.[57] The vertical lines in the table mark breaks between panels, which generally correspond to important differences in question wording, sample design, and the geographic area covered. Because of these differences, some care should be used in comparing statistics across panels both in this table and in table 5 below.

Across samples, low-status households in the Boston area were fairly evenly split between owner and renter occupation. Average housing costs rose steadily for this group after correcting for general inflation, with the exception of slight drops in the recession years of 1981 and 1993.[58] Real median incomes for the group remained steady, fluctuating around $30,000 in 1998

57. Over time, this set of individuals represents a smaller share of the overall population of heads of household. In 1977, more than half of all households are included in this group; by 1998, only the lowest 36 percent of the educational attainment distribution is represented here. This trend may in part explain any evidence of increasing relative disadvantage shown here. This group is also consistently older than the overall sample of heads of household, though the median age is roughly constant over time. Each set of statistics utilizes AHS sample weights for the survey year.

58. Monthly housing costs have been computed by the AHS since 1985. These costs include rent; utility payments and other heating costs; trash removal fees; condominium, homeowners association, or mobile home park fees; principal and interest of up to three outstanding mortgage loans; property taxes; and insurance payments. In 1977 and 1981, I replicate this monthly housing cost calculation using the same criteria.

Table 4. Summary Statistics for Households Headed by Individual with No More than a High School Diploma[a]

Household characteristic	1977	1981	1985	1989	1993	1998
Percent owner-occupier	50.4	50.9	53.5	54.8	55.7	53.8
Median number of rooms	5	5	5	5	5	5
Median household size	2	2	2	2	2	2
Income and housing costs (1998 dollars)						
Median monthly housing costs	476	459	600	670	593	717
Median annual family income	30,804	28,895	31,855	34,974	28,820	30,000
Tenth percentile of family income	9,241	8,384	8,086	8,329	7,924	4,900
Median annual income left over after housing costs	24,472	22,987	23,413	25,815	20,495	21,760
Tenth percentile of annual income left over after housing costs	4,469	3,920	3,216	3,471	2,941	-1,860
Housing unit quality rating						
Excellent (after 1981: 10)	39	41	50	42	44	35
Good (after 1981: 7–9)	43	44	36	43	42	49
Fair (after 1981: 5 or 6)	14	12	10	10	10	12
Poor (after 1981: 4 or below)	4	3	3	3	3	2
Unweighted sample size (N)	6,865	2,480	1,793	1,479	1,776	1,278

a. Vertical lines indicate breaks in American Housing Survey panels. AHS sample weights are used in the computation of all statistics. Housing unit rating percentages may not sum to 100 because of rounding and nonresponse.

dollars.[59] Households at the lower end of the income distribution tended to drift further down, especially between 1993 and 1998, when the reported 10th percentile of real income for this group fell by approximately 38 percent.

Affordable housing studies frequently focus on measures of a household's housing costs as a percentage of income. Rather than use that statistic, table 4 presents an alternative measure, equal to the amount of annual income left over after a household pays its housing costs. This measure comes closer to capturing the concept of a household's living standard: it is possible for a family to spend a greater share of its income on housing and still be able to afford more nonhousing goods, if both its income and housing costs increase. Between 1977 and 1998, the median low-status household had between $20,495 and $25,815, in constant 1998 dollars, left over after paying for housing. While this statistic fluctuates considerably, two patterns are worth noting here. First, the rapid escalation in housing costs was accompanied by a more rapid increase in income during the 1980s, implying that the median low-status household had more income left over at the end of the period.[60] Second, the recession that occurred between 1989 and 1993 reduced income more than housing costs for this group. In 1998, the median less educated household earned about 800 fewer inflation-adjusted dollars than in 1977, but had nearly $3,000 less to spend after paying for housing.

At the low end of the income distribution, decreasing income and steady or rising housing costs combine to paint a bleak picture. Between 1977 and 1989, even as leftover income rose slightly at the median of the distribution, the value for 10th percentile households fell by roughly $1,000, or nearly 25 percent. By 1998, over 10 percent of the less educated population faced annual housing costs higher than their reported income for the year.

There is some evidence that low-status households responded to higher housing costs by selecting lower quality housing units. In 1985, when asked to rate their housing unit on a scale from one to ten, fully half of less educated respondents gave their unit the top ranking. By 1998, that proportion had fallen to 35 percent. There is a corresponding increase in the fraction of respondents who gave ratings between seven and nine. While this subjective rating scale shows a decline, table 4 shows no change in more objective meas-

---

59. All dollar values reported in this paper are deflated using the Consumer Price Index.

60. Increased household income may have come at the expense of household leisure consumption. For this reason, the leftover income measure might misrepresent utility changes for households that do not change their housing consumption over time. Unfortunately, the AHS data do not provide information on hours or weeks worked.

ures of quality at the median of the distribution: housing size, in terms of number of rooms, or the number of persons per household.

For the average less-educated resident of the Boston area then, the period between 1977 and 1998 brought housing costs that first rose and then failed to fall along with real income after 1989, without any noticeable increase in quality. Interestingly, this pattern suggests that much of the harm associated with gentrification may occur after the fact, when some owner-occupying low-status households experience income declines after having locked in their housing costs at the peak of a boom. However, this source of harm most likely affects households at all points in the income distribution.

Even if households have less income to spend after paying for housing, their living standards might improve if the goods that come along with residential location—local public services and neighborhood characteristics—improve. The following section evaluates this argument.

Satisfaction with Neighborhood and Services

Table 5 presents additional statistics for AHS households headed by a less educated individual between 1977 and 1998.[61] A quick glance at the table shows that many of the reported neighborhood and service-quality statistics vary dramatically from panel to panel. Much of this variation can no doubt be attributed to differences in question wording and skip patterns between panels of the survey. It is somewhat implausible, for example, that the prevalence of abandoned buildings in Boston neighborhoods dropped by more than half between 1981 and 1985, then almost tripled between 1993 and 1998.

Subjective neighborhood quality ratings, measured on a ten-point scale, decline noticeably between 1985 and 1998. The trend parallels the change in subjective housing unit ratings revealed in the previous table: nearly half of respondents gave their neighborhood the top rating in 1985, while less than one-third did so in 1998. This decrease in satisfaction might reflect changes in a number of attributes, including "character," as discussed above.

Satisfaction with public services does not appear to follow any neat trend during this time. The dramatic fall in reported bothersome street crime after 1981 is most likely an artifact of survey techniques, especially as problems with crime rose steadily before and after that date.[62] The number of individ-

61. As in the previous table, all statistics reflect the use of AHS sample weights.
62. Beginning in 1985, respondents were only asked about bothersome street crime if they first reported that something in the neighborhood was bothersome to them.

Table 5. Neighborhood and Public Service Statistics for Households Headed by Individual with No More than a High School Diploma[a]

Percent unless otherwise indicated

Household characteristic	1977	1981	1985	1989	1993	1998
Living within 300 feet of abandoned buildings	10.3	8.3	3.3	2.0	2.4	6.5
Living in neighborhoods with accumulations of trash, litter, or junk	18.1	17.7	30.8	25.2	20.4	10.4
Reporting bothersome crime in neighborhood	14.8	19.7	3.8	6.3	6.3	6.9
Rating public services as "bothersome"	n.a	n.a.	1.5	1.2	1.3	1.2
Rating schools as inadequate (1977–89) or unsatisfactory (1998)	4.6	7.3	n.a.	3.2	n.a.	1.2
Living on streets in need of repair	18.1	14.3	37.8	28.9	25.0	48.0
Rating public transportation as inadequate	17.9	20.6	n.a.	3.0	n.a.	2.5
Neighborhood quality rating						
Excellent (after 1981: 10)	34	33	48	40	42	30
Good (after 1981: 7–9)	46	48	33	39	39	51
Fair (after 1981: 5 or 6)	16	15	13	14	12	12
Poor (after 1981: 4 or below)	4	4	5	5	6	4
Unweighted sample size (N)	6,865	2,480	1,793	1,479	1,776	1,278

a. Vertical lines indicate breaks in American Housing Survey panels. Question wording and skip patterns often vary between panels. AHS sample weights are used in the computation of all statistics. Neighborhood rating percentages may not sum to 100 because of rounding and nonresponse.

Table 6. Evidence on Changes in the Composition of "Poor" Neighborhoods[a]
Percent college educated in matched census tracts

Year	Boston metro area		Detroit metro area	
	Poverty-weighted	*Overall*	*Poverty-weighted*	*Overall*
1970	11.6	14.3	5.8	9.4
1980	18.2	22.5	8.0	14.3
1990	24.2	30.8	9.4	18.1
Ratio of 1990 to 1970	2.1	2.2	1.6	1.9

Source: Data compiled from the Urban Institute, Urban Underclass Database, which uses a constant set of census tract boundaries in 1970, 1980, and 1990.

a. "Poverty-weighted" statistics use the number of persons in poverty as weights. "Overall" statistics use the population over 25 in each tract as weights.

uals bothered by poor public services is small whenever it is measured; the number dissatisfied with the public schools is similarly small and appears to decrease over time. Satisfaction with local streets improves within panels but falls between them, and satisfaction with public transportation appears incomparable because of changes in the survey instrument after 1981. Thus the AHS data prove to be a disappointing source of intertemporal data on service satisfaction. On the basis of the statistics reported in table 5, however, it is difficult to argue that the escalation in housing prices in the Boston area has been accompanied by significantly greater satisfaction with public services among less advantaged residents.

Has gentrification contributed to the socioeconomic integration of urban neighborhoods or exacerbated residential separation between rich and poor households? To consider this issue, table 6 presents evidence collected from decennial census reports in 1970, 1980, and 1990. The table compares the demographic composition of census tracts with high concentrations of poverty to overall metropolitan characteristics.[63] To assist in determining the impact of gentrification, the table presents statistics for two metropolitan areas: Boston, which experienced considerable central city revitalization during this time period, and Detroit, which did not.[64]

In 1970, the average individual in a poverty household in the Boston metropolitan area lived in a census tract where 11.6 percent of individuals over 25 had a college degree. This is less than the overall percentage of the over-

63. To eliminate concerns that changes in census tract boundaries might influence these statistics, this table uses the Urban Institute's Urban Underclass Database, which reports tract characteristics for fixed-boundary areas across the three census samples.

64. Wyly and Hammel (1999) conducted fieldwork in both Boston and Detroit in 1998. They report twenty-five "core" or "fringe" gentrifying tracts in Boston, and only seven in Detroit, a city about 60 percent larger in terms of the 2000 population.

25 population with a college degree, which stood at 14.3 percent. This pattern can be observed in each census sample in both Boston and Detroit; households on the lower end of the income distribution tend to live in neighborhoods with a disproportionately small number of college graduates.

In both Boston and Detroit, the college-educated proportion of the population grew steadily between 1970 and 1990, generally doubling over the twenty-year period. In Boston, the average individual in poverty also witnessed a doubling of the share of college-educated residents within his or her own neighborhood. Poor individuals in the Boston area in 1990 had more college-educated neighbors, on average, than the typical household did in 1980. In Detroit, the change was significantly smaller for individuals in poverty. Instead of doubling, the proportion of college-educated residents in the typical poor person's neighborhood went up by 62 percent, to a value equivalent to the overall average share in 1970. In Boston, the number of college-educated residents in the typical poor person's neighborhood has remained relatively steady at 80 percent of the metropolitan average. In Detroit, by contrast, the proportion has fallen from 60 percent of the metropolitan average to 52 percent.

The process of demographic change within neighborhoods is clearly visible in the set of Boston census tracts Wyly and Hammel identify as gentrifying.[65] In these tracts, outlined in figure 7, the number of college educated individuals tripled between 1970 and 1990, from just over 10,000 to over 33,000. During the same time period, the number of persons in poverty declined by only 15 percent, from 21,680 to 18,223.[66]

Based on this evidence, it is difficult to argue that gentrification has accelerated the segregation of households by socioeconomic status. By introducing more high-status households to central city neighborhoods, the process has had the opposite effect.

Summary of the Boston Evidence

As a final exercise, this section analyzes consecutive AHS samples to determine whether households with definitively lowered living standards can be identified in the Boston metropolitan area and, if so, whether these reductions seem consistent with the hypothesized effects of gentrification. This exercise

---

65. Wyly and Hammel (1999).

66. Author's calculations from the Census of Population and Housing, as tabulated in the Urban Institute's Urban Underclass Database.

departs greatly from most analyses of gentrification's effects by focusing on individuals who remained in the same housing unit between samples, rather than those who moved out of gentrifying areas. Households facing high moving costs may respond to gentrification by increasing their housing expenditure rather than exiting the neighborhood. Additionally, households outside of gentrifying areas can still be affected by the process, to the extent that increased demand for housing in one area creates upward pressure on prices in substitutable neighboring areas. Consequently, this analysis considers stayer households in all parts of the metropolitan area, not just in gentrified zones.

To be identified as having lowered living standards that might relate to gentrification, a household must meet six criteria. First, its housing costs must rise faster than inflation. Second, its real income, left over after paying housing costs, must decrease. Third, the household must not be living in a higher-quality housing unit, as revealed by questions on improvements and subjective quality ratings. Fourth, the household must report no increase in its rating of neighborhood quality. Fifth, the household must report no increase in its satisfaction with public services. Finally, the household must report no decrease in size, since it may be possible to achieve higher living standards with less income if a household has fewer members to support.

This exercise necessarily makes some errors of omission. Households may report an increase in neighborhood quality, for example, but the effect of this increase might not be sufficient to offset the effect of higher housing costs. The estimated fraction of stayer households with lower living standards must therefore be considered a lower bound. Nonetheless, the households identified in this exercise may be considered representative of the entire group.

Table 7 reports the results of the exercise, which begins with the set of housing units that did not switch occupants between 1985 and 1989 or between 1989 and 1993. For both time periods, this creates an initial sample of roughly 1,500 unweighted observations. In both periods, the majority of households faced no increase in real housing costs—many homeowners are doubtlessly eliminated in this step.[67] Of those respondents facing higher costs, the majority earned enough additional income to offset the increase. Just under 20 percent of the sample in both time periods faced higher costs without an offsetting increase in income.[68]

67. Proposition 2 1/2, which limits both the overall tax rate and the rate of growth for each municipality's tax levy, may have protected some owners from property tax increases resulting from rapid growth in assessed value.

68. It is possible that reduced income for some households was accompanied by increased leisure consumption. The AHS does not contain information on hours or weeks worked.

Table 7. Identifying Households with Reduced Living Standards in the American Housing Survey[a]

Set description	Set number	1985–89	1989–93
All "stayer" households (*N*)	(1)	1,506	1,493
Subset of (1) with increase in real housing costs	(2)	678	557
Subset of (2) with decrease in real income after housing costs	(3)	286	284
Subset of (3) with no significant improvements to housing unit in last two years of time period	(4)	139	75
Subset of (4) reporting no increase in satisfaction with housing unit	(5)	107	55
Subset of (5) reporting no increase in satisfaction with neighborhood	(6)	81	45
Subset of (6) reporting no increase in satisfaction with public services	(7)	65	37
Subset of (7) reporting no decrease in household size	(8)	49	28
Set (8) as percentage of set (1)		3.3	1.9
Summary statistics for set (8)			
Percent owner-occupier		0	0
Percent in poverty at beginning of period		12	7
Percent with high school diploma or less		78	75
Percent in single-person households		61	54
Median age of householder at beginning of period		65	70
Number of AHS zones containing a set (8) household (maximum = 30)		22	19

a. Counts and summary statistics do not use AHS sample weights. "Significant improvements" include new or remodeled kitchens, new siding, roofs, other major repairs or improvements costing more than $500 in current dollars, added or remodeled bathrooms, replaced or added major equipment (heating, air conditioning, and so forth), new storm windows or doors, and new insulation. The most common improvement in both samples was a new roof. The number of households dropped for the last four reasons (bathrooms, major equipment, storm windows, and insulation) equals zero in both samples.

Within this set, the majority of respondents reported either an increase in housing quality, neighborhood quality, public service quality, or some combination of the three. While it is not possible to tell whether these quality increases justify the additional housing costs, the relatively strict standards of this exercise mandate the exclusion of these households. After taking out households that decreased in size between survey years, the set of respondents experiencing reductions in living standards as defined by these criteria amounts to 2 or 3 percent of the initial sample.

Table 7 reports some characteristics of these households; the relatively small sample size implies that only a limited amount of weight should be placed upon them. The worse-off households include no owner-occupiers, a modest number of households initially in poverty, and a disproportionate number of less educated heads of household. The majority are single-person households, and the heads of household are disproportionately older—most are 65 years of age or older in the initial sample. The households are also fairly dispersed; in each case, approximately two-thirds of the thirty Boston AHS zones contain at least one worse-off household.

Are these households victims of gentrification? Would their standards of living have been higher in the absence of gentrification? Arguments can be made either way. In some respects, this collection of households corresponds to the stereotypical view of groups vulnerable to gentrification pressures. They are relatively old, less educated renters, frequently living on their own. It is likely that for these households, the physical and psychic costs of moving are quite high. More mobile groups—especially younger households— may have responded to the same housing price pressures by relocating.

On the other hand, the relative geographic dispersion of these households suggests that they might simply be a collection of individuals who have fallen on personal hard times. It is also interesting to note that the number of worse-off households between 1989 and 1993, when real housing prices were declining in the Boston area, is of the same order of magnitude as the number recorded between 1985 and 1989, when upward pressure on prices was acute.

The relative ambiguity surrounding the results of this exercise encapsulates the lessons derived from the Boston case study. The difficulty of estimating what would have happened in the absence of gentrification makes it nearly impossible to determine the distributional implications of the process. Rather than examine the outcomes of the poor relative to this counterfactual scenario, this study has focused on absolute trends in outcomes. The data suggest that an absolute decline in living standards can be identified for only a small number of households. It is at best speculative to refer to these declines as the result of gentrification.

Conclusion

Rather than answer the question of whether gentrification harms the poor, this paper has illuminated the difficulties involved in arriving at an answer. In order to determine whether low-socioeconomic-status households in an urban area are worse off as a result of gentrification, and to determine the proper policy response—if any—researchers must ask the following questions:

What is the underlying cause of gentrification? Gentrification can occur when the preferences of high-status households change, or when the income disparity between high- and low-status households increases. In the latter case, policy responses to gentrification may be best subsumed under general policy responses to increasing income inequality.

Does revitalization increase the amount that poor households are willing to pay for housing? Gentrification might make central city neighborhoods more attractive to low-status households for several reasons. Employment prospects in the city might improve. Increases in the city's tax base might promote higher quality public services. The upgrading and socioeconomic integration of revitalizing neighborhoods might make them better places to live. On the other hand, decreases in neighborhood "character," as perceived by initial residents, might decrease willingness to pay. Gentrification might also decrease poor households' willingness to pay if the process leads to land value decreases in other parts of the urban area.

Does revitalization increase housing costs beyond what poor households are willing to pay? If neighborhood improvements are insufficient to compensate low-status households for the associated cost increases, one of two things might happen. If the costs of relocating are relatively low, displacement will occur. If relocation costs are high, households will accept cost increases, suffering a decreased standard of living in the process. In either case, the consequences of gentrification will be felt well beyond the neighborhoods directly involved. Increased demand in other neighborhoods, from households that have either been displaced or are new to the urban area, will generate this broader impact.

While this study does not definitively conclude that gentrification has harmed poor residents of Boston, it is worthwhile to consider proper policy responses, should some future study produce evidence that is more conclusive. Neighborhood revitalization is not a market failure; as modeled here, it is an efficient outcome of changes in preferences or the income distribution in a local economy. Rather, it is an equity issue; any redistributive policy response will necessarily improve the well-being of some households while harming others. Moreover, to the extent that gentrification follows the income-driven model, the appropriate policy responses should be conceived in the context of broad efforts to address income disparities.

Preference-driven gentrification can be addressed with measures aimed specifically at the housing market. These measures will, by necessity, entail some sacrifice of market efficiency for distributional equity. Previously proposed responses to gentrification include moratoriums on building and price controls in the rental housing market. These policies can be faulted on two fronts. First, they are notoriously ineffective at targeting the intended benefi-ciary population.[69] Moreover, these policies may have negative long-run consequences, as the curtailment of supply responses to increased demand creates further upward pressure on prices, shortages, and reductions in the quality of housing.

A more appropriate strategy for public policy would directly target those households deemed vulnerable to the pressures of gentrification—in the Boston case, this group would include older individuals, especially those liv-ing alone, in rental units. Targeted households might become eligible for rent subsidies or assistance in finding and moving into a new, less expensive res-idence. Ideally, such a program would be financed by states or other regional governments, since the demand pressure associated with gentrification can easily spill over across local jurisdictional boundaries, and locally financed redistribution might serve to reignite divestment from central city neighbor-hoods. A subsidy program would spread the costs of providing affordable housing throughout the population, rather than imposing it on the suppliers of housing. Analysts may not agree on whether gentrification harms the poor; however, they should agree that *in the event* that gentrification causes harm, the remedy ought to reflect basic economic principles.

69. Households living in rent controlled units in the Boston AHS samples of 1985, 1989, and 1993 had roughly the same median income as renter households in market rate units. Poverty rates of households in rent controlled units were significantly lower than the metro-politan average. The sample of rent controlled units is relatively small: 56, 59, and 61 in the three surveys.

Comments

Douglas S. Massey: I have always been skeptical of gentrification's critics. The way some of them carry on, you'd think that gentrification involved a massive in-migration of whites from suburbs to cities and the large-scale displacement of poor minorities from urban neighborhoods. In fact, cities continue to lose white residents, and white Americans are overwhelmingly concentrated in suburbs. To the extent that *some* whites are entering or staying in central cities, they are small in number and highly selected in characteristics. Compared to the continued large outflow of whites to suburbs and the well-established proclivity of white movers to avoid inner city locations, gentrification is truly a drop in the bucket. That is, gentrification is relatively small compared to the other major flows of population into and out of cities.

Another reason for my skepticism is the difficulty of defining "gentrification." At the most general level, the term seems to imply the replacement of poor people by a new "gentry" of affluent households. But who are the poor people and who are the gentry? Is any socioeconomic upgrading of a neighborhood considered a gentrification? Does a neighborhood gentrify if its own residents get richer and better educated over time, or do the gentry have to move in from outside? Is some class-mixing good but too much, a bad thing? Is it enough that the class standing of in-movers is greater than out-movers, or do they have to be of different races as well? The imagery that generally accompanies stories on gentrification generally selects from two extremes of America's socioeconomic distribution: pairing a black welfare family with a white professional couple. But such juxtapositions must be rare indeed.

Finally, I have always thought that complaints about gentrification are fundamentally hypocritical. On the one hand, liberal urban specialists rail against the suburbanization of America and the abandonment of the cities by the nation's whites. On the other hand, when a very few and highly selected whites buck the trend and stake a claim in the city, they are berated as opportunists and decried for gentrifying the inner city. But liberals can't have it both ways. If the middle and upper classes are to remain in the city to shore up the tax base and play leadership roles in civic affairs, they have to live somewhere.

Another element in the hypocrisy pertains to the recent fascination of social scientists with the concentration of poverty—the social isolation of the poor in predominantly poor neighborhoods. If this is a bad thing—and much empirical evidence suggests that it is—then how can it be remedied without the presence of middle-class and affluent households in places also inhabited by the poor? I suspect that much of the gentrification debate is actually a coded reference to the contestation of blacks and whites for urban space. After all, affluent and middle-class blacks are generally blamed for the concentration of urban poverty through their "abandonment" of poor black neighborhoods. It is hard to imagine people complaining about gentrification if it were to involve middle class and affluent black families moving into or remaining within poor black neighborhoods. This, it seems, would be good. Apparently class-mixing within neighborhoods only becomes evil when it crosses racial as well as socioeconomic lines, although this fact is never explicitly stated.

Not surprisingly, therefore, Vigdor barely touches on the issue of race in his careful analysis of gentrification using American Housing Survey data from Boston, despite the fact that the Boston metropolitan area is far more segregated by race than by class. Indeed, throughout the United States, the degree of segregation between blacks and whites vastly exceeds that between rich and poor. Although the spatial isolation of the poor may have increased in American cities, it is nothing compared to the spatial isolation of African Americans, particularly those who are poor. As is so often the case, the action in gentrification probably stems from an *interaction* between race and class in the urban environment.

Because of this interaction, it is difficult to comprehend the effect of one without taking into account the other. Despite his glossing over the issue of race, however, there is much to like in Vigdor's analysis, for it clearly demonstrates the difficulties and glaring inconsistencies in the gentrification debate. Using reliable data for a well-understood case, he shows just how hard it is to define gentrification in the first place, to model the process of class change theoretically, and to measure its consequences empirically. As is often the case, the answer one obtains depends to a large degree on the assumptions and theories with which one begins; and if measuring the first order effects of gentrification on poor households is difficult, taking into account higher order effects at equilibrium is even more difficult. In the end, Vigdor concludes that we cannot really know whether gentrification harms the poor. The most important lesson seems to be that if any harm occurs, it is through increased housing costs rather than involuntary displacement.

Thus gentrification in the end appears to be a non-issue. The debate itself is fraught with inconsistencies and contradictions: When one attempts to measure the consequences of gentrification strictly along the lines of socioeconomic status, the main problem appears to be rising housing costs for the poor. However, policies of tax abatements or housing subsidies for poor households in neighborhoods undergoing revitalization have the potential to resolve that problem easily. Furthermore, I suspect that much of the friction in the debate stems from the unstated factor of race, with African Americans implicitly portrayed as victims of racially structured real estate processes that are beyond their control. To tackle that issue, however, Vigdor would have to bring race more centrally into his analysis and consider shifts over time in racial as well as class composition within neighborhoods.

Alice M. Rivlin: Professor Vigdor addresses an apparently straightforward, policy-relevant question in his paper: "Does Gentrification Harm the Poor?" Many people are asking this question, and some are alleging that the answer is clearly "yes." Policymakers ought to know whether these allegations are correct, and, if so, what they can do to mitigate the injury. Unfortunately, as with many seemingly straightforward questions, the answers turn out to be difficult to pin down.

Vigdor has done an extremely thorough job of thinking through how gentrification comes about, its potential positive and negative effects on low-income people, and how to detect whether the poor are being harmed or not. He points out that gentrification can result either from a change in preferences of upper-income people for the amenities of a particular part of a city or from a shift in the distribution of income toward the higher end. Rising rents and property taxes caused by gentrification might force low-income people to move out of the area. The fact that a household moves out, however, does not prove that gentrification is the cause or that the household has been harmed by the move. On the other hand, even a household which elects not to move may suffer harm in the form of rising housing costs. Moreover, the effects of gentrification are not limited to housing. The poor may benefit from increased services or retail jobs created by gentrification, from improved public services financed by increased tax revenues, and from increased economic integration of the neighborhood. They may also perceive themselves to be either benefited or harmed by changes in the "character" of the neighborhood. In short, Vigdor has provided a balanced and analytically useful framework for examining the question of whether gentrification harms the poor.

As I read Vigdor's paper I find myself switching back and forth between two lenses: that of the academic policy analyst and that of the policymaker. Through my academic lens, I find Vigdor's framework well articulated and his empirical analysis stunningly ingenious. Through the policymaker lens, my view is somewhat more skeptical. For example, Vigdor stresses the distinction between gentrification caused by a widening disparity in the distribution of income and that caused by a shift in the preferences of upper-income people for formerly less desirable parts of the city. My first reaction: "Good point!" both from an analytical and a policy perspective—but on reflection I am less sure.

Vigdor argues that gentrification that is a by-product of a widening gap between rich and poor should be addressed directly, either through tax and transfer policies designed to redistribute income or through gap-narrowing investment policies, not through its housing market side effects. Gentrification that reflects a shift in preferences, on the other hand, might be a "root cause of harm" and therefore a candidate for being offset by mitigating housing policies.

In an actual neighborhood, however, it is hard to distinguish between the two causes of gentrification, since they often occur together. If skilled professionals are making more money, they will seek better housing. Some of them will add to sprawl in the suburbs—where they will distress environmentalists, but not displace many poor people—and others will gentrify the inner city, which may suddenly seem to them a more desirable place to live.

Does it really matter whether the impetus for gentrification is more income or changing taste? Local politicians respond to low-income residents, who perceive themselves harmed by rising rents and property taxes, or simply resent change and newcomers. These politicians can influence zoning regulations, rent controls, or property tax provisions, but do not perceive that they control the larger forces that affect income distribution. Even policies that might mitigate rising disparity in incomes—income taxes, transfer programs, and targeted investments in education and training—are not tools that are available at the local level. Hence, the policymaker may consider the causes of the gentrification totally irrelevant.

The author searches the literature on gentrification and concludes that it is pretty ambiguous. Most studies that focus on displacement as the measure of harm fail to recognize that people who are not displaced may be worse off, and do not even demonstrate that those who do move have been displaced by gentrification or harmed by moving.

Vigdor then treats the reader to an extremely interesting case study of gentrification in the Boston area. He weaves together several data sources in intriguing and imaginative ways, and comes to some encouraging conclusions. Focusing on housing units containing poor households in an initial period, he finds the household is more likely to have moved out of poverty than to have been displaced by a non-poor household. He finds little evidence that low-status households have been more likely than others to move out of gentrifying neighborhoods. Almost all of those who stayed had incomes rising at least as fast as their housing costs. The small minority that did not move (mostly older singles) might have been harmed by gentrification, although their situations might have deteriorated without it. Vigdor also goes beyond the housing information and attempts to explore whether gentrification affects labor markets, neighborhood quality, and satisfaction with public services. Unfortunately, the evidence does not add up to much.

Refocusing through my policymaker lens, I am struck by a huge omission in the paper: scarcely any attention is paid to race and ethnicity. The anxiety voiced in Washington's revitalizing neighborhoods has strong racial overtones. Some of Washington's African American majority fear they will be pushed out by an influx of higher-income white invaders. The newcomers not only look different, but also are seen as threatening the "character" of the neighborhood. They listen to different music, happily pay four dollars for a cup of coffee, don't go to church, and mostly don't have kids in the neighborhood schools. Many African American Washingtonians believe in the existence of "the plan," said to be a secret strategy by which the white, upper-income establishment intends to get control of property in the city and return the government to majority white rule. A long-standing legacy of mismanaged urban renewal, with well-documented displacement of low-income African Americans in earlier decades, feeds their distrust of government and white interlopers.

In the rapidly gentrifying neighborhood of Columbia Heights, the threatened group is Hispanic, often newly arrived immigrants. Recent well-intentioned, but heavy-handed efforts of the city to go after landlords with egregious housing code violations caused outraged protests in the affected neighborhoods. Community residents view the enforcement, not as an effort to improve their housing, but as part of a plot to displace low-income Hispanic tenants, renovate the buildings, and raise the rents to levels affordable only by Anglo yuppies.

On the local policy firing line, the debate is dominated by the perceptions of those who fear they are about to be harmed, invaded, or displaced. It does not take many people moving out of gentrifying neighborhoods to escalate the fears of people who feel the world is hostile to them and whose history suggests they might be right.

Hence despite the careful reasoning and reassuring evidence of Professor Vigdor's paper, those of us who want to revitalize cities are confronted with a policy challenge. We believe that rising property values and an increased proportion of higher earners in city neighborhoods will ultimately benefit everyone, including the poor. We argue that better public services can be financed with a higher tax base and that benefits will flow from reducing the concentration of poverty, especially in the schools. Nevertheless, to win community support we need to design policies to deal with real and perceived harm flowing from gentrification.

In principle, it should be possible to capture the revenues from the rising property values in gentrifying areas in a community fund of some sort and channel them into improved public services, especially schools, recreation, and other benefits to residents of the area. Some of these revenues could also be used to defer property tax increases falling on existing low-income residents and to hold them harmless against above-trend rent increases resulting from gentrification. If Vigdor is right that only a small number of older residents are likely to be harmed by gentrification, such policies need not be very expensive. However, they would be difficult to design so they are perceived to be fair, simple, and minimally intrusive.

I share Vigdor's implicit conclusion: that gentrification does not harm many low-income people, and may well benefit most of them. However, well-reasoned, solidly researched academic papers like this one are not likely to convince poor residents of gentrifying neighborhoods, who feel threatened by hostile forces—or their elected representatives—that all is for the best.

Hence, policy analysts are faced with the need to design new strategies: First, to capture the value that gentrification creates and channel it into visible benefits for the whole community and, second, to reduce harm to low-income residents who want to remain in their homes.

References

Atkinson, Rowland. 2000. "Measuring Gentrification and Displacement in Greater London." *Urban Studies* 37 (1): 149–65.

Bane, Mary J., and David Ellwood. 1986. "Slipping into and out of Poverty: The Dynamics of Poverty Spells." *Journal of Human Resources* 21 (1): 1–23.

Berry, Brian J. L. 1985. "Islands of Renewal in Seas of Decay." In *The New Urban Reality*, edited by Paul E. Peterson, 69–96. Brookings.

———. 1999. "Comment on Elvin K. Wyly and Daniel J. Hammel's 'Islands of Decay in Seas of Renewal: Housing Policy and the Resurgence of Gentrification'" *Housing Policy Debate* 10 (4): 783–88.

Bourne, L.S. 1993. "The Myth and Reality of Gentrification: A Commentary on Emerging Urban Forms." *Urban Studies* 30 (1): 183–89.

Brooks-Gunn, Jeanne, Greg J. Duncan, and J. Lawrence Aber, eds. 1997. *Neighborhood Poverty, Volume I: Context and Consequences for Children*. New York: Russell Sage Foundation.

Case, Anne C., and Lawrence F. Katz. 1991. "The Company You Keep: The Effects of Family and Neighborhood on Disadvantaged Youths." Working Paper 3705. Cambridge, Mass.: National Bureau of Economic Research.

Cullen, Julie B., and Steven D. Levitt. 1999. "Crime, Urban Flight, and the Consequences for Cities." *Review of Economics and Statistics* 81 (2): 159–69.

Ellen, Ingrid Gould, and Margery Austin Turner. 1997. "Does Neighborhood Matter? Assessing Recent Evidence." *Housing Policy Debate* 8: 833–66.

Freeman, Richard B.1995. "Are Your Wages Set in Beijing?" *Journal of Economic Perspectives* 9 (3): 15–32.

Glaeser, Edward L. 1999. "Learning in Cities." *Journal of Urban Economics* 46 (2): 254–77.

Glaeser, Edward L., Matthew Kahn, and Jordan Rappaport. 2000. "Why Do the Poor Live in Cities?" Working Paper 7636. Cambridge, Mass.: National Bureau of Economic Research.

Henig, Jeffrey R. 1980. "Gentrification and Displacement within Cities: A Comparative Analysis." *Social Science Quarterly* 61: 638–52.

Ihlanfeldt, Keith R., and David L. Sjoquist. 1998. "The Spatial Mismatch Hypothesis: A Review of Recent Studies and Their Implications for Welfare Reform." *Housing Policy Debate* 9 (4): 849–92.

Jackson, Kenneth T. 1985. *Crabgrass Frontier: The Suburbanization of the United States*. Oxford University Press.

Kain, John F. 1968. "Housing Segregation, Negro Employment, and Metropolitan Decentralization." *Quarterly Journal of Economics* 82 (2): 175–97.

———. 1992. "The Spatial Mismatch Hypothesis: Three Decades Later." *Housing Policy Debate* 3 (2): 371–460.

Katz, Lawrence F., Jeffrey R. Kling, and Jeffrey B. Liebman. 2001."Moving to Opportunity: Early Results of a Randomized Mobility Experiment." *Quarterly Journal of Economics* 116 (2): 607–54.

Kennedy, Maureen, and Paul Leonard. 2001. "Dealing with Neighborhood Change: A Primer on Gentrification and Policy Choices." Discussion Paper. Brookings Institution Center of Urban and Metropolitan Studies.

Lee, Barret A., and David C. Hodge. 1984. "Social Differentials in Metropolitan Residential Displacement." In *Gentrification, Displacement and Neighborhood Revitalization*, edited by John J. Palen and Bruce London, 140–69. Albany: SUNY Press.

LeGates, Richard T., and Chester Hartman. 1986. "The Anatomy of Displacement in the United States." In *Gentrification of the City,* edited by Neil Smith and Peter Williams, 178–203. Boston: Allen and Unwin.

Ludwig, Jens, Greg J. Duncan, and Paul Hirschfeld. 2001. "Urban Poverty and Juvenile Crime: Evidence from a Randomized Housing-Mobility Experiment." *Quarterly Journal of Economics* 116 (2): 665–69.

Ludwig, Jens, Greg J. Duncan, and Joshua C. Pinkston. 2000. "Neighborhood Effects on Economic Self-Sufficiency: Evidence from a Randomized Housing-Mobility Experiment." Unpublished manuscript. Georgetown University.

Ludwig, Jens, Helen F. Ladd, and Greg J. Duncan. 2001. "Urban Poverty and Educational Outcomes." *Brookings-Wharton Papers on Urban Affairs*: 147–201.

Marcuse, Peter. 1986. "Abandonment, Gentrification, and Displacement: The Linkages in New York City." In *Gentrification of the City*, edited by Neil Smith and Peter Williams, 153–77. Boston: Allen and Unwin.

Margo, Robert A. 1992. "Explaining the Postwar Suburbanization of Population in the United States: The Role of Income." *Journal of Urban Economics* 31: 301–10.

Mieszkowski, Peter, and Edwin S. Mills. 1993. "The Causes of Metropolitan Suburbanization." *Journal of Economic Perspectives* 7 (3): 135–47.

Morrill, Richard. 2000. "Geographic Variation in Change in Income Inequality among U.S. States, 1970–1990." *Annals of Regional Science* 34: 109–30.

Nelson, Kathryn P. 1988. *Gentrification and Distressed Cities*. University of Wisconsin Press.

Pack, Janet R. 1998. "Poverty and Urban Public Expenditures." *Urban Studies* 35 (11): 1995–2019.

Palen, John J., and Bruce London, eds. 1984. *Gentrification, Displacement and Neighborhood Revitalization.* Albany: SUNY Press.

Ruggles, Steven, and others. 1997. *Integrated Public Use Microdata Series: Version 2.0.* Minneapolis: Historical Census Projects, University of Minnesota.

Schill, Michael H., and Richard P. Nathan. 1983. *Revitalizing America's Cities: Neighborhood Reinvestment and Displacement*. Albany: SUNY Press.

Stevens, Ann H. 1994. "The Dynamics of Poverty Spells: Updating Bane and Ellwood." *American Economic Review* 84 (2): 34–7.

————. 1999. "Climbing out of Poverty, Falling Back in: Measuring the Persistence of Poverty over Multiple Spells." *Journal of Human Resources* 34 (3): 557–88.

Thurston, Lawrence, and Anthony M. J. Yezer. 1994. "Causality in the Suburbanization of Population Employment." *Journal of Urban Economics* 35 (1): 105–18.

U.S. Department of Housing and Urban Development. 1981. "Residential Displacement—An Update." Report to Congress, October.

Vigdor, Jacob L. 2001. "Median Voters, Marginal Residents, and Property Tax Limitations." Unpublished manuscript. Duke Working Paper Series SA 1–07 (June). Duke University.

Wheaton, William. 1977. "Income and Urban Residence: An Analysis of Consumer Demand for Location." *American Economic Review* 67 (4): 620–31.

Wilson, William J. 1987. *The Truly Disadvantaged.* University of Chicago Press.

Wyly, Elvin K., and Daniel J. Hammel. 1999. "Islands of Decay in Seas of Renewal: Housing Policy and the Resurgence of Gentrification." *Housing Policy Debate* 10 (4): 711–71.

INGRID GOULD ELLEN
New York University

KATHERINE O'REGAN
New York University

AMY ELLEN SCHWARTZ
New York University

LEANNA STIEFEL
New York University

Immigrant Children and New York City Schools: Segregation and Its Consequences

IMMIGRANT CHILDREN REPRESENT a large and growing proportion of school children in the United States, especially in urban areas. An estimated 10.4 percent of the U.S. population is now foreign born, the highest percentage since 1930, and in central cities, the proportion has risen to 16 percent.[1] Yet we know surprisingly little about the experience or isolation levels of foreign-born students. While there is considerable research on the degree to which racial minorities are isolated in U.S. schools and on the disturbing consequences of this segregation, there is no parallel research concerning immigrants.

The goal of this paper is to examine this issue, looking at evidence from the New York City school system. In particular, we address two main questions: First, how segregated are immigrant students in New York's schools and how does that segregation vary across groups with differing language skills and from different regions of the world? Second, to the extent we do see segregation, how different are the schools attended by immigrant children (either overall or from particular regions) in terms of student characteristics, teachers, and funding levels?

We thank Dylan Conger for her expert research assistance and the Rockefeller Foundation and the Russell Sage Foundation for financial support. We also thank conference participants, especially our two discussants, for their helpful comments.

1. Lollock (2001); Schmidley and Gibson (1997).

183

New York City is an especially apt place to study immigrant students because the city's public schools educate so many immigrants from more than 200 countries, speaking more than 120 languages. In addition, we have been able to assemble an extraordinarily detailed data set, which allows us to exploit the cultural richness of New York City's student population.

The paper is organized as follows: In the first section, we review the literature on school segregation and explore the ways in which segregation might affect immigrant students. In section two, we describe our data and provide a brief statistical portrait of immigrant students in New York City. In section three, we lay out our methods and hypotheses, while in section four, we present our analysis of segregation of immigrant students. We then present our conclusions in section five.

Theory and Previous Literature

It is worth discussing why we might be concerned about segregation in the first place. Through a variety of avenues, segregation may affect the educational and social outcomes of children. For example, many studies have found that a lack of interracial contact in elementary or secondary school can be harmful to black children, especially in the longer run.[2] Whether the same holds for immigrant children is not at all clear. The few studies that address this question find that ethnic isolation has either little effect or somewhat positive effects on immigrant children, but most of these studies rely on very small samples and use subjective assessments of either students or school personnel to describe the ethnic composition of peers.[3] Moreover, most studies of residential segregation find that immigrant families are not nearly as segregated as blacks, that they tend to assimilate over time, and that first-generation immigrants from a particular country or region are more segregated than their later-generation counterparts.[4] Therefore, even if segregation were

2. See Hanushek and others (2001a); Kain and O'Brien (1999); Mahard and Crain (1983); Wells and Crain (1994). One notable exception to the finding that segregation of minorities may have a negative impact on their educational outcomes can be found in Rivkin (2000). Using data on public school students from large, urban districts from the sophomore cohort of the High School and Beyond Longitudinal Survey, Rivkin (2000) finds that exposure to white students has little effect on a black student's subsequent test scores, years of education, or earnings.

3. Matute-Bianchi (1986); Rumbaut (1995); Rodriguez (1999).

4. Lieberson (1963); White, Biddlecom, and Guo (1993); Allen and Turner (1996); White and Omar (1996). One exception is Borjas (1994), who finds that even third generation Hispanic immigrants are nearly as isolated as those who are first generation.

to have an impact, it might be much smaller for immigrants, and might disappear with time.

Nonetheless, the evidence on the significance of segregation for blacks and the many theoretical reasons we outline for why concentration might have an effect on immigrant students suggest that their segregation merits study. We discuss below three key ways in which school segregation might affect immigrant students: through peer effects, through differential resources, and through network effects.

Peer Effects

Whether and how much peers influence student performance has been studied extensively in education.[5] The hypothesis is that a student's decisions about how much to study, how to behave in the classroom, and what kinds of classes to take are very much shaped by interactions with other students and those students' parents, and moreover, the level of discussion and instruction in a classroom is determined by one's peers.[6] If a group is highly segregated, its members will interact more intensively with other members of their own group and less with outsiders. The implication, as Cutler, Glaeser, and Vigdor point out, is that the impact of segregation on performance may depend critically on the characteristics of the segregated group in question.[7] More specifically, isolation should lead to better outcomes for students from relatively advantaged groups and worse outcomes for students from disadvantaged groups. What they do not point out is that because segregation is not complete, the characteristics of the other students who attend schools with the segregated group are also critical in determining peer effects.

For blacks, who have significantly lower levels of education and earnings than the national average, segregation has meant that they typically live in higher poverty neighborhoods and attend schools with a greater share of students who are poor and from less educated families.[8] Considering racial prejudice and the relatively low incomes of blacks, it is also probably true that

5. See, for example, Hanushek and others (2001b); Zimmer and Toma (2000); Argys, Rees, and Brewer (1996).

6. While there is a fair degree of consensus that peers can shape the performance of low-achieving students, there is less consensus about the relevance of peers to high-achieving students. Some studies find that tracking, that is, segregating high-performing children, benefits high-achieving students; see Argys, Rees, and Brewer (1996). Other studies find that tracking makes little difference to their performance; see Slavin (1990).

7. Cutler, Glaeser, and Vigdor (2000).

8. Massey and Denton (1993); Jargowsky (1997).

the non-blacks who attend schools with large numbers of blacks come from relatively poor and disadvantaged backgrounds, compared to the average non-black.

For immigrant groups, whether segregation leads to less advantaged peers is not as clear. On average, immigrants in the United States are not as educated as the native born. In 2000, 86.6 percent of native-born adults 25 and over had at least a high school degree as compared to just 67 percent of the foreign-born population in this age group.[9] However, some researchers hypothesize that immigrants embrace education as a strategy for upward mobility, and that immigrant children may thus encourage their peers to spend more time on their schoolwork.[10] This positive peer effect may be particularly salient for immigrants living in high-poverty, inner-city neighborhoods where schools are often troubled and where native-born youth are regarded as more alienated from mainstream educational culture.[11]

Moreover, we see tremendous diversity in the backgrounds of parents immigrating from different parts of the world. For example, 84 percent of Asian immigrants 25 and over had at least a high school education in 2000, nearly the same proportion as the native born. By contrast, only 37 percent of immigrants this age from Central America had completed high school.[12] Therefore, if peers (or their parents) exert an influence, this aspect of segregation is likely to have more harmful consequences for children born in Central America compared to those born in Asia.[13] Cutler, Glaeser, and Vigdor find the effects of residential segregation on adults vary significantly across immigrant groups from different countries.[14] Additionally, they find that living in a more highly segregated city correlates with lower incomes and educational outcomes only for groups with low initial skill levels (as measured by standardized occupation scores).

Again, because segregation is not complete, it is also important to consider which other demographic groups attend schools with immigrants. Bearing in mind that many immigrants to the United States are racial minorities and that high levels of racial segregation characterize our schools, race is likely a key factor. For example, we would expect to see Hispanic immigrants sharing

---

9. Lollock (2001).
10. McDonnell and Hill (1993).
11. Portes (1995); Portes and Zhou (1994).
12. Lollock (2001).
13. The quality of the educational systems in the countries of origin is also likely to play a role here.
14. Cutler, Glaeser, and Vigdor (2000).

schools disproportionately with native-born Hispanics, students whose families are typically poorer and less educated compared to native-born whites.

Resources

Allocations of resources within school districts reflect the interplay of politics, differences in costs, and, more generally, the accumulated decisions of teachers, principals, parents, and students, all of whom enjoy some measure of school choice. Accordingly, whom one goes to school with can also affect the resources in a school. Political pressures may mean a segregated group gains access to schools with greater or fewer resources, such as number and quality of teachers and overall levels of funding.[15]

Once again, there is some evidence that schools with greater representation of blacks or Hispanics are allocated fewer resources.[16] In New York State, recent court hearings have ruled in favor of analyses showing that school districts in the state with greater shares of minorities receive less state aid and expenditures per pupil.[17] While evidence on the intradistrict relationship between resources and race is thinner, Iatarola and Stiefel, and Schwartz and Gershberg both find evidence that schools with more black students receive fewer of some resources in New York City, other things being equal.[18]

As for immigrants, there are certainly reasons to believe that immigrants would have relatively little political power. Many parents, for instance, may not be citizens and therefore do not participate in the political process.[19] Moreover, foreign-born citizens may vote less frequently than the native born, due to language barriers. Verba, Schlozman, and Brady, for example, find that voter turnout in the United States is significantly lower among Hispanic citizens than it is among non-Hispanic whites and blacks.[20]

---

15. There is an enormous literature on whether resources, and which ones, affect student achievement and other student outcomes, with not much consensus about the answer. One of the earliest studies by Coleman and others (1966) states that family background is more important than school inputs in the determination of achievement. Since then, prominent researchers such as Hanushek (1986, 1997), Greenwald and others (1996), and Hedges and others (1994) have come to conflicting conclusions. Burtless (1996) summarizes much of this literature.

16. Kain and Singleton (1996).

17. *Campaign for Fiscal Equity, Inc. v. State of New York,* 187 misc. 2d 1, 719 NYS 2d 475, 175, 178 (NY Sup 2001).

18. See Iatarola and Stiefel (forthcoming) and Schwartz and Gershberg (2001).

19. Eligibility for enrollment in New York City public schools is unaffected by immigration status.

20. Verba, Schlozman, and Brady (1995, pp. 228–39).

That said, it might be true that ethnic concentration can enhance political power. Clustering may also allow for the targeting of specialized resources that benefit immigrants, such as bilingual programs. Both the New York State and federal governments provide additional resources for districts serving large limited English proficiency (LEP) populations. In 1996–97 approximately $81 million in state aid and $23.5 million in federal aid were provided to fund English as a Second Language (ESL) and bilingual education programs for LEP students.[21] The New York City Board of Education allocates funds for bilingual classes if there are fifteen or more students in the same grade speaking the same language.[22] Consequently, the resources a school receives to provide services to its LEP population depend, in part, on whether there is a critical mass of students speaking a particular language.

In sum, it is not clear a priori whether segregation should predict greater or lesser resources for immigrant children. Evidence on differentials is limited. Iatarola and Stiefel find that higher proportions of recent immigrants are associated with lower per-pupil spending, higher pupil-teacher ratios, but more experienced teachers.[23] As explained in Schwartz and Gershberg, there is relatively little in the way of additional funding aimed directly at providing services to immigrant children.[24] Instead, existing policies and sources of funding focus on addressing LEP students. Consistent with this policy, they find that school-level resources generally increase with the representation of LEP students, but decline with the proportion of immigrants, other things being equal. As a result, immigrant groups with stronger English skills, such as Caribbean immigrants, appear to receive fewer resources.

Networks and Norms

Even if resources and peers are similar across schools, the isolated children may still be disadvantaged by their lack of connection to the mainstream culture. This is likely to be a long-term effect—one that becomes apparent as children grow older and begin to navigate the labor market. At that point, they may find they have fewer connections to jobs, less practice interacting

21. See Schwartz and Gershberg (2001) for more.
22. When there are fewer than fifteen pupils in the same language category and grade, ESL teachers are allocated at the ratio of one teacher per seventy-five students.
23. Iatarola and Stiefel (forthcoming).
24. According to Gershberg (2000), a small federal program, the Emergency Immigrant Education Program (EIEP), is aimed explicitly at immigrants. With approximately $5 million in funding in 1996–97, however, the EIEP is too small to significantly affect the distribution of resources.

with the dominant group, and less familiarity with cultural norms. Wells and Crain find that black Americans who attend desegregated schools benefit greatly over the long term, but not because their test scores were any higher. Rather, they benefited from the superior connections they made to the white world and the greater ease they felt when interacting with whites.[25]

That said, ethnic isolation might, in fact, provide children with denser networks of connections within their group and provide far greater opportunities for within-group trade and interaction through ethnic networks. In the case of immigrants, ethnic clustering may also help ease their transition to the United States, providing an opportunity to interact with others who share their language and customs, and who can help them maneuver in this new society.

Since these effects will not appear immediately and are primarily observed outside of the school environment and outside of our data, our work focuses on the first two ways segregation may affect immigrants' school outcomes. Nevertheless, any differences we find in peers and school resources may also have implications for networks and norms.

In summary, there are several reasons to believe that segregation may well affect immigrant children, for better or for worse. There are, of course, more normative reasons why we might care about segregation, per se. For one thing, segregation often implies coercion or a lack of choice. For another, such segregation may help to sustain cultural barriers and prejudice and further the balkanization of the American population.[26]

Data Description and Statistical Portrait of Immigrant Students

New York City educates more than one million students each year in more than 1,100 schools. In this study, we use a rich database that includes academic and socioeconomic information on all children in New York City's 870 public elementary and middle schools, linked to institutional information on the schools themselves, for the academic year 1998–99.[27] More than 600,000 children attend these schools in any single year, representing a wide range of cultures, languages, and backgrounds.

25. Wells and Crain (1994).

26. See Warren Hoge, "British Life Is Fractured along Racial Lines, a Study Finds," *New York Times*, December 12, 2001, p. A3, for a recent report in Great Britain which expresses great concern that the country will suffer balkanization as a result of its growing segregation.

27. The data have been generously provided by the New York City Board of Education.

Table 1. Characteristics of All Students, 1998–99

Groups of students	Number	Proportion
Total enrollment	611,479	. . .
Native born	513,043	0.839
Foreign born	98,436	0.161
Black	217,174	0.355
White	95,506	0.156
Hispanic	231,313	0.378
Asian	65,524	0.107
Eligible for free or reduced-price lunch[a]	501,238	0.866

Source: Authors' calculations
a. Eligibility based on 578,773 students.

The student-level data, which we aggregate to the school level for this study, include eligibility for free or reduced-price lunch (our proxy for poverty), race and ethnicity, and test scores.[28] Most relevant for our study, the student-level data also include detailed information on student country of birth, an indicator identifying "recent immigrants" (that is, immigrants who have entered the school system within the last three years), and performance on the Language Assessment Battery (LAB).[29] This set of tests is used to assess English proficiency and eligibility for specialized instructional services and allows us to identify students with varying English skills. School-level data include information on teachers, such as percentage certified and percentage with master's degrees, and expenditure data by function of expenditure, such as classroom and non-classroom. By combining these data, we can directly assess both the peer and resource environments.

Table 1 presents descriptive statistics for all students attending school in the 1998–99 school year, the latest available year of data. The overwhelming majority of students, 84 percent, are non-white, and 16 percent are foreign born. Nearly 87 percent of students are also "poor," or more accurately, qualify either for free or reduced-price lunch by having family resources below 130 or 185 percent of the federal poverty line. Throughout the remainder of the paper, we will refer to this financially vulnerable position as poor.

Table 2 provides some information on immigrant students themselves. As shown, 46 percent of these foreign-born students are recent immigrants and

28. In contrast to census data, *Hispanic* is a distinct race-ethnicity group in this data, as in other administrative data. There are five mutually exclusive race-ethnicity categories in the data: white, black, Asian, Hispanic, or other.

29. We refer to students born abroad (outside the United States and its territories) as immigrants, even if their parents are U.S. citizens.

Table 2. Characteristics of Foreign-Born Students, 1998–99

	Number	*Proportion*
Foreign born	98,436	1.000
Recent immigrant	45,673	0.464
Limited English skills (LES)	30,738	0.312
Six largest regions of student birth		
Dominican Republic	18,742	0.190
Mexico, Central America, or Spanish South America	15,839	0.161
Other Caribbean	15,081	0.153
Former Soviet Union	10,118	0.103
South Asia	9,721	0.099
China, Hong Kong, or Taiwan	7,238	0.074
Black	19,527	0.198
White	17,743	0.180
Hispanic	35,052	0.356
Asian	25,883	0.263
Eligible for free or reduced-price lunch[a]	84,063	0.903

Source: Authors' calculations.
a. Eligibility is based on 93,112 students.

31 percent scored less than 40 on the Language Assessment Battery. We will refer to this latter group as immigrants with limited English skills (LES).[30] To make the geographic diversity of these students manageable, we have grouped the more than 200 countries by region, based on geographic proximity and similarities in language and race and ethnicity. The six largest regions, representing 78 percent of immigrant students, are presented separately. The single largest group, including approximately 18,700 elementary and middle school children and 19 percent of all foreign-born students, comes from the Dominican Republic. Students from Mexico, Central America, or Spanish South America represent the second largest group, over 15,800 students. The third largest group comprises more than 15,000 students from Caribbean countries, while the fourth largest group is the more than 10,000 students who come from "Soviet" countries, that is, countries from the former Soviet Union.[31] Compared to the overall student population, foreign-born students are much more likely to be Asian and less likely to be black. Immigrants as a group are also somewhat more likely to be poor.

Table 3 reveals some differences among these immigrant subgroups. Recent immigrants, for instance, are both more likely to have limited English

30. A score of 40 is one criterion used to determine eligibility for services aimed at Limited English Proficiency (LEP).
31. Caribbean countries include countries in the Caribbean other than the Dominican Republic.

Table 3. Characteristics of Foreign-born Subgroups, 1998–99

| | Proportion of group | | |
Origin	Eligible for free or reduced-price lunch	Recent immigrant	LES
Foreign born	0.903	0.464	0.312
Recent immigrant	0.917	1.000	0.442
LES	0.967	0.657	1.000
Six largest regions of student birth			
Dominican Republic	0.984	0.373	0.533
Mexico, Central America, or Spanish South America	0.946	0.430	0.452
Other Caribbean	0.945	0.475	0.071
Former Soviet Union	0.736	0.416	0.158
South Asia	0.910	0.573	0.356
China, Taiwan, or Hong Kong	0.902	0.555	0.478

Source: Authors' calculations.

skills and somewhat more likely to be poor than the foreign-born population as a whole. Poverty is even more common among LES immigrants. In fact, less than 4 percent of LES immigrants are not poor, suggesting that this group might be particularly vulnerable. The table also shows striking differences across regions. While more than half of Dominican immigrants are LES, only about 7 percent of Caribbean immigrants and less than 16 percent of Soviet immigrants are LES. In terms of poverty, about three quarters of Soviet immigrants are poor, making Soviet students even less likely to be poor than are the native born. Meanwhile Dominican students, with a poverty rate exceeding 98 percent, are virtually all poor. As suggested in the previous section, these differences may affect the segregation and school environment of these groups. We exploit the size and diversity of these immigrant groups throughout the remainder of the paper.

Hypotheses and Methods

As noted above, our primary motivation for examining the segregation of immigrants in schools is its potential impact on school performance and other outcomes. Therefore, we first examine the degree to which different immigrant groups are segregated in the New York City schools. Second, we provide evidence about the consequences of this segregation by considering two key aspects of immigrants' school environment shaped by segregation: peers and resources.

To accomplish the first aim, we rely on conventional measures of segregation such as the dissimilarity index, which best captures the overall unevenness of a population's distribution and has been used extensively in both the residential and school literatures.[32] Intuitively, the dissimilarity index indicates the percentage of one group of students that would have to change schools in order to be evenly distributed across all schools. We also use two versions of interaction indices to capture the potential contact between groups. Specifically, we use the exposure index to capture the extent to which the average student from one group is exposed to, or likely to interact with, students from another group and the isolation index to show how much she is likely to interact with students from her own group.[33] We look at the exposure of each population to the native born, and at their isolation.

While there is little systematic evidence on the segregation of immigrants in schools, based on the evidence from residential segregation and the strong link between residential location and primary schools, we expect to see somewhat greater segregation for more recent immigrants and those with limited English skills.

The second key aim in the paper is to explore the consequences of this segregation. We are not directly testing how student performance is affected by segregation levels; we are providing information about how segregation shapes the school environments of particular groups of immigrants through two avenues found relevant in previous literature: peers and resources. Here, we provide some important groundwork for testing whether immigrants are helped or hurt by segregation by exploring the extent to which such isolation has meant that immigrants or particular groups of immigrants face a different set of peers and experience a different level of resources.

We again use the exposure index to describe the composition of the student body, and to measure exposure to peers. In consideration of the existing literature on peer effects cited previously, we focus on four characteristics of peers that might be important and that are available in our data: poverty, race, language skills, and test scores.

Our resource analysis focuses on teacher qualifications and per student spending, commonly used measures in analyses of school performance. For

32. For a discussion of the dimensions of segregation and an assessment of best-associated measures, see Massey and Denton (1988). For examples of use of measures, see Clotfelter (1998); Orfield (1993); Orfield and Yun (1999). For residential segregation, see Massey and Denton (1993); White and Omar (1996); Rivkin (1994); and Frey and Farley (1996).

33. For the average student of group A, the exposure index tells us the share of her school's population that belongs to group B, while the isolation index tells us the share of her school's population that also belongs to group A.

those who find that some resources do matter, teachers are often cited as important.[34] We also report expenditures, including classroom and non-classroom, because at least some researchers find that spending can have positive marginal effects, and there is some evidence that the impact differs between classroom and other types of spending. We examine whether these resources differ for either immigrant students as a whole or for particular subgroups of immigrants.

As for hypotheses, while we have no clear expectations for immigrants as a whole (other than greater exposure to LES students), we would expect certain groups of immigrants to experience different peers. As Cutler, Glaeser, and Vigdor point out, those who come from a less advantaged group (in terms of general human capital) will have peers with higher rates of poverty and LES.[35] Moreover, we also expect immigrants to share schools disproportionately with native-born students of their same race, which means we expect black and Hispanic immigrants to be exposed to somewhat higher poverty rates and lower test scores. For resources, we would expect LES immigrants to receive somewhat greater funding although less experienced teachers, because of the difficulty in finding teachers with appropriate language skills. Finally, through a combination of peers and school resources, we may expect immigrants with fewer human and financial resources to attend schools with lower average test scores.

Empirical Evidence

Our empirical work begins by examining the degree of segregation of various immigrant groups before moving on to consider peers and resources.

Segregation of Immigrants

Table 4 shows three segregation indices for our various groups.[36] The first column presents dissimilarity indices, showing the degree to which various groups are separated from the rest of the population. The dissimilarity index for foreign born versus native born is 0.328 for 1998–99, indicating that just about one-third of foreign-born students would need to change schools to

34. Ferguson (1991); Ferguson and Ladd (1996).
35. Cutler, Glaeser, and Vigdor (2000).
36. Note that we compare segregation levels in 1995–96 to levels in 1998–99 and find that the indices are fairly stable over time.

Table 4. Segregation and Exposure of Students, 1998–99

Origin	Dissimilarity index	Corrected dissimilarity index	Exposure to native born	Isolation index	Students (N)
Native born	0.328	0.328	0.854	0.854	0.839
Foreign born	0.328	0.328	0.763	0.237	0.161
Recent immigrant	0.306	0.308	0.767	0.117	0.073
LES	0.376	0.394	0.750	0.106	0.050
Six largest regions of student birth					
Dominican Republic	0.483	0.545	0.803	0.105	0.031
Mexico, Central America, or Spanish South America	0.405	0.424	0.758	0.071	0.026
Other Caribbean	0.498	0.564	0.811	0.093	0.024
Former Soviet Union	0.504	0.778	0.669	0.175	0.017
South Asia	0.441	0.608	0.723	0.066	0.016
China, Taiwan, or Hong Kong	0.471	0.702	0.696	0.134	0.012
Non-white	0.677	0.683	0.841	0.904	0.844
Eligible for free or reduced-price lunch	0.556	0.570	0.836	0.904	0.866

Source: Author's calculations.

achieve a completely even distribution. Foreign-born students, in other words, are only about half as segregated as are non-white students from white, who have a dissimilarity index of 0.683. Segregation is also much higher along poverty lines, with a dissimilarity index of 0.570. Contrary to expectations, recent immigrants are not more segregated than immigrants overall. Those with limited English skills, however, are more segregated.

When considering immigrants from specific regions, we see that each of these groups is far more segregated than immigrants as a whole.[37] Students from the former Soviet Union and those from China, Hong Kong, or Taiwan are the two most segregated, with dissimilarity indices of 0.778 and 0.703 respectively. For each of these groups, segregation is even higher than that found between white and non-white students. The two regions with the lowest levels of segregation are the Dominican Republic and Mexico, Central America, and Spanish South America. Perhaps not coincidentally, the students from these regions are Hispanic, entering a school system in which the largest racial/ethnic group is also Hispanic.

The next column shows exposure to the native born. It more directly measures potential interaction with native-born students. The average foreign-born student attends a school in which 76 percent of students are native born. By contrast, the typical native-born student attends a school in which 85 percent of students are native born. Looking across regions, we see that exposure to the native born varies from a high of 81 percent for other Caribbean immigrants, a group with relatively low segregation, to a low of 67 percent for Soviet immigrants, the most segregated subgroup.

The third column presents a final dimension of segregation, each group's level of isolation, or exposure to its own members. Soviet immigrants, who have the highest dissimilarity index, also have the highest level of isolation, 0.175, indicating that the average Soviet immigrant goes to a school in which almost 18 percent of the population was also born in the former Soviet Union. This high isolation is not simply driven by a large population; as the last column shows, Soviet immigrants make up less than 2 percent of all students. Consider that Dominican immigrants, who make up a larger share of the population, are not nearly as isolated.

---

37. The dissimilarity index is a dichotomous measure of exhaustive categories. Therefore, these region indices measure the degree to which students born in a particular region are separated from all other students, not simply the native born.

Table 5. Exposure to Peer Group Race, Poverty, and LES, 1998–99

Exposure of and to	White	Black	Hispanic	Asian	Eligible for free or reduced-price lunch	LES
Proportion of total population	0.156	0.355	0.378	0.107	0.866	0.050
Native born	0.154	0.371	0.375	0.096	0.861	0.045
Foreign born	0.168	0.272	0.393	0.163	0.872	0.078
Recent immigrant	0.164	0.272	0.388	0.174	0.876	0.078
LES	0.128	0.206	0.501	0.163	0.908	0.106
Six largest regions of student birth						
Dominican Republic	0.039	0.218	0.686	0.053	0.960	0.094
Born in Mexico, Central America, or Spanish South America	0.138	0.188	0.518	0.154	0.891	0.095
Other Caribbean	0.056	0.665	0.208	0.067	0.919	0.035
Former Soviet Union	0.461	0.135	0.193	0.210	0.770	0.076
South Asia	0.204	0.165	0.366	0.264	0.843	0.086
China, Taiwan, or Hong Kong	0.207	0.090	0.275	0.427	0.833	0.132

Source: Authors' calculations

Peers

Table 5 provides a summary portrait of the peers experienced by a typical member of each of our immigrant groups. Specifically, it shows exposure to various student characteristics, such as poverty, race, and limited English skills. For reference, the first row provides the percentage of the total population that is white, black, and so on. If students were evenly distributed across schools, the exposure index to any group would always equal its share of the population.

Starting with poverty, the table shows that native-born students, immigrants, and recent immigrants all typically attend schools where between 86 and 88 percent of the students are poor. LES immigrants face somewhat higher poverty rates, but the more striking differences emerge when we look at region subgroups. As shown, the typical Dominican student attends a school where 96 percent of students are poor; the typical Soviet immigrant, by contrast, attends a school where 77 percent of students are poor.

These differences are partly driven by the differential poverty rates of the groups themselves; table 3 indicates that 98 percent of Dominican immigrants are poor compared to only 74 percent of Soviet immigrants. But these immigrant groups are simply not that isolated. Even in the case of Soviet immigrants—the most isolated group—only 17 percent of their peers on average are also Soviet immigrants. So most of these differences are driven by the poverty rates of the other students these immigrants go to school with. Consider Dominicans: the typical Dominican immigrant attends a school where just over 10 percent of students were born in the Dominican Republic, and 96 percent of students are poor. This suggests that the other students in the schools attended by Dominican immigrants have poverty rates of nearly 96 percent.

The table also shows that, fitting with the high levels of racial segregation in the New York City schools, immigrants tend to go to schools with students of their own race. For example, the average immigrant from the Dominican Republic and from other Caribbean countries attends a school that has almost no white students. (Dominican immigrants in our sample are 98 percent Hispanic, and other Caribbean immigrants are 88.5 percent black.) Soviet immigrants, however, who are virtually all white, attend schools where nearly half of all students are white. We will return to distinctions in race again, below.

Finally, the last column of table 5 considers exposure to students with limited English skills. As expected, foreign-born students have greater exposure to students with limited English skills than do the native born, particularly foreign-born students with limited English skills themselves. Immigrants from all regions, with the exception of other Caribbean countries, attend schools where more students have limited English skills than do native-born students. To the extent that exposure to students with better English skills is beneficial, isolation of these groups could have a negative effect, particularly for those groups whose own language skills are more limited. Notice that these exposure levels, however, are much lower than the prevalence of LES among these groups themselves. For example, almost half of students born in China, Taiwan, or Hong Kong have limited English skills, but they typically attend schools where the percentage of LES students is only 13 percent.

Perhaps the most direct measure of relevant peer characteristics would be the average test scores of a student's peers. While this measure may capture a critical characteristic of one's peers, it is itself shaped by the school environment, both through peers and resources. Recognizing the interdependency between this peer characteristic and the rest of the school environment, we construct a separate table, table 6, showing test scores in the schools attended by the average student in each of the subgroups. Note that to help separate peer characteristics from the effect of the school environment, we show the test scores the students received at the end of the previous school year, when they were in the third and sixth grades rather than the fourth and seventh grades.

Table 6. Test Scores of Peers in Previous Year Means Weighted by Share of Group in Current School, 1998–99

| | *Previous year standardized test score* | | | |
| | *Current 4th graders* | | *Current 7th graders* | |
	Reading	*Math*	*Reading*	*Math*
Native born	-0.011	0.004	-0.033	-0.045
Foreign born	0.033	0.078	-0.017	0.011
Recent immigrant	0.032	0.079	-0.039	-0.011
LES	- 0.060	-0.021	-0.106	-0.082
Six largest regions of student birth				
Dominican Republic	-0.233	-0.250	-0.269	-0.266
Mexico, Central America, or Spanish South America	-0.024	-0.005	-0.075	-0.062
Other Caribbean	-0.091	-0.092	-0.141	-0.150
Former Soviet Union	0.357	0.498	0.291	0.420
South Asia	0.146	0.230	0.126	0.175
China, Taiwan, or Hong Kong	0.234	0.398	0.217	0.270

Source: Authors' calculations

Test Scores

The first row of table 6 provides the average or normalized test scores for students in schools attended by the native born. Immigrants do not appear to attend schools with students with noticeably different test scores from native-born students, including more recent immigrants or LES immigrants, although the test scores for seventh grade appear somewhat lower for LES immigrants.

The largest differences are by region of birth, and these are striking. Students born in the Dominican Republic, who had the highest level of own poverty and exposure to poverty, attend schools where test scores are the lowest of any of the groups in the table. These low scores occur for both sets of tests. At the other extreme are the very high test scores in schools attended by Soviet immigrants, a low poverty and low LES group. While Soviet immigrants are the most segregated of all of our immigrants, this segregation appears to increase their contact with a relatively advantaged student population. Note that the Chinese and South Asian immigrants, the second and third most segregated immigrant groups, also attend schools where test scores are higher than the average scores in schools attended by the native born.

Resources

Table 7 provides weighted means of school resources by immigrant groups. It documents the resources offered at the schools attended by the average stu-

Table 7. School Resources Means Weighted by Share of Group in School, 1998–99

| | Percent of teachers | | | Per-pupil spending | |
	Fully licensed or permanently assigned	With more than five years teaching	With Master's degree or higher	Classrooms	Aggregate
Native born	0.826	0.620	0.789	$3,892.95	$8,652.41
Foreign born	0.834	0.632	0.807	$3,912.00	$8,351.79
Recent immigrant	0.843	0.627	0.810	$3,857.71	$8,287.54
LES	0.809	0.620	0.797	$3,962.04	$8,463.94
Six largest regions of student birth					
Dominican Republic	0.745	0.588	0.753	$3,930.29	$8,605.53
Mexico, Central America, or Spanish South America	0.829	0.616	0.808	$3,907.05	$8,335.81
Other Caribbean	0.796	0.610	0.770	$3,868.09	$8,350.10
Former Soviet Union	0.904	0.678	0.853	$4,018.70	$8,363.55
South Asia	0.884	0.649	0.842	$3,834.57	$8,022.74
China, Taiwan, or Hong Kong	0.896	0.696	0.866	$4,040.31	$8,454.42

Source: Authors' calculation.

dent in each of the subgroups. The first three columns report, for the average student in each group, the proportion of teachers in a variety of tenure and educational categories. The final two columns contain per-pupil expenditure data. Classroom expenditures primarily go to teacher salaries. Thus differences in classroom spending across schools reflect both differences in the number of teachers per pupil as well as differences in the average salaries of teachers, which, in turn, reflect differences in experience and education. Aggregate spending includes spending on a wide range of school resources, such as libraries, guidance counselors, principals, food service, school safety, and building maintenance, in addition to classroom teachers.

The table provides no evidence that foreign-born students are in schools with less experienced or less educated teachers than native-born students. Instead, slightly more of the teachers in these schools are licensed, have been teaching for at least five years, and have master's degrees. While there is little difference in classroom spending, the schools attended by foreign-born students average about $300 less per pupil in aggregate spending. The same pattern obtains for recent immigrants. Whether or not these differences are important depends, in part, on the services provided outside the classroom and their efficacy. Unfortunately, we know of no evidence on the impact of these resources on school performance.

We hypothesize above that LES immigrants would receive more resources based on existing policies and sources of funding, which focus on addressing English proficiency and not nativity status per se. Our analyses indicate that, as compared to other immigrants, LES immigrants do attend schools with higher classroom spending. But the table also shows that they attend schools with less educated and less experienced teachers, suggesting that the schools with less experienced teachers may be compensated by having a larger number of teachers.[38] Whether this reflects the lesser experience of teachers fluent in the languages spoken by recent immigrants or teacher preferences for certain schools or locations, for example, is unclear.

We again find our largest differences in resources when looking at immigrants born in specific regions. Students from the Dominican Republic and other Caribbean countries enjoy particularly low measures of teacher quality. Students born in these regions, when compared to other foreign-born or to native-born students, attend schools in which teachers are noticeably less educated and experienced, although their schools' overall spending is higher than for these other groups. The Soviet immigrants are once again at the other extreme. Their schools enjoy nearly the highest measures of teacher experience and education across all measures, considerably higher than found in schools attended by the native born. Surprisingly, the differences in teacher qualifications do not result in higher per-pupil spending overall, although we do observe differences in classroom spending, suggesting a trade-off between spending inside and outside the classroom. Finally, South Asian immigrants attend schools that receive fewer resources than any other group: almost $600 less per pupil in aggregate spending compared to Dominicans and the native born.

In summary, aggregate per-pupil spending is at lower levels for all groups of immigrants compared to the native born, and among immigrants, spending is highest for those with limited English skills. When looking at teacher characteristics, we see greater variation and learn that the immigrants whom we would categorize as more disadvantaged are taught by less qualified teachers. Soviet immigrants, however, the most isolated of our immigrant groups, enjoy a relatively advantaged student population and attend schools with teachers who are more qualified than those found in the schools of the native born, even though spending is low.

38. This is also consistent with findings by Iatarola and Stiefel (forthcoming) that show higher pupil-teacher ratios for recent immigrants; this group of students has slightly more senior and educated teachers but fewer of them per pupil, leading to lower per-pupil spending.

The Role of Race

The high degree of racial segregation that characterizes New York City's schools suggests that immigrants of different races will face peers of different races. Table 5 points out that our immigrant subgroups attend schools in which the other students are disproportionately of their same race. Dominican immigrants, for example, who are virtually all Hispanic, attend schools in which over 90 percent of students are black or Hispanic.[39] Soviet immigrants, meanwhile, who are virtually all white, attend schools in which less than a third of students are black or Hispanic. To some extent, then, the disparities we see across immigrant groups seem to be driven by racial differences, rather than by differences in language or other educational characteristics.

Table 8 reflects the relationship between race and school environment, measured, as before, by poverty levels, test scores, and resources. The first column shows exposure to poverty and indeed shows large racial differences—differences that generally swamp any disparities by nativity status.[40] As compared to both white and Asian immigrants, black and Hispanic immigrants attend schools that have far higher rates of poverty. The main story appears to be that black and Hispanic immigrants, whose own poverty rates are high, are clustered in schools that are also populated by native-born students of similar race and ethnicity, whose poverty rates are similarly high.

The test scores seem to indicate clear racial patterns. Asian and particularly white students, regardless of nativity, attend schools with fourth grade students whose scores are well above average on the previous year's third grade reading tests, and the same patterns hold for other tests as well. Black and Hispanic students, by contrast, attend schools with students whose test scores are well below average. Again, the differences across nativity status are small compared to the differences across race.

Teacher characteristics differ greatly, too, with the racial and ethnic composition of the school. White students, whether foreign born or not, attend schools with the most experienced and educated teachers. Asian students attend schools with teachers with more experience and higher levels of education than do other minorities, while all black and Hispanic students, of any nativity, compete for the lowest levels. Once again, foreign-born white and

39. On the census, Dominicans typically describe themselves as both black and Hispanic.
40. While foreign-born whites attend schools with poverty rates more than 15 percent higher than native-born whites, the disparity between foreign- and native-born Asians is less than 6 percent and the difference between schools attended by foreign- and native-born blacks and Hispanics is 1 percent or less.

Table 8. School Peers, Test Scores, and Resources by Nativity and Race, 1998–99

	Exposure to free or reduced-price lunch (0.866 of total population)	*Previous year standardized reading for current 4th graders*	*Teachers with Master's degree or higher (proportion)*	*Per-pupil spending (aggregate)*
Native born				
White	0.610	0.415	0.860	$8,363.03
Black	0.921	-0.125	0.760	$8,810.17
Hispanic	0.918	-0.126	0.777	$8,720.13
Asian	0.770	0.285	0.859	$8,086.42
Foreign born				
White	0.771	0.312	0.848	$8,329.64
Black	0.920	-0.108	0.765	$8,465.52
Hispanic	0.929	-0.138	0.778	$8,472.45
Asian	0.828	0.178	0.849	$8,114.78

Source: Authors' calculations.

Asian students have slightly lower levels than their native-born counterparts, but differences across other races are far more pronounced.

As noted previously, higher measures of teacher quality do not necessarily translate into greater spending, because of a combination of differences in teacher-pupil ratios, as well as differences in non-classroom spending across schools. Again, the largest differences are seen between racial groups rather than between the native-born and foreign-born groups of the same race. Black and Hispanic students, whether foreign born or native born, attend schools with the highest level of spending, exceeding the spending in schools attended by white children by as much as $450 and by Asian children by as much as $750. Whether these spending disparities reflect the greater political power of black and Hispanic communities, or greater educational needs of students in the schools attended by black and Hispanic children, due, for example, to poverty, LES, or other special needs, is unclear and left for future research. Note, however, that Iatarola and Stiefel, and Schwartz and Gershberg, find little consistent evidence that race per se is associated with differences in expenditures across schools in New York City, controlling for LES, poverty, and other school variables.[41]

41. Iatarola and Stiefel (forthcoming) and Schwartz and Gershberg (2001).

Conclusions

In summary, we find that foreign-born students as an aggregate group are not especially segregated from native-born students, at least compared to levels of segregation of non-whites and poor. While there are some differences in terms of peer and school resource environments, there is little clear evidence that immigrants as a whole experience sizable effects from segregation, at least through the avenues we explore.

Nonetheless, when looking at particular groups of foreign-born students, especially students from the former Soviet Union and China, Hong Kong, and Taiwan, we see significantly higher levels of segregation. The schools attended by these different groups, even within a single, large urban school district, are strikingly dissimilar, suggesting that the consequences of segregation are quite different across groups. At one extreme, the typical Soviet immigrant attends a school where students are far less likely to be poor or non-white, have stronger English skills, and achieve mean standardized test scores that are significantly above the citywide average. Teachers in these schools also have more experience and are better educated than the teachers found either in the schools of other immigrant groups or of the native born. By contrast, Dominican immigrants attend schools with students who are virtually all poor, virtually all black or Hispanic, and more likely to be LES. They also attend schools where test scores are significantly below average and where the teachers are less experienced and less educated compared to the teachers for all other groups. Nonetheless, spending is highest in the schools attended by these groups, reflecting, perhaps, a trade-off between numbers of teachers and teacher experience or higher non-classroom spending.

If these school environment characteristics are important, the experience of Soviets and Dominicans underscores how school segregation may benefit or harm specific immigrant groups. While the high level of isolation of Soviet immigrants, an advantaged group, appears to benefit them, the isolation of Dominicans increases their contact with a disadvantaged population, presumably to their detriment. Because these two groups make up a relatively small share of the student population, their peer environments are also substantially determined by the other students with whom they go to school who were not born in their country or region. Racial segregation in the school system appears to play a significant role in determining who those other students are. For Soviet students, a predominantly white group, racial segregation means they attend schools with other students who are also white and therefore enjoy lower poverty rates, more experienced teachers, and higher test scores, albeit with lower spending. For Dominican immigrants, by contrast, racial segregation appears to place them in schools where almost every child is poor.

Ultimately, then, there are two forms of segregation that shape the school environments of immigrants. First is own-group segregation. Whether such own-group clustering is harmful or helpful depends, at least in part, on the characteristics of the particular group. But equally important is racial segregation, which profoundly affects who else is attending these schools and has starkly different implications for immigrants of different races.

Comments

Derek Neal: This paper seeks to determine whether or not immigrant school children in New York City are isolated from native-born students, and further determine whether or not there are any negative effects of isolation on the access of immigrant students to resources in schools. I believe that the overall patterns in the results suggest three conclusions. First, race or ethnicity and not immigrant status is the force that drives the sorting of students among schools in New York. Second, students in New York City schools have roughly equal access to the resources that drive classroom spending. Third, the vast majority of students in New York City schools are economically disadvantaged. Here, I review the evidence for these three conclusions. Then, I discuss the implications of these conclusions for broader issues concerning research agendas in urban education.

Table 4 provides ample evidence that foreign-born students are not isolated from the native-born population. All immigrant groups experience considerable exposure to native-born students and also experience low levels of isolation. However, the penultimate row of table 4 foreshadows the most important pattern in the data. Non-white students as a group are quite isolated from white students. Table 5 shows that race and ethnicity exert a strong influence on sorting patterns among all immigrant groups. In short, immigrant school children in New York City are most likely to attend school with people who look like them. How long one has been in the United States is not the important factor for understanding sorting. Rather, race and ethnicity appear to be much more important.

Table 7 describes resources. The classroom spending column is most important. Any large differences in the class sizes experienced by students in different categories should be reflected in this variable. The education production function literature provides little evidence that non-classroom spending or the observed teacher characteristics in columns one through three are associated with higher levels of student achievement. Per-pupil classroom spending appears to vary little with the composition of class by immigrant status. It is unfortunate that the authors do not provide the exact same set of statistics in table 8, which deals with stratification by race. But there is no evidence in this paper, or apparently in related work by some of the authors, that race is correlated with the distribution of resources among New York City schools.

The most striking result in the paper involves the fact that more than 85 percent of the students in New York City's elementary and middle schools are eligible for free or reduced-price lunch. Further, table 8 demonstrates that students from all backgrounds attend schools that, on average, contain a majority of students who are economically disadvantaged.

These results are so striking that one must ask whether it would be better to divert future research efforts away from the experiences of immigrants and towards the broader question of the isolation of economically disadvantaged children in urban public schools. The distribution of household income within the city cannot account for the number of free-lunch-eligible children in the public schools. According to the Agriculture Department guidelines, children must be from families within 185 percent of the federal poverty line in order to be eligible for reduced-price or free lunches. In 1998, this meant that children from a family of four were eligible if their family income was below $30,433 dollars per year.[1] I have not been able to find income distribution data for New York City that is broken down by both age of children and family size, but based on 1990 census data, $30,433 in 1998 dollars is well below the real value of median income among all family households within New York City.[2]

How can 86 percent of children in New York City public schools be eligible for reduced-price or free lunches given the overall distribution of household income in the city? Two factors come straight to mind. To begin-First, private schools in New York have a significant share of the elementary school market. Second, middle- and upper- income persons with children are likely over-represented in the suburbs of New York as opposed to the city. It would be interesting to know more about the relative contribution of these two

1. See www.fns.usda.gov/cnd/.
2. See http://factfinder.census.gov/. The median family income for New York City in the 1990 census was $34,360. This is more than $45,000 in 1998 dollars given the CPI-U inflation numbers.

factors. Specifically, can we document clear evidence that supports anecdotes we hear about the tendency of young families to move out of large cities as soon as their oldest child reaches school age?

After reading this paper, I did some exploratory tabulations with the *Common Core of Data* for 1998–99.[3] In the vast majority of cities and towns in the New York metropolitan area, far less than half of all students are eligible for free or reduced-price lunches. However, poverty levels are often quite high in the largest school districts. For example, there are only two school districts outside New York City but within the New York metropolitan area that educate more than 20,000 elementary school students. These districts are Jersey City and Newark. According to the CCD, the fractions of elementary school students eligible for free or reduced-price lunches in these districts are 0.79 and 0.86 respectively.

In terms of future research on public school segregation, the most pressing order of business must be to understand exactly why the current equilibrium sorting involves such a striking concentration of economically disadvantaged children in inner-city public schools. Further, we need to make more progress in our attempts to understand how this sorting would change under different systems of school finance and governance.

Ironically, critics of voucher schemes often charge that vouchers would inevitably lead to more segregation among schools by race and income. However, given the data, it takes some creativity to imagine how schools in the New York area could get "more segregated."

Thomas Nechyba: This paper provides a nice overview of the levels of segregation experienced within schools by immigrant children from different backgrounds, and it reports the degree to which measurable school inputs vary among immigrant groups. By breaking the data into statistics for subgroups of immigrants, the analysis highlights the importance of not treating "immigrants" as a single group but rather recognizing the considerable heterogeneity in the experience of immigrant families. Much of this heterogeneity is, of course, linked to socioeconomic and racial differences, and to that extent, issues related to the segregation of immigrants are closely related to the more studied issues surrounding racial and income segregation. Still, as the authors note, additional concerns—especially those surrounding English language proficiency—might arise in the immigrant context.

---

3. Data available at http://nces.ed.gov/ccd/.

This careful description of the data is an important first step in understanding issues faced by immigrant families. While answering some questions, such a description does not, however, provide all the answers policy makers are likely to ask. In my comments below, I would therefore like to focus on two broader questions raised by the stimulating analysis of Ellen, O'Regan, Schwartz, and Stiefel. First, what can we conclude about school *quality* from the descriptive analysis of the differences in public school *inputs* devoted to different immigrant groups in New York? And second, how can what we have learned regarding immigrant concentrations within schools ultimately inform policy?

What Can We Say about School Quality Differences?

The empirical challenges of measuring school quality using school inputs are well known. Broadly speaking, school inputs can be divided into three categories: the quantity of resources, the quality of resources, and peer quality.

A long and unsettled debate surrounds the importance of marginal additions in the measurable *quantity* of school resources. The debate regarding the degree to which the *quality* of resources can be meaningfully measured is similarly unsettled. Additionally, the role of peer quality, while judged important by many, is notoriously difficult to isolate empirically and thus remains poorly understood. In short, it is extraordinarily difficult to come to judgments about the output "school quality" by observing school inputs.

Nevertheless, the authors report several tables of statistics related to measures of these three types of inputs. Those related to the quantity and quality of resources are highlighted in table 7 where relatively small differences are found for different immigrant groups. Furthermore, to the extent that there are differences, they seem to be driven by race and ethnicity rather than whether or not children were native or foreign born.

Table 8 in the paper reports several measures of such inputs for native- and foreign-born children of different ethnicities. Both the measure of quantity of resources—per pupil spending—and the measure of quality of resources—percent of teachers with master's degrees—are virtually identical for native- and foreign-born children. This suggests that differences in measurable school inputs for immigrant groups are largely driven by differences in race and ethnicity.

More pronounced are the differences in average reading and math abilities (peer quality) in schools frequented by different immigrant groups (table 6). The overall picture that emerges, therefore, is that the quantity and quality of resources are relatively similar for different immigrant groups within New York City, but the peer compositions differ in the predictable direction (with black and Hispanic immigrants attending schools with lower peer quality than white and Asian immigrants).

What, then, can we say about school quality differences? While I suppose it is comforting to know that measurable inputs (aside from peer quality) do not differ dramatically for different groups of children, we have little indication from the evidence that even relatively equal levels of these measurable inputs produce anything close to parity in school quality for children of different backgrounds. Teacher quality is difficult to measure and shows little correlation with measurable characteristics of teachers (such as whether they have a master's degree). In the presence of union contracts that prohibit other forms of compensation, good teachers are typically rewarded with "good" jobs in schools with few disadvantaged children. Other resources of unobservable high quality likely flow in similar directions. Thus quite apart from peer differences, it is likely that true input quality differences are substantially wider than suggested by the data that the authors focus on—implying considerable public school quality differences for different immigrant groups in the predictable directions (that is, black and Hispanic immigrants experiencing substantially worse school quality than white and Asian immigrants).

What Policy Inferences Should We Draw from the Data on Immigrant Concentrations?

Given the difficulty of quantifying school quality difference from observed input differences, an alternative way of viewing the problem is as one of revealed preference. If it were the case that *all* parents had true access to *all* public schools, then we could conclude that the observed school choice that parents are making for their children is optimal in some sense. Choices regarding schooling, however, are not unconstrained. Which schools are within a parent's choice set depends on where the household has chosen to live—a choice which is in turn constrained by parental resources and housing markets. In addition, immigrant families in particular are often dependent on local networks that further tie households to particular geographic areas. And more explicit barriers to entry into certain neighborhoods and schools may exist as well.

In judging whether the concentrations of immigrants in particular schools is desirable or not, it is therefore important to understand to what extent these concentrations are driven by parental *preferences* and to what extent they are driven by parental *constraints*. To the extent that they are an expression of unconstrained choice, it would be difficult to argue that the segregated outcome requires policy intervention in the direction of reducing the levels of immigrant concentrations. After all, a Chinese mother who chooses to send her child to a school with children of predominantly Chinese ancestry may have very good reasons for doing so. On the other hand, to the extent that the observed levels of concentrations are due to constraints faced by parents—that is, to the extent that immigrant parents are not truly exercising choice when it comes to their children's schooling, policy makers might be much more concerned.

The evidence presented in this paper suggests that some immigrant groups probably fall into the former category while others fall into the latter. In particular, it seems plausible that black and Hispanic immigrants are much more constrained than white and Asian immigrants, and that concentrations of black and Hispanic immigrant children in certain schools are therefore less likely to be pure expressions of parental satisfaction with those schools' levels of quality. Given the widespread view that busing for purposes of desegregation has run its course and is unpopular with parents of all races, the challenge to policymakers is then to find ways of providing additional choice to groups that are geographically constrained and have access to relatively bad schools. In the absence of massive income redistribution that alleviates such mobility constraints, the key to any meaningful increase in choice would then seem to lie in facilitating the process of bringing additional school options to low income immigrant areas. Such options may come in the form of charter and magnet schools within the public system or increased private school choice through vouchers.

Ultimately, much of what we can take from the paper is therefore still very much speculation. My reading suggests that school quality differences experienced by different immigrant groups are likely to be substantially bigger than the reported differences in school inputs, and my tentative policy conclusion is that these differences can ultimately best be addressed through the increase of choice for those who currently face constraints that imply little or no choice of schools for their children. Both these conclusions are tentative and based in large part on a whole literature that deals with the link between school and residential choices, and both would require more rigorous testing than was possible for the authors in this one paper. Such testing is likely to require a structural approach that arrives at firm estimates of underlying preference and production parameters and then investigates policy options within a single analytic framework that holds these estimated parameters constant.

References

Allen, James P., and Eugene Turner. 1996. "Spatial Patterns of Immigrant Assimilation." *Professional Geographer* 48 (2): 140–55.

Argys, Laura M., Daniel I. Rees, and Dominic J. Brewer. 1996. "Detracking America's Schools: Equity at Zero Cost?" *Journal of Policy Analysis and Management* 15 (4): 623–45.

Borjas, George. 1994. "Ethnicity, Neighborhoods, and Human Capital Externalities." Working Paper 4912. Cambridge, Mass.: National Bureau of Economic Research (November).

Burtless, Gary. 1996. "Introduction and Summary." In *Does Money Matter? The Effect of School Resources on Student Achievement and Adult Success,* edited by Gary Burtless, 1–42. Brookings.

Clotfelter, Charles T. 1998. "Public School Segregation in Metropolitan Areas." Working Paper 6779. Cambridge, Mass.: National Bureau of Economic Research.

Coleman, James S., and others. 1966. *Equality of Educational Opportunity.* Government Printing Office.

Cutler, David M., Edward L. Glaeser, and Jacob L. Vigdor. 2000. "Ghettos and the Transmission of Ethnic Capital." Unpublished manuscript. Cambridge, Mass.: Harvard University and National Bureau of Economic Research.

Ferguson, Ronald F. 1991. "Paying for Public Education: New Evidence on How and Why Money Matters." *Harvard Journal on Legislation* 28 (Summer): 465–98.

Ferguson, Ronald F., and Helen F. Ladd. 1996. "How and Why Money Matters: An Analysis of Alabama Schools." In *Holding Schools Accountable: Performance-Based Reform in Education,* edited by Helen F. Ladd, 265–98. Brookings.

Frey, William, and Reynolds Farley. 1996. "Latino, Asian and Black Segregation in U.S. Metropolitan Areas: Are Multi-Ethnic Metros Different?" *Demography* 33 (1): 35–50.

Gershberg, Alec Ian. 2000. "New Immigrants and the New School Governance in New York: Defining the Issues." New York: New School University. Mimeo.

Greenwald, Rob, Larry V. Hedges, and Richard D. Laine. 1996. "The Effect of School Resources on Student Achievement." *Review of Educational Research* 66 (3): 361–96.

Hanushek, Eric A. 1986. "The Economics of Schooling: Production and Efficiency in Public Schools." *Journal of Economic Literature* 24 (3): 1141–77.

———. 1997. "Assessing the Effects of School Resources on Student Performance: An Update." *Educational Evaluation and Policy Analysis* 19 (2): 141–64.

Hanushek, Eric A., John F. Kain, Jacob M. Markman, and Steven G. Rivkin. 2001a. "Does Peer Ability Affect Student Achievement?" Working Paper 8502. Cambridge, Mass.: National Bureau of Economic Research (October).

Hanushek, Eric A., John F. Kain, and Steven G. Rivkin. 2001b. "How Much Does School Integration Affect Student Achievement." Prepared for the annual meetings of the American Economic Association. New Orleans, La., January 5–7.

Hedges, Larry V., Richard D. Laine, and Rob Greenwald. 1994. "Does Money Matter? A Meta-analysis of Studies of the Effects of Differential School Inputs on Student Outcomes." *Educational Researcher* 23: 5–14.

Iatarola, Patrice, and Leanna Stiefel. Forthcoming. "Intradistrict Equity of Public Education Resources and Performance." *Economics of Education Review* 22 (2).

Jargowsky, Paul. 1997. *Poverty and Place: Ghettos, Barrios, and the American City.* New York: Russell Sage.

Kain, John F., and Daniel M. O'Brien. 1999. "Minority Suburbanization in Texas Metropolitan Areas and Its Impact on Student Achievement." Working Paper. University of Texas at Dallas: Cecil and Ida Green Center for the Study of Science and Society.

Kain, John F., and Kraig Singleton. 1996. "Equality of Educational Opportunity Revisited." *New England Economic Review* (May-June): 87–114.

Lieberson, Stanley. 1963. *Ethnic Patterns in American Cities.* New York: Free Press.

Lollock, Lisa. 2001. "The Foreign-Born Population in the United States." *United States Bureau of the Census, Current Population Reports*: 20–534.

Mahard, Rita E., and Robert L. Crain. 1983. "Research on Minority Achievement in Desegregated Schools." In *The Consequences of School Desegregation,* edited by Christine H. Rossell and Willis D. Hawley, 103–25. Temple University Press.

Massey, Douglas S., and Nancy Denton. 1988. "The Dimensions of Racial Segregation." *Social Focus* 67: 281–315.

———. 1993. *American Apartheid: Segregation and the Making of the Underclass.* Harvard University Press.

Matute-Bianchi, Maria Eugenia. 1986. "Ethnic Identities and Patterns of School Success and Failure among Mexican-Descent and Japanese American Students in a California High School: An Ethnographic Analysis." *American Journal of Education* 95 (November): 233–55.

McDonnell, Lorraine M., and Paul Hill. 1993. *Newcomers in American Schools: Meeting the Educational Needs of Immigrant Youth.* Santa Monica, Calif.: Rand.

Orfield, Gary. 1993. "The Growth of Segregation in American Schools: Changing Patterns of Separation and Poverty since 1968." The Harvard Project on School Desegregation. Harvard University.

Orfield, Gary, and John T. Yun. 1999. "Resegregation in American Schools." The Civil Rights Project. Harvard University.

Portes, Alejandro. 1995. "Children of Immigrants: Segmented Assimilation and its Determinants." In *The Economic Sociology of Immigration: Essays on Networks, Ethnicity, and Entrepreneurship*, edited by Alejandro Portes, 1–41. New York: Russell Sage Foundation.

Portes, Alejandro, and Min Zhou. 1994. "Should Immigrants Assimilate?" *The Public Interest* (116): 1–17.

Rivkin, Steven G. 1994. "Residential Segregation and School Integration." *Sociology of Education* 67 (4): 279–92.

————. 2000. "School Desegregation, Academic Attainment, and Earnings." *Journal of Human Resources* 35 (2): 333–46.

Rodriguez, Tom D. 1999. "The Effect of School Ethnic Context upon the Psychosocial and Academic Performance of Second-Generation Youths." Ph.D. dissertation, Johns Hopkins University.

Rumbaut, Ruben G. 1995. "The New Californians: Comparative Research Findings on the Educational Progress of Immigrant Children." In *California's Immigrant Children: Theory, Research, and Implications for Educational Policy*, edited by Ruben G. Rumbaut and Wayne Cornelius, 17–69. Center for U.S.-Mexican Studies. University of California at San Diego.

Schmidley, A. Dianne, and Campbell Gibson. 1999. "Profile of the Foreign-Born Population in the United States, 1997." *U.S. Census Bureau.* Current Population Reports, Series P23–195. Government Printing Office.

Schwartz, Amy Ellen, and Alec Ian Gershberg. 2001. "Immigrants and Education: Evidence from New York City." *National Tax Association (Proceedings, 2000)*: 125–34.

Slavin, Robert E. 1990. "Achievement Effects of Ability Grouping in Secondary Schools: A Best Evidence Synthesis." *Review of Educational Research* 60 (3): 471–99.

Verba, Sidney, Kay Lehman Schlozman, and Henry E. Brady. 1995. *Voice and Equality: Civic Voluntarism in American Politics*. Harvard University Press.

Wells, Amy Stuart, and Robert L. Crain. 1994. "Perpetuation Theory and the Long-Term Effects of School Desegregation." *Review of Educational Research* 64 (4): 531–55.

White, Michael J., Ann E. Biddlecom, and Shenyang Guo. 1993. "Immigration, Naturalization, and Residential Assimilation among Asian Americans in 1980." *Social Forces* 72 (1): 93–118.

White, Michael J., and Alaf Omar. 1996. "Segregation by Ethnicity and Immigrant Status in New Jersey." In *Keys to Successful Immigration: Implications of the New Jersey Experience,* edited by Thomas J. Espenshade, 375–94. Washington: Urban Institute.

Zimmer, Ron, and Eugenia F. Toma. 2000. "Peer Effects in Private and Public Schools across Countries." *Journal of Policy Analysis and Management* 19 (1): 75–92.